CAT

PRACTICE & REVISION KIT

Level C Paper 2

Information for Management

BPP is the **official provider** of training materials for the ACCA's CAT qualification. This Practice & Revision Kit forms part of a suite of learning tools, which also includes CD-ROMs for tuition and computer based assessment, and the innovative, internet-based 'virtual campus'.

In this February 2003 edition

- **DO YOU KNOW**? Checklists to test your knowledge and understanding of **Information for Management** topics

- **QUESTIONS WITH HELP** and questions with **HELPING HANDS**

- Feedback on examiner's comments in **WHAT THE EXAMINER SAID** and **EXAMINER'S MARKING SCHEMES**

- **TWO MOCK EXAMS -** the June 2002 and December 2002 examinations

FOR JUNE 2003 AND DECEMBER 2003 EXAMS

BPP Professional Education
February 2003

First edition September 1998
Sixth edition February 2003

ISBN 0 7517 1080 6 (previous edition 0 7517 5208 8)

British Library Cataloguing-in-Publication Data
A catalogue record for this book
is available from the British Library

Published by

BPP Professional Education
Aldine House, Aldine Place
London W12 8AW

www.bpp.com

Printed in Great Britain by W M Print
45-47 Frederick Street
Walsall, West Midlands
WS2 9NE

We are grateful to the Association of Chartered Certified Accountants for permission to reproduce the syllabus, the pilot paper and past examination questions of which the Association holds the copyright. The suggested solutions have been prepared by BPP Professional Education.

We are also grateful to the Chartered Institute of Management Accountants, the Association of Accounting Technicians, the Institute of Chartered Secretaries and Administrators and the Association of Chartered Certified Accountants for permission to reproduce past examination questions in this kit. The suggested answers have been prepared by BPP Professional Education.

Page

BPP
PROFESSIONAL EDUCATION

		Page reference	Done

PART F: DECISION MAKING

HOW TO USE THIS PRACTICE & REVISION KIT

Aim of this Practice & Revision Kit

> To provide the practice to help you succeed in the examination for C2 *Information for Management*.

To pass the examination you need a thorough understanding in all areas covered by the syllabus and teaching guide.

Recommended approach

- Make sure you are able to answer questions on **everything** specified by the syllabus and teaching guide.

- Learning is an **active** process. Use the **DO YOU KNOW?** Checklists to test your knowledge and understanding of the topics covered in C2 *Information for Management* by filling in the blank spaces. Then check your answers against the **DID YOU KNOW?** Checklists. Do not attempt any questions if you are unable to fill in any of the blanks - go back to your **BPP Interactive Text** and revise first.

- When you are revising a topic, think about the mistakes that you know that you should avoid by writing down **POSSIBLE PITFALLS** at the end of each **DO YOU KNOW?** Checklist.

- Once you have completed the checklists successfully, you should attempt all of the questions in this Practice & Revision Kit. Each section has one **QUESTION WITH HELP**, and one question without any help or guidance. All of the other questions have **HELPING HANDS** which you should use in order to help you answer the question in the best way. There are 28 past examination questions in this Practice and Revision Kit.

  - Each answer gives feedback on **WHAT THE EXAMINER SAID.**

  - There is an **EXAMINER'S MARKING SCHEME** at the end of each answer.

  - There is a mark allocation for each question. Each mark carries with it a time allocation of 1.8 minutes (including time for selecting and reading questions). A 20 mark question should therefore be completed in 36 minutes.

- Once you have completed all of the questions in the body of this Practice & Revision Kit, you should attempt both of the **MOCK EXAMS** under examination conditions. Check your answers against our answers and apply the ACCA's Official marking scheme to find out how well you did.

This approach is only a suggestion. You or your college may well adapt it to suit your needs.

CURRENT ISSUES

A recent article by the examiner is reproduced on the following pages. You are strongly advised to read through it carefully.

TECHNICAL

Management control using variances and ratios

NIGEL COULTHURST

RELEVANT TO PAPER C2

The calculation and interpretation of variances, which measure the performance of a business (business unit) in comparison with standard / budget, and the ensuing control action are an important aspect of the Paper C2, *Information for Management* syllabus. Session 14 of the Teaching Guide covers the analysis of variances (variance calculations, investigation, causes and inter-relationships), Session 15 is concerned with management control using variances and ratios. This article covers Session 15 material, specifically:

* the concept and use of control limits and control charts;
* control actions that may be taken in response to a reported variance;
* calculation and evaluation of control ratios.

CONTROL LIMITS

Standards are set in advance as a basis for comparison with actual results to reveal variation from expected performance. However, standards set should not be viewed too rigidly because:

* standards may be set at different levels (i.e. basic, current, attainable or ideal') and thus variances from standard (favourable or adverse) may be expected;
* standards are only estimates;
* standards reflect the average performance that is expected over a period of time.

As a consequence:

* variance limits may be established. A limit would be an allowance for a variance (adverse or favourable) that would not trigger investigation and control action unless and until exceeded;

* cumulative (rather than single period) variances may be compared with the control limit.

The variance allowance (or control limit) tries to allow for:

* the level at which the standard has been set (e.g. basic);
* the difficulties of establishing the standard performance;
* normal (or random) variations around average performance (as opposed to a consistent trend), especially if the cumulative variance is used for control purposes;
* minor operational variances that are too small to justify the cost of investigation and control action.

While the concept of a variance allowance is relatively straightforward, the setting of the limit in practice, allowing for the several factors outlined above, is difficult. A combination of experience / judgement and the application of statistics (e.g. standard deviation) may be used.

CONTROL CHARTS

Control charts are a useful way of presenting variance data over a period of time, in relation to the control limits set (whether single period or cumulative). This is illustrated in **Figure I**.

CONTROL ACTION

Whether to take action will generally depend upon whether a variance identified (especially if cumulative) is outside the control limits. If outside the limit, the variance will be material and a trend is likely to have been established. Further analysis and investigation would then follow, subject to:

* whether the underlying cause is already known or whether it is likely to be controllable, i.e. lead to the possibility of control action being taken;
* the likely cost of investigation. Judgement needs to be made as to whether likely benefits resulting from investigation will exceed the cost;
* behavioural considerations e.g. the effect on staff motivation.

The result could be:

* more informed performance management;
* corrective action;
* a change to the standard / budget;
* no action / no change to target.

CONTROL RATIOS

Any business, to be successful, will need to obtain the right resources at minimum cost and use these resources efficiently to produce the desired outputs. This is the essence of the 3 Es (Economy, Efficiency and Effectiveness).

The setting of standards and comparison of actual with standard / budgeted performance can be an important part of the measurement of economy, efficiency and effectiveness. Variance analysis, in the form of monetary values, measures the impact on profit of differences between actual and standard / budget. Control ratios measure performance against standard / budget in relative (%) terms. There are three key control ratios: capacity (resource input), efficiency (productivity of resource usage) and activity (output volume).

The basis of performance measurement via these control ratios is the concept of the standard hour (the amount of work achievable,

FIGURE 1: CONTROL CHARTS

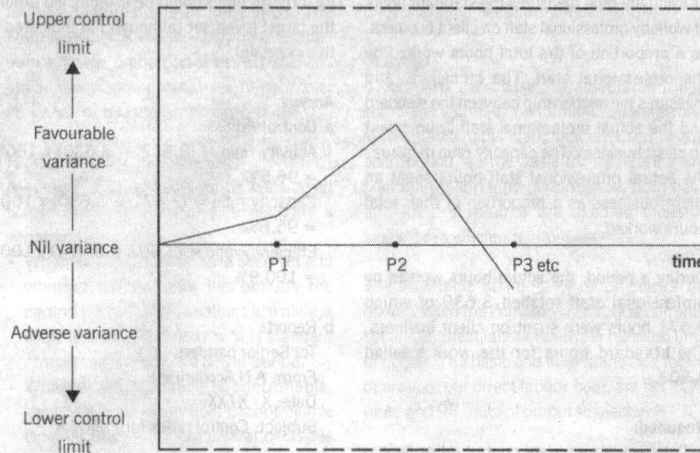

at standard efficiency levels in an hour[1]). The standard hour provides a common basis for the measurement of work done, typically in a production (factory) environment. Actual hours worked on a variety of tasks can be compared with budgeted hours, and with the output achieved measured in standard hours.

The **capacity** ratio typically measures the utilisation of labour resource in terms of total hours worked in comparison with those budgeted. The usual formula for the calculation of the capacity ratio is:

Actual hours worked x 100%
  Budgeted hours

A capacity ratio of 100% would mean that budgeted hours were worked. A ratio of <100% would indicate hours worked < budget and a ratio >100% would indicate hours worked > budget.

The **efficiency** ratio measures how well the labour resource has been used in comparison with the standard set. The formula for the calculation of the efficiency ratio is:

Standard hours of output x 100%
  Actual hours worked

An efficiency ratio of 100% would mean that the productivity of labour was exactly on standard. An efficiency ratio <100% would indicate productivity < standard and an efficiency ratio >100% would indicate productivity > standard.

The **activity** (also called **volume** or **production volume**) ratio typically measures the output achieved compared with budget. The usual formula for the calculation of the activity ratio is:

Standard hours of output x 100%
  Budgeted hours

An activity ratio of 100% would mean that output was on budget. A ratio of <100% would indicate output < budget and a ratio >100% would indicate output > budget.

The activity ratio is a function of the resources utilised (capacity ratio) and how well they are used (efficiency ratio) and thus the ratio can be expressed as:

TECHNICAL

$Activity = Capacity \times Efficiency$

$$\frac{\text{Standard hours of output}}{\text{Budgeted hours}}$$

$$=$$

$$\frac{\text{Actual hours worked}}{\text{Budgeted hours}}$$

$$\times$$

$$\frac{\text{Standard hours of output}}{\text{Actual hours worked}}$$

The June 2001 and December 2001 Paper C2 examinations included questions featuring the calculation and evaluation of control ratios. These two questions are used in the following examples.

EXAMPLE 1

Question 4 in the June 2001 examination required the calculation of control ratios, but in a non-production setting (i.e. a firm of accountants). It should be noted that the capacity and activity ratios were used differently to the typical production environment formulae described above.

Candidates were required to apply their knowledge and understanding of control ratios. Clear instructions were given as to the meaning and basis for calculation of each of the ratios.

Question

A firm of accountants uses the standard hours worked by professional staff on client business as the basis for client charging, and for cost control. The standard hours for each client job are established in advance, based on the expected amount of time required for each task. Some of the hours worked by professional staff are not on client business and are thus not chargeable.

Target control ratios are:

Activity	96.9%
Efficiency	102.0%
Capacity	95.0%

The activity ratio measures the standard hours of work by professional staff on client business, as a proportion of the total hours worked by the professional staff. The efficiency ratio measures the relationship between the standard and the actual professional staff hours spent on client business. The capacity ratio measures the actual professional staff hours spent on client business as a proportion of their total hours worked.

During a period, the actual hours worked by professional staff totalled 3,630 of which 3,471 hours were spent on client business. The standard hours for the work totalled 3,502.

Required:

a Calculate appropriate control ratios for the period (each to one decimal place of a percent).

b Prepare a brief report for the firm's senior partners that:

 i interprets the control ratios calculated in (a) above;

 ii identifies possible causes of any variation from target.

c Describe the factors that should be considered before a decision is made to investigate a variation from target.

Comment

As can be seen from the question, the fact that some of the hours worked by professional staff are not on client business, and thus not chargeable, means that target ratios set for capacity and activity (as defined in this particular example) are below 100%. The target activity ratio is higher than the target capacity ratio because an efficiency ratio >100% is expected:

Activity	=	Capacity	x	Efficiency
0.969	=	0.95	x	1.02

Thus 100% is not expected for any of the control ratios and thus some variances from 100% would be regarded as normal i.e. allowed

for. Control limits could be established around the target levels set (although not indicated in this example).

Answer

a Control ratios:

Activity ratio = $(3{,}502 \div 3{,}630) \times 100\%$
= 96.5%

Capacity ratio = $(3{,}471 \div 3{,}630) \times 100\%$
= 95.6%

Efficiency ratio = $(3{,}502 \div 3{,}471) \times 100\%$
= 100.9%

b Report:

To: Senior partners
From: A N Accountant
Date: X / X / XX
Subject: Control ratios for Period X

Set out below is a summary of performance (as measured by the activity, efficiency and activity ratios) for Period X, and a description of the possible causes of variation from target (currently under investigation).

Control ratios:
The proportion of the total hours worked by professional staff in the period, that were charged to clients, was 96.5%. This was 0.4 percentage points below target. A greater proportion of hours than target were actually spent on client business (at 95.6% a favourable capacity variance of 0.6 percentage points). However, below target efficiency (despite being above 100% it was nevertheless 1.1 percentage points below the target of 102.0%) meant that the work achieved was not converted into sufficient chargeable output.

The link between activity, capacity and efficiency ratios is as follows:
Activity (0.965) = Capacity (0.956) x Efficiency (1.009)

Reasons for variation:
Possible reasons for the favourable capacity variance versus target are improved

scheduling of client business and reduced training requirements in the period. The adverse efficiency variance may have resulted from a greater proportion of less experienced junior staff hours, problems with particular jobs and / or a rather demanding target.

c) Factors affecting investigation:
A number of factors should be considered before deciding whether to investigate a variation from target:

- Whether control limits have been set and whether the variance lies outside the control limit. Small variations are always likely to occur (in £ and / or % of standard / target) especially in a single period.
- Whether the variance is controllable. Variations may result from uncontrollable external factors or from central decisions (e.g. a pay award). Such variations may call for a change in the standard / target for the future, not an investigation into the past.
- Whether a trend has been established. Variations from standard / target are more likely to justify investigation if they are repeated over several periods. Fluctuation either side of target may simply be an inevitable consequence of fluctuating business conditions.
- Whether expected benefits are likely to exceed the cost of investigation, including the effect on staff motivation / morale. All of the above factors will have a bearing on whether the potential benefit from investigation of a variance is likely to outweigh the cost. However, there may also be other factors to consider (e.g. past experience, nature of the expense item, responsibility area) which are likely to influence the net outcome of an investigation.

EXAMPLE 2

Question 2(b) in the December 2001 examination focused on the efficiency ratio in a situation where standards were set at different levels (i.e. basic, attainable and ideal) and used for different purposes. Candidates were required to apply their knowledge and understanding of control ratios flexibly.

Question

A company uses basic, attainable and ideal standards within its performance management system. Attainable standards are used, within each period, as the basis for monitoring and controlling short term performance. Both basic and ideal standards are used to measure longer-term efficiency improvements.

The attainable standard time for one of the operations in the company's factory is currently set at 1.2 direct labour hours per hundred units of output. The basic and ideal standards for the operation, per direct labour hour, are set at 75 units and 90 units of output respectively.

During the period just ended, 163,085 units were manufactured in 1,930 direct labour hours. The standard direct labour rate is £7.50 per hour.

Required:

Calculate for the operation described above:
i the direct labour efficiency variance (£) and the efficiency ratio (%) for the period;
ii the % improvement achieved to date, based on the actual performance in the most recent period compared with the basic standard;
iii the further % improvement possible, based on a comparison of the ideal and the attainable standards.

Comment

Attainable standards are used in the above example as the basis for monitoring and controlling short-term performance. In the absence of any information to the contrary, a ratio of 100% (actual hours versus attainable standard) is presumably the target. If attainable hours are seen as difficult to achieve, a target of slightly less than 100% could be set with control limits. Basic and ideal standards may, at the same time, be set and used but with a different purpose (as seen in this example) viz. to measure longer-term changes in efficiency.

Answer

Standard hours of output	
=	163,085 units
x	1.2 direct labour hours per unit
	100
=	1,957 standard direct labour hours

i Efficiency variance (£)
= (1,957 std hrs - 1,930 actual hrs)
x £7.50 per hr
= £203 favourable

Efficiency ratio (%)
= (1,957 std hrs ÷ 1,930 actual hrs)
x 100%
= 101.4%

ii Improvement achieved:
Most recent period
= 163,085 units ÷ 1,930 hours
= 84.5 units per direct labour hour
Achievement (actual versus basic standard)
= [(84.5 ÷ 75) - 1] x 100%
= 12.7% improvement achieved

iii Improvement possible:
Attainable standard
= 100 units ÷ 1.2 hours
= 83.3 units per direct labour hour
Potential (ideal versus attainable standard)
= [(90 ÷ 83.3) - 1] x 100%
= 8.0% further improvement possible

REFERENCE

1 Performance measurement by Nigel Coulthurst, *student accountant* September 2001 □

Nigel Coulthurst is Examiner for Paper C2

(x)

SYLLABUS

INFORMATION FOR MANAGEMENT

To develop knowledge and understanding of the application of management accounting techniques to support the management processes of planning, control and decision making.

OBJECTIVES

On completion of this module candidates should be able to:

1	Discuss the use and limitation of accounting based management information
2	Prepare forecasts of income and expenditure
3	Produce draft budget proposals
4	Prepare and present budget variance reports
5	Analyse financial data for management control purposes
6	Analyse financial data for decision making purposes
7	Make recommendations for cost reduction and value enhancement

CONTENT

(a)	**Accounting for management:** management processes, nature of decision making, management information requirements, contribution and scope of management accounting, maintenance and improvement of accounting information systems.

(b)	**Product and service costing:** evaluation of methods, activity based systems for allocating costs, cost drivers, reporting implication of full-absorption and marginal (variable) costing approaches.

(c)	**Responsibility accounting:** relating the design of cost collection and reporting to the control structure of the organisation, cost, revenue, profit and investment centres.

(d)	**Budgetary planning:** budget types, budget development processes, co-ordination of sub-budgets, principal budget factors, incremental and zero based approaches, budget review, use of computer based models.

(e)	**External information:** sources of economic and financial information, use of and limitations of published statistics, adjusting data for price movements. Cost and value management: cost reduction methods, value analysis, activity based costing, quality assurance processes, TQM.

(f)	**Budgetary control:** capacity variations, flexible budgets, calculating and analysing variances, budgets and employee motivation.

(g)	**Variance analysis:** the significance of and identification of possible reasons for standard cost variances and control ratios.

(h)	**Performance measurement:** use of indicators to measure productivity, unit costs, resource utilisation, profitability, quality of service.

(i)	**Pricing policies and procedures:** preparation of cost estimates, tendering and quotations, pricing methods (full cost plus, demand based, marginal).

(j)	**Decision making:** cost behaviour, opportunity costs and relevant cost concepts, cost volume profit analysis, breakeven charts, 'make or buy' type situations.

THE EXAMINATION PAPER

Assessment methods and format of the paper

Questions based on demonstrating that the candidates have acquired the necessary skills with all questions to be answered.

Number of marks

Four compulsory questions   100

Time allowed: 3 hours

Prerequisite knowledge

Successful completion of Levels A and B.

Development of Paper C2

This paper builds on the knowledge acquired in Paper B2 enabling students to apply a wide range of management accounting techniques in order to plan and control activities as well as make decisions.

Analysis of past papers

The analysis below shows the topics which have been examined under the current syllabus and the CAT Pilot paper.

Marks

December 2002

		Marks
1	Cost and profit calculations; value analysis and quality control and assurance	40
2	Absorption costing and activity based costing	20
3	Pricing	20
4	Budgeting and variance calculation	20

June 2002

		Marks
1	Process costing-joint products; relevant costing	40
2	Planning and control systems; ZBB and incremental budgeting	20
3	Marginal costing, absorption costing and variance calculation	20
4	Breakeven analysis, decision making and limiting factor analysis	20

What the examiner said

'There were some very good performances across the whole paper and on individual questions. However, the performance of candidates overall continued to disappoint.' A large number of candidates did not appear to be prepared for the exam and where the basics appeared to be known, narrative answers showed that there was a serious lack of understanding. Candidates continue to fail to read the contents and requirements of questions carefully – marks will not be gained by answering a question of a candidate's own liking (rather than the question being set).

Marks

December 2001

1	Absorption costing, marginal costing and unit costing	40
2	Cost control and cost reduction; standard costing and variance analysis	20
3	Decision making	20
4	Budgeting	20

What the examiner said

'The performance of candidates overall was disappointing across all questions and was below the standard achieved at the previous examination sitting.' Many candidates demonstrated a lack of knowledge and understanding of the basic concepts tested across the paper. The examiner also reported that presentation of answers was often poor and there was evidence that candidates failed to read the content and requirements of questions carefully.

June 2001

1	Marginal costing; absorption costing and breakeven analysis	40
2	Data presentation and management information	20
3	Activity based costing	20
4	Control ratios	20

What the examiner said

Well-prepared candidates achieved good marks, though a large number of candidates did demonstrate a lack of understanding of the basics of the syllabus for Paper C2.

Common errors

- Poor organisation
- Poor presentation
- Ignoring instructions (regarding rounding)
- Lack of workings
- Failure to manage time effectively

December 2000

1	Calculation of standards and associated finished stock value; preparation, commentary on and explanation of budgeted profit and loss account and cash budget; identification of factors impacting on cash flow	40
2	Discussion on various aspects of management accounting	20
3	Calculation of margin-based selling price; performance appraisal	20
4	Various aspects of contract costing	20

What the examiner said

It was disappointing to see so many basic errors in candidates' answers. Some candidates were obviously not sufficiently prepared to deal with some of the key topics in this syllabus. Candidates who were well-prepared achieved some good marks.

BPP
PROFESSIONAL EDUCATION

Marks

June 2000

1	Preparation of marginal costing profit and loss accounts; evaluation of pricing options; breakeven analysis	40
2	Decision making	20
3	Information and monitoring of performance	20
4	Performance appraisal	20

What the examiner said

- Although some candidates were better prepared for this sitting and took more care with layout and presentation, many did not understand the basic concepts of management accounting and did not give enough thought to the presentation of their answers.

- The range of marks achieved was wide. A small number of candidates gained excellent marks.

- *All* workings should be done in the answer booklet and then neatly crossed through. Credit can sometimes be given for workings that contain the basic logic of the principle being tested but where errors might have crept into the calculations.

- Many candidates missed numerous opportunities to gain marks by not clearly stating what their decisions were or by not demonstrating the logic they had used in arriving at their answers.

- Credit can sometimes be given when formulae are stated correctly even if subsequent calculations are incorrect.

- Many candidates ignored requirements to round answers.

- Candidates must be aware that management accounting involves the use of monetary values and physical measures (litres, kilograms, passengers and so on).

December 1999

1	Management accountant and the value provided by the management accountant; labour payment systems	40
2	Absorption costing versus marginal costing; budgeted versus actual profit	20
3	Decision making	20
4	Batch costing	20

What the examiner said

- Many candidates had difficulty with some of the basic concepts of management accounting.

- Overall, candidates continued to take greater care with the presentation of answers although many missed opportunities to pick up marks throughout the paper by not putting the correct headings on their answers and by not giving sufficient thought to the most appropriate layout of their work.

June 1999

1	Budget preparation	40
2	Cost volume profit analysis; external sources of information	20
3	Cost reduction	20
4	Absorption costing	20

What the examiner said

There was a noticeable overall improvement in the standard of answers and the examiner was particularly pleased that candidates were taking more care with presentation (see article on (vii) to (x)). Many candidates missed opportunities to pick up marks throughout the paper, however, by not putting the correct headings on their answers and by not giving significant thought to the most appropriate layout of their work.

Given the title of the paper, candidates must organise their work so that it has meaning for another person (probably a non-financial specialist). Final answers should be presented in a manner which facilitates management understanding (neat layout, use of tables and diagrams, headings and so on).

Marks

December 1998

1	High-low method, marginal costing income/expenditure statement, breakeven analysis	40
2	Absorption costing, variance analysis	20
3	Budget preparation process	20
4	Tenders	20

What the examiner said

The standard of answers showed a significant improvement compared with the first sitting of the exam. Most candidates attempted all four questions but there was evidence that wider coverage of the syllabus is required by candidates.

There were a number of easy marks to be gained throughout the paper for presentation.

June 1998

1	Budget preparation using absorption costing, marginal costing and ABC	40
2	Responsibility accounting and performance measures	20
3	Flexible budgeting and variance analysis	20
4	Decision making and TQM	20

What the examiner said

The examiner was disappointed with the pass mark for this exam, many candidates struggling with one or more of questions 2, 3 and 4.

Candidates tended to be very competent in the parts of the examination that required computational analysis but the majority were unable to interpret the results of computations or to offer advice to management.

A theme of the paper is the analysis and interpretation of management accounting information for presentation to management and so candidates must be able to organise and present their work so that it can be understood by somebody else (probably a non-accountant). For example, there were a number of easy marks available in the paper for using tables for figures and for using headings and so on for explanations and reports.

The examination paper

Examiners' approach to Paper C2

The following extract is from an article published in the December 1997 issue of the *ACCA Technician Bulletin*.

'Approach to the paper

The central theme of the paper is the accountant's role in supporting management decision making, through the techniques of analysis, planning and control. The cost accounting methods, introduced in paper **B2**, are developed into a more comprehensive range of management accounting processes in this paper.

Candidates should note that the stated aim of the syllabus is to "develop knowledge and understanding of the application of management techniques". This means that it is not sufficient for candidates merely to perform the mechanics of various computational techniques, but they must also understand how those techniques might be applied in practical situations. This will involve drawing conclusions and making recommendations to management.

Syllabus

As the title of the paper suggests, the purpose of management accountancy is to present information to management. Information should be presented in a business-like way, enabling management to readily understand both the advice being given and the analysis supporting that advice. The use of graphs, tables and charts will be expected, where these are appropriate to demonstrate the point being made.

While many of the basic techniques of management accounting have changed little over the years, candidates should note that there are a number of more recent developments which are included in the syllabus for this paper. Activity-based costing, total quality management, the use of computer based models, are examples of techniques that are now entering the work place. Students should be familiar with these techniques and be able to suggest how they might be applied in organisations. There are many topical articles on these subjects in journals and magazines.

Questions will generally be based on practical scenarios and these will be drawn from manufacturing, service and not-for-profit organisations.

Job, batch, contract and process costing methods appear in paper **B2**. In this paper (**C2**) it is not intended to test the mechanics of preparing accounts and costings at length, however candidates should be able to demonstrate the effect of absorption and marginal costing on these techniques. In addition the preparation of estimates for future jobs and batches may be tested.

Performance measurement is a wide ranging and growing subject within management accounting. In this paper candidates will only be expected to understand how the performance of various activities in an organisation might be monitored by the use of simple financial and non-financial measures. For example a production department might have targets for unit costs, reject rates, the number of orders completed on time, or the number of hours lost as a result of machine breakdowns.

Statistical analysis of data for use in the preparation of forecasts will not include regression analysis but analysis using scatter diagrams, moving averages and time series analyses will be expected.

Questions on variance analysis will not include multiple product lines, thereby requiring mix variances to be calculated, except in the area of sales.

Setting prices for products and services is a key area of management decision making; management accountants have a significant role to play in providing analysis to inform such decisions. Candidates should be able to prepare cost-based approaches to setting prices and should also understand how the concept of demand elasticity may also impact on selling prices and volumes. Calculations involving the use of elasticity formulae will not be required.

Examination format

The examination will consist of 4 compulsory questions. The first question will carry a weighting of 40% and will involve analysis of accounting data in a practical scenario. The remaining 3 questions will be equally weighted, each accounting for 20% of the total marks available for the paper.

There will be a mix of computational and discursive questions.'

Questions and answers

DO YOU KNOW? – MANAGEMENT ACCOUNTING AND INFORMATION

- *Check that you can fill in the blanks in the statements below before you attempt any questions. If in doubt, you should go back to your BPP Interactive Text and revise first.*

- Management involves five basic tasks.
  - ....
  - ....
  - ....
  - ....
  - ....

- Management accounting is concerned with the collection of .... (from both internal and external sources), its analysis and processing into .... , and the interpretation and communication of that .... so as to assist management with ...., ... and ....

- Useful management information should be:
  - ....
  - ....
  - ....
  - ....
  - ....
  - ....
  - ....
  - ....
  - ....

- The steps in the decision-making process are as follows.
  - *Step 1*....................................
  - *Step 2*....................................
  - *Step 3*....................................
  - *Step 4*....................................
  - *Step 5*....................................
  - *Step 6*....................................

- External sources of information might be .... (such as an organisation's files of invoices and letters) or .... (such as governments, banks, newspapers and trade journals).

- A short formal report may be broken down into the following sections.
  - ....
  - ....
  - ....
  - ....
  - ....

- A short informal report may be divided into three parts.
  - ....
  - ....
  - ....

- .... are a simple way of presenting information about two variables.

- .... often convey the meaning or significance of data more clearly than would a table. There are three main types of bar chart.
  - ....
  - ....
  - ....

- A .... is the distribution of the number of times the value of a particular variable occurs. A .... is the distribution of the number of times a variable, the value of which falls within a particular range, occurs. A .... shows the total number of times that a variable with a value above or below a certain amount occurs.

- A histogram is the pictorial representation of a .... The number of observations in a class is represented by the .... covered by the bar, rather than by its ....

  TRY QUESTIONS 1-3

- *Possible pitfalls*

  Write down the mistakes you know you should avoid.

DID YOU KNOW? – MANAGEMENT ACCOUNTING AND INFORMATION

- *Could you fill in the blanks? The answers are in bold. Use this page for revision purposes as you approach the exam.*

- Management involves five basic tasks.
  - **Planning**   ○ **Controlling**   ○ **Decision making**
  - **Organising**   ○ **Motivating**

- Management accounting is concerned with the collection of **data** (from both internal and external sources), its analysis and processing into **information**, and the interpretation and communication of that **information** so as to assist management with **planning, control** and **decision making**.

- Useful management information should be:
  - **relevant**   ○ **confidence inspiring**
  - **timely**   ○ **complete**
  - **appropriately communicated**   ○ **manageable in terms of volume**
  - **clear to the manager using it**   ○ **provided at a cost which is less than the**
  - **accurate**   **value of its benefits**

- The steps in the decision-making process are as follows.
  - *Step 1.* **Identify objectives**
  - *Step 2.* **Search for alternative courses of action**
  - *Step 3.* **Collect data about the alternative courses of action**
  - *Step 4.* **Select the appropriate course of action**
  - *Step 5.* **Implement the decision**
  - *Step 6.* **Compare actual and planned outcomes and take any necessary corrective action**

- External sources of information might be **primary** (such as an organisation's files of invoices and letters) or **secondary** (such as governments, banks, newspapers and trade journals).

- A short formal report may be broken down into the following sections.
  - **Terms of reference/introduction**   ○ **Procedure/method**
  - **Findings**   ○ **Conclusions**
  - **Recommendations**

- A short informal report may be divided into three parts.
  - **Background/situation/introduction**
  - **Findings/analysis of the situation**
  - **Action/solution/conclusion**

- **Tables** are a simple way of presenting information about two variables.

- **Charts** often convey the meaning or significance of data more clearly than would a table. There are three main types of bar chart.
  - **Simple**   ○ **Component (including percentage component)**
  - **Multiple (or compound)**

- A **frequency distribution** is the distribution of the number of times the value of a particular variable occurs. A **grouped frequency distribution** is the distribution of the number of times a variable, the value of which falls within a particular range, occurs. A **cumulative frequency distribution** shows the total number of times that a variable with a value above or below a certain amount occurs.

- A histogram is the pictorial representation of a **frequency distribution**. The number of observations in a class is represented by the **area** covered by the bar, rather than by its **height**.

  TRY QUESTIONS 1-3

- *Possible pitfalls*
  - **Failing to use a report format when asked to do so**
  - **Not labelling diagrams**
  - **Drawing very small, untidy or unclear diagrams**

1   QUESTION WITH HELP: PRESENTING INFORMATION

You are one of the assistant management accountants for Lever Ltd, a car manufacturer. The company has undertaken an attitude survey of recent buyers of small cars in Great Britain. As a part of this study, 100 recent buyers of British cars and 100 recent buyers of German cars were asked to agree or to disagree with a number of statements. One of the summary tables from the survey is shown below.

Statements	Buyers of British cars		Buyers of German cars	
	Agree	*Disagree*	*Agree*	*Disagree*
British cars are:				
easy to get serviced	65	35	46	54
economical	81	19	55	45
reliable	76	24	48	52
comfortable	69	31	61	39
German cars are:				
easy to get serviced	32	68	60	40
economical	61	39	83	17
reliable	74	26	85	15
comfortable	35	65	58	42

Required

Draft an appraisal of the most significant features of these data, illustrating your analysis with tables and diagrams.   **(20 marks)**

> *If you are stuck, look at the next page for detailed help as to how you should tackle this question.*

APPROACHING THE ANSWER

Step 1.   Begin by looking at the overall opinions of the people surveyed. Calculate the percentages of people who agreed with each of the four statements about British cars and then analyse the results.

Step 2.   Calculate the percentages of people who agreed with each of the four statements about German cars and then analyse the results.

Step 3.   Draw up a multiple/compound bar chart of the results of your calculations in Steps 1 and 2. The four statements should be represented on one axis and the percentage of people who agreed with the statements on the other. The attitudes of respondents to each statement should be represented by two separate bars, one for British cars and one for German cars. Don't forget to include a key. Analyse the diagram.

Step 4.   Then draw up a multiple/compound bar chart of the opinions of buyers of British cars and carry out an analysis.

Step 5.   Likewise, draw up a multiple/compound bar chart of the opinions of buyers of German cars and analyse the diagram.

1   ANSWER TO QUESTION WITH HELP: PRESENTING INFORMATION

Let us first look at the **overall opinions** of the 200 people surveyed regarding both British and German cars. For **British cars**, the percentages who agreed with each of the four statements made were as follows.

British cars are:	*% Agree*
easy to get serviced	55.5
economical	68.0
reliable	62.0
comfortable	65.0

It can be seen from these figures that the overall percentages who were happy about the economy, reliability and comfort of British cars were more or less the same, but rather fewer people agreed that servicing was easy.

Turning to **German cars**, the **overall opinions** expressed were as follows.

German cars are:	*% Agree*
easy to get serviced	46.0
economical	72.0
reliable	79.5
comfortable	46.5

The picture here is somewhat different in that about the same proportion (46%) agreed that the cars were easy to get serviced and that they were comfortable whereas a markedly higher proportion (about 75%) were happy with economy and reliability.

Comparing British and German cars overall, the picture can be represented by the following **bar chart.**

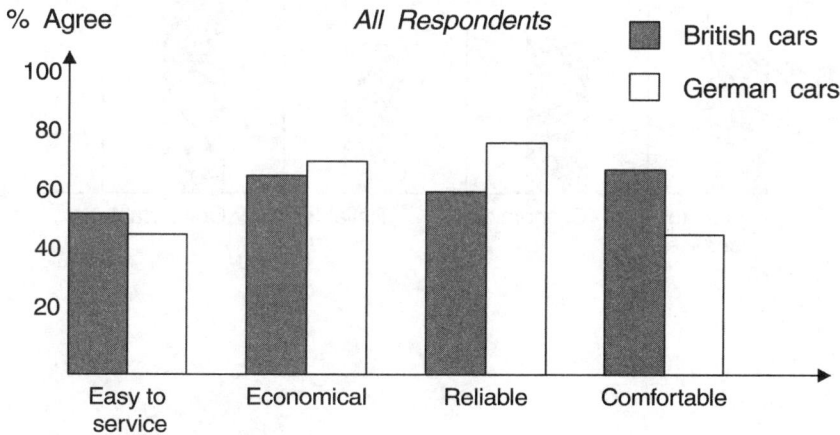

It can be seen that there is not much difference in terms of both ease of servicing and economy, but German cars seem to score more highly for reliability whereas British cars seem to be more acceptable as regards comfort.

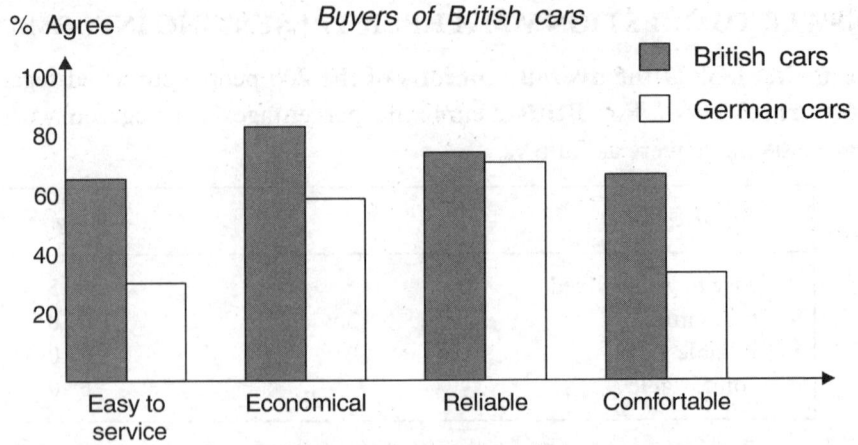

Buyers of British cars

% Agree

Looking more closely at the data, it is possible to **contrast the opinions of those respondents who bought British cars with those who bought German cars**. For the purchasers of British cars, their attitudes as regards British and German cars are represented in the following bar chart.

As would be expected, the attitudes of this group are biased towards British cars, and the only factor where British and German cars are at all close is reliability. When one looks at the purchasers of German cars, the same sort of picture emerges. As can be seen from the following bar chart, buyers of German cars favour German cars for all features except comfort where, as with reliability in the previous case, there is very little to choose between British and German cars.

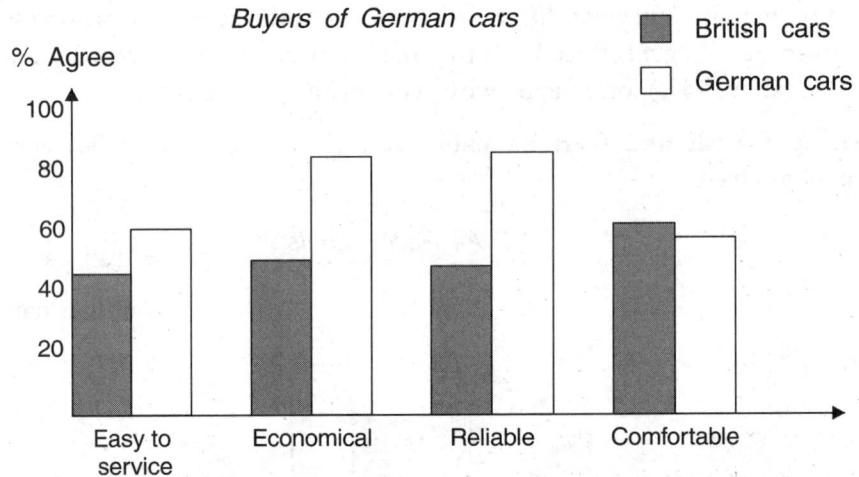

Buyers of German cars

% Agree

2   REPORT TO EMPLOYEES (6/01)

The following information is to be used as the basis for reporting sales performance in a UK company's Report to Employees.

The business is split into three regions. Of the total sales for the year of £399.0 million, 57.1% were in the UK, 31.8% in the rest of Europe and the remainder in the Rest of the World. Customers are also classified by type as either 'domestic' or 'industrial'. UK sales were divided in the ratio 2:5 (domestic: industrial). Domestic sales for the whole company were 31.0% of total sales for the year. 12.5% of total industrial sales were in the Rest of the World region.

Required

(a) Tabulate the sales revenue in as much detail as possible (to one decimal place of £m).

(5 marks)

(b) Prepare a component bar chart of the tabulated information for inclusion in the report to employees. (6 marks)

(c) Outline the features of good presentation of information in tabular or diagrammatic form. (3 marks)

(d) List the features of useful management information and identify possible links between them. (6 marks)

(20 marks)

2   ANSWER: REPORT TO EMPLOYEES

What the examiner said

This question was generally the best answered on the paper. Some candidates ignored the instructions to tabulate the figures to 1 decimal place of £1m.

(a)

Helping hand

Make sure you read a question's requirements very carefully, ie make sure that you tabulate the data in your table to the correct number of decimal places.

	Sales region		
	UK	*Rest of Europe*	*Rest of World*	*Total*
Customer type	£m	£m	£m	£m
Domestic	65.1	48.7	9.9	123.7
Industrial	162.7	78.2	34.4	275.3
	227.8	126.9	44.3	399.0

(b)

Helping hand

Make sure that you use a ruler and a sharp pencil when drawing graphs in examinations. Marks are usually awarded for presentation.

Component bar chart showing sales analysis by region

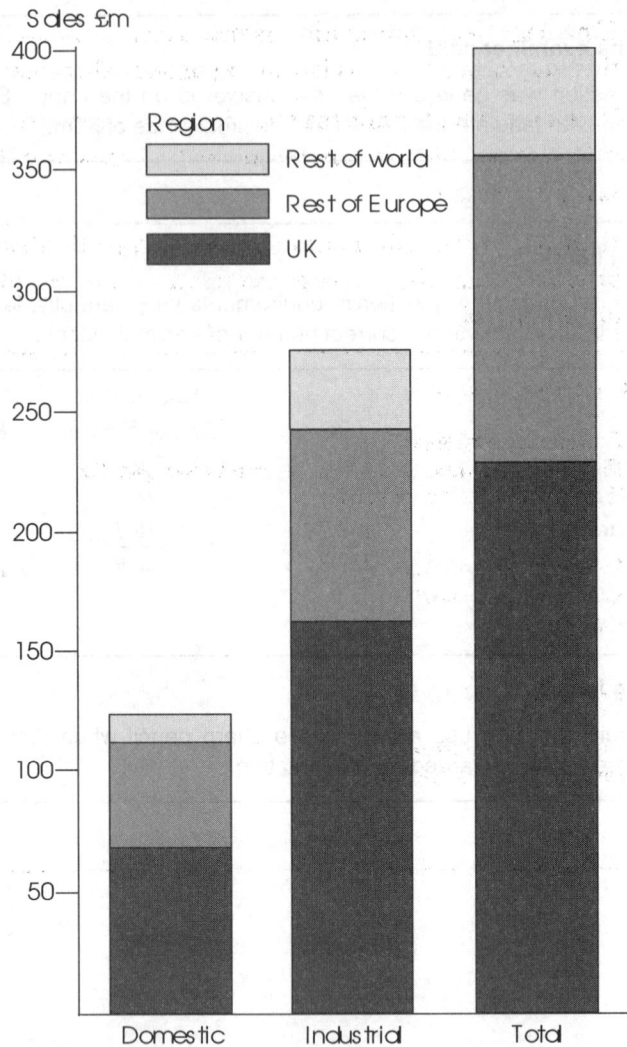

(c) **Features of good presentation of information**

- Clear title
- Clearly labelled columns/rows for tables
- Information accurately presented
- Sub totals and totals where applicable (and add up)
- Identify source of data
- Rounding – to the correct number of significant figures or decimal places
- Neat presentation

(d) **Features of useful management information**

- It should be **relevant** for its purpose
- It should be **complete** for its purpose
- It should be sufficiently **accurate** for its purpose
- It should be **clear** to the manager using it
- The manager should have **confidence** in it
- It should be **communicated** to the appropriate manager
- It should not be excessive – its volume should be **manageable**
- It should be communicated at the most **appropriate time** (timely)
- It should be communicated by an appropriate **channel of communication**
- **Value of benefits** should be greater than costs

Possible links

(i)   If management information is produced to such a high degree of accuracy, then this may mean that it is late being delivered and therefore not timely.

(ii)   If management information is 'too complete' and contains unnecessary information, then it may be so costly to produce that costs are greater than the value of benefits.

(iii)   If management information is 'too complete' then the volume of information produced may be so large so as to make it difficult to understand and/or unmanageable.

Examiner's marking scheme

		Marks	
(a)	Format/presentation	1	
	Figures calculated directly from data in the question	2	
	Figures calculated indirectly	2	
			5
(b)	General presentation	2	
	Components shown	3	
	Accuracy	1	
			6
(c)	Features (4 for max marks)		3
(d)	Features (4 for max marks)	3	
	Links (up to 1½ for each)	3	
			6
			20

---

3   QUALK LTD ALSO (12/00, amended)   *36 mins*

Qualk Ltd designs and assembles specialist personal computers (PCs) from components bought in through a single wholesaler – who buys all the individual parts from a variety of manufacturers. The industry is expanding and the specification of new models is changing rapidly, as technology and customer expectations increase. Qualk designs a new model every six months to go on sale from either January or July. Each model is sold through the company's web site for six months, at which point it is withdrawn and replaced by the next model.

During each model cycle, the purchase price of the components tends to fall significantly. Because some of the components are specific to Qualk's requirements, a single purchase order has to be placed before the start of the model cycle. It is then not possible to vary the quantity without significant penalties. The wholesaler makes up the components for delivery into minimum batches of at least 200 sets of computers. The component kits are assembled into computers in the month in which they are sold. At the end of each six-month cycle the surplus stock of PCs has to be sold quickly before the computers become totally obsolete.

The directors of Qualk Ltd are considering the future management of the company as it continues to grow. They have plans to design and offer a range of five different models. This would mean that at any one time there would be five models at different stages of their life cycles, thus reducing the peaks and troughs associated with a single model.

So far, they have employed the services of a firm of chartered certified accountants, Mallow and Scrunch, to produce the statutory accounts and to assist them in outline budgeting. A friend in the trade with a much larger company has told one of the directors that as their business grows and becomes more complex, Qualk will need both a financial accountant and a management accountant.

The managing director is confused by this suggestion as he had not previously thought there would be a need for any type of accountant. 'Now it seems I need two!' he exclaimed to Marjorie Mallow at the annual review meeting. 'It's all a conspiracy. Why do I 'need' two types of accountant? Don't they both do the same thing? In any case, what would all this accounting do for my business?' he added, with a clear sense of irritation.

Required

Assuming the role of the certified accountant, Mrs Mallow, write a report to the managing director of Qualk Ltd. Your report should include reference to the following.

(a) A table summarising the principal differences between financial accounting and management accounting   (6 marks)

(b) A description of how both financial accounting and management accounting, might be of assistance to a business such as Qualk Ltd   (8 marks)

(c) An outline of the different time periods to which management accounting information relates and an explanation of the difference between summary and detailed management information   (6 marks)

     You may find it useful to illustrate your answer with a diagram.   **(20 marks)**

3   ANSWER: QUALK LTD ALSO

What the examiner said

It appeared that many candidates did not appreciate how the emphasis of management accounting is different to financial accounting.

Helping hand

You are required to use a table in part (a). The examiner often reports that candidates use inappropriate methods of presentation: make sure you're not one of those candidates.

REPORT

To: Managing director, Qualk Ltd
From: Mrs Mallow, Certified Accountant, Mallow and Scrunch
Date: 15 December 20X0

Subject: The need for both a financial accountant and a management accountant

This report is intended to clarify the role and value of employing a management accountant now that Qualk Ltd is expanding and plans to be engaged in a more complex production pattern and offer a wider product mix.

Contents

(a)   A table summarising the principal differences between financial accounting and management accounting

(b)   A description of how both financial accounting and management accounting might be of assistance to a business such as Qualk Ltd

(c)   An outline of the different time periods to which management accounting information relates and an explanation of the difference between summary and detailed management information

(a)   **Principal differences between financial accounting and management accounting**

Characteristic	Management accounting	Financial accounting
Legal/statutory basis	None	Companies Acts/tax laws/SSAPs/FRSs
Users of the information provided	Primarily internal management	Primarily external stakeholders
Timescale/time horizon	Past, present and up to several years into the future	Entirely historic
Data	Non-financial as well as financial. Often estimated and not part of the formal accounting system	Entirely financial and contained in the accounting system
Level of detail/accuracy	Approximations and estimates are acceptable	Precise, although reports may round data to £'000, £m and so on
Operational uses	Aid to decision making, planning and control	Raising credit, monitoring debt, credit management
Strategic value	High	Low
Dynamic	Yes - adaptable to needs of the organisation	No – constrained by laws and customs

BPP
PROFESSIONAL EDUCATION

(b)   **How financial accounting and management accounting may assist a business such as Qualk Ltd**

As is clear from the table above, financial accounting and management accounting **fulfil different operational needs.**

Financial accounting

Financial accounting is supported by a **rigorous and accurate double entry system.**

(i)   This system records the business's assets, liabilities and capital.

(ii)   It forms the basis for credit control, helping to ensure that debtors meet their terms and helping to minimise bad debts.

(iii) It provides the records necessary to ensure that the business meets its obligations to creditors.

(iv)   It records the organisation's current cash position and maintains a record of stocks and fixed assets, providing a basis for their verification and acting as a deterrent to fraud.

Regular financial statements (profit and loss account, balance sheet and cash flow statement) provide management with tools for assessing the current and immediate past performance of the business.

Finally, the financial accounting system provides some of the **data** used in management accounting.

Management accounting

Management accounting provides **information for decision making, planning, control and performance appraisal.**

(i)   Decisions on pricing, investment in new assets, launching new products and cutting back or expanding operations can all be assisted by the information provided by a management accountant.

(ii)   Budgeting and budgetary control (monitoring performance against plan) can be used to formalise delegation and to appraise managers' performance.

It would be difficult to expand Qualk Ltd's business successfully or to maintain a larger product range without the insights provided by management accounting information.

(c)   **Time periods to which management accounting relates**

As noted in (a) above, management accounting concentrates on the **immediate past** (how much did our products cost to make, how much profit did we make?) and on the **future.**

(i)   Comparisons between actual and budgeted results will, typically, be made on a monthly basis and will cover past periods of at most one year.

(ii)   Immediate forecasts which are used for short-term planning will cover one to three months into the future.

(iii) Medium-term plans and budgets will, typically, cover one to three years.

(iv)   Longer-term strategic management accounting will look as far into the future as may be required by the business. Some businesses may regard two years as long term (consumer products), while others concerned with infrastructure, pharmaceuticals and so on will have ten- to fifteen-year planning horizons. Qualk Ltd would benefit from a two- to five- year forward plan.

Level of detail in information

The level of detail in management accounting information will **decrease** both the **higher the recipient of the information** is within the organisation and the **further it looks into the future.**

(i)   Short-term standard costing reports monitoring the performance of sections of the manufacturing shop floor may be very detailed.

(ii)   Monthly summaries and long-term forecasts provided to top management will be summarised to provide just the key information required.

The aim of management accounting is to **provide information in a form and at a level of detail appropriate to its purpose and to the user.**

Examiner's marking scheme

		Marks
(a) Differences between financial and management accounting		
- 4 differences (both sides shown) (1½ marks × 4)		6
(b) 2 marks each aspect	to 4	
Report format	to 1	
Reference to Qualk scenario	to 3	
		8
(c) Timing of management information		
- past v future	to 3	
- summary v detail	to 3	
		6
		20

DO YOU KNOW? - COST ACCUMULATION

- *Check that you can fill in the blanks in the statements below before you attempt any questions. If in doubt, you should go back to your BPP Interactive Text and revise first.*

- Absorption costing involves three steps.

   - ....
   - ....
   - ....

- Apportionment involves two stages.

   - The apportionment of .... overheads (using bases of apportionment such as floor area for rent and rates)
   - The apportionment of .... overheads (using bases of apportionment such as (for the stores department) number of materials requisitions)

- Service department overheads can be apportioned using one of the following methods.

   - ....
   - ....
   - ....

- Overheads are absorbed into products using an absorption rate (estimated overhead divided by budgeted activity level). ....-absorbed overhead will occur when overheads incurred are less than overheads absorbed. ....-absorbed overhead will occur when overheads incurred are greater than overheads absorbed. ....-absorbed overhead is added to profit, ...-absorbed overhead is deducted from profit.

- Activity based costing (ABC) is an alternative to the traditional absorption costing approach. ABC involves the identification of the factors which cause the costs of an organisation's major activities to change. These factors are known as ....Support overheads are charged to products on the basis of their usage of an activity.

- When using ABC, for costs that vary with production levels in the short term, the cost driver will be volume related (labour or machine hours). Overheads that vary with some other activity (and not volume of production) should be traced to products using transaction-based cost drivers such as ....

- In marginal costing, only ....costs are charged to the cost of making a product or providing a service. Fixed costs are deducted from ....and are written off in the period incurred without being absorbed into product/service costs.

- In marginal costing, stocks are valued at .... cost whereas in absorption costing they are valued at .... cost and hence, if the opening and closing stock levels differ, the profit reported for the accounting period under the two methods will be different. In the long run, however, total profit will be the same whatever method is used.

- The difference between absorption costing and marginal costing profits = ...

- There are arguments for and against both costing methods. Although either can be used for internal purposes, ... costing must be used for external reporting.

   TRY QUESTIONS 4 – 8

- *Possible pitfalls*

   Write down the mistakes you know you should avoid.

DID YOU KNOW? - COST ACCUMULATION

- *Could you fill in the blanks? The answers are in bold. Use this page for revision purposes as you approach the exam.*

- Absorption costing involves three steps.

  - **Allocation**
  - **Apportionment**
  - **Absorption**

- Apportionment involves two stages.

  - The apportionment of **general** overheads (using bases of apportionment such as floor area for rent and rates)
  - The apportionment of **service department** overheads (using bases of apportionment such as (for the stores department) number of materials requisitions)

- Service department overheads can be apportioned using one of the following methods.

  - **Directly**
  - **Using the repeated distribution (continuous allotment) method**
  - **Using algebra**

- Overheads are absorbed into products using an absorption rate (estimated overhead divided by budgeted activity level). **Over**-absorbed overhead will occur when overheads incurred are less than overheads absorbed. **Under**-absorbed overhead will occur when overheads incurred are greater than overheads absorbed. **Over**-absorbed overhead is added to profit, **under**-absorbed overhead is deducted from profit.

- Activity based costing (ABC) is an alternative to the traditional absorption costing approach. ABC involves the identification of the factors which cause the costs of an organisation's major activities to change. These factors are known as **cost drivers**. Support overheads are charged to products on the basis of their usage of an activity.

- When using ABC, for costs that vary with production levels in the short term, the cost driver will be volume related (labour or machine hours). Overheads that vary with some other activity (and not volume of production) should be traced to products using transaction-based cost drivers such as **number of production runs or number of orders received.**

- In marginal costing, only **variable** costs are charged to the cost of making a product or providing a service. Fixed costs are deducted from **contribution** and are written off in the period incurred without being absorbed into product/service costs.

- In marginal costing, stocks are valued at **variable production** cost whereas in absorption costing they are valued at **full production** cost and hence, if the opening and closing stock levels differ, the profit reported for the accounting period under the two methods will be different. In the long run, however, total profit will be the same whatever method is used.

- The difference between absorption costing and marginal costing profits = **change in stock level × overhead absorbed per unit**.

- There are arguments for and against both costing methods. Although either can be used for internal purposes, **absorption** costing must be used for external reporting.

TRY QUESTIONS 4 – 8

- *Possible pitfalls*

  - **Including direct costs in the costs to be apportioned and absorbed**

  - **Using an activity level other than the normal level of activity when calculating absorption rates**

  - **Being unclear on how to reconcile absorption costing and marginal costing profits**

4   ENGINEERING COMPANY (6/01)

(a)   Describe briefly the reasons for the development of activity-based costing.   (4 marks)

An engineering company is in the process of preparing production overhead budgets and apportioning the overheads to products, where feasible, using activity-based costing (ABC).

There are two production centres (machining and assembly) and one service centre (maintenance) in the factory.

Budgeted production overhead costs (£) are as follows.

	Total £	Machining £	Assembly £	Maintenance £
Indirect labour	96,176	34,338	32,058	29,780
Maintenance materials	17,792	16,475	1,317	
Power	16,800			
Machine depreciation	77,300	72,000	5,300	
Other indirect materials	11,600	9,200	2,400	
Rent and rates	32,600			
Buildings insurance	5,120			
Heat and light	6,780			

The following additional information is provided to enable the ABC analysis to be carried out.

(i)   Indirect labour, in each production centre, comprises the following separate activities.

Machining	£	
Setting-up	25,525	(424 set-ups)
Inspection	8,813	(1,360 inspection hours)
	34,338	

Assembly	£	
Component handling	17,136	(180 batches)
Inspection	14,922	(180 batches)
	32,058	

Each of the bracketed items above indicates the key driver of that particular activity's costs.

(ii)   The proportion of the maintenance centre indirect labour cost relating to each production centre is:

Machining	85%
Assembly	15%

(iii)   Power usage is:

Machining	89%
Assembly	11%

(iv)   The total maintenance costs of each production centre (ie maintenance materials plus a share of maintenance centre indirect labour) are put into cost pools, along with the cost of power and machine depreciation, all driven by the machine usage of:

Machining	14,730 machine hours
Assembly	1,060 machine hours

(v)   The key driver of 'other indirect materials' costs, in each of the production centres, is the value of direct materials used (which totals £340,000).

(vi)   Space costs (rent and rates, buildings insurance, and heat and light) are **not** to be included in the ABC analysis as there is no causal link with final products.

Required

(b)   Determine activity-based production overhead absorption rates (eg a cost per set-up in the machining centre).   (11 marks)

The following information relates to the manufacture of 1,000 units of Product X, one of the engineering company's products:

Direct materials	£3,700

Machining	75 machine hours
	14 set-ups
	60 inspection hours
Assembly	50 machine hours
	10 batches

(c)   *Required*

Determine the production overhead cost of Product X (£ per 1,000 units).   (5 marks)

(20 marks)

4   ANSWER: ENGINEERING COMPANY

What the examiner said

According to the examiner, part (a) was rarely well-answered with many candidates describing how activity based costing operates rather than the reasons for its development and use. In part (b) many candidates ignored the absorption of 'other indirect materials'. In part (c) a common mistake was to include the direct materials at cost as part of the production overheads.

(a) **Reasons for the development of ABC**

Absorption costing was developed at a time when most organisations produced only a narrow range of products and when overhead costs were only a small fraction of total costs. Total costs were mainly composed of **direct labour** and **direct material** costs. As such, under- and over-absorbed overheads were relatively insignificant.

These days, however, overheads are generally far more important. Manufacturing industries are now more complex and automated with more broad ranges of products being produced and heavier reliance on service departments.

- Direct labour may account for as little as 5% of a product's cost
- Computers allow for sophisticated overhead allocation methods, such as ABC

In today's business environment, it is difficult to justify the use of direct labour or direct material as the basis of allocating overheads. It is for this reason that ABC has developed.

(b)

Helping hand

Remember to set out your workings clearly so that it is obvious how you have calculated the activity-based overhead absorption rates in your answer.

ACTIVITY-BASED OVERHEAD ABSORPTION RATES

	Units	*Machining* £	*Units*	*Assembly* £
Indirect labour				
Set-up costs (W1)	Per set-up	60.20		
Inspection costs (W2)	Per inspection hour	6.48	Per batch	82.90
Component handling costs (W3)			Per batch	95.20
Maintenance (W4)	Per machine hour	8.74	Per machine hour	12.20
Other indirect materials (W5)	Per £/direct material	0.027	Per £/direct material	0.007

Workings

1   **Indirect labour set-up costs – Machining department**

$$\frac{\text{Set - up costs}}{\text{Number of set - ups}} = \frac{£25,525}{424 \text{ set - ups}}$$

$$= £60.20 \text{ per set-up}$$

2   **Indirect labour inspection costs – Machining department**

$$\frac{\text{Inspection costs}}{\text{Number of inspection hours}} = \frac{£8,813}{1,360 \text{ inspection hours}}$$

$$= £6.48 \text{ per inspection hour}$$

Indirect labour inspection costs – Assembly department

$$\frac{\text{Inspection costs}}{\text{Number of batches}} = \frac{£14,922}{180 \text{ batches}}$$

$$= £82.90 \text{ per batch}$$

3 **Indirect labour component handling costs – Assembly department**

$$\frac{\text{Component handling costs}}{\text{Number of batches}} = \frac{£17,136}{180 \text{ batches}}$$

$$= £95.20 \text{ per batch}$$

4 **Maintenance**

Maintenance costs relevant to Machining department

	£
Materials	16,475
Labour (85% × £29,780)	25,313
Power (89% × £16,800)	14,952
Machine depreciation	72,000
Cost pool total	128,740

$$\text{Overhead absorption rate} = \frac{\text{Cost pool total}}{\text{Total machine hours}}$$

$$= \frac{£128,740}{14,730 \text{ machine hours}}$$

$$= £8.74 \text{ per machine hour}$$

Maintenance costs relevant to Assembly department

	£
Materials	1,317
Labour (15% × £29,780)	4,467
Power (11% × £16,800)	1,848
Machine depreciation	5,300
Cost pool total	12,932

$$\text{Overhead absorption rate} = \frac{\text{Cost pool total}}{\text{Total machine hours}}$$

$$= \frac{£12,932}{1,060 \text{ machine hours}}$$

$$= £12.20 \text{ per machine hour}$$

5 **Other indirect materials**

The key driver of 'other indirect materials' costs in each of the production centres is the value of direct materials used which is £340,000 as stated in the question.

Machining department

$$\frac{£9,200}{£340,000} = £0.027 \text{ per £ direct material}$$

Assembly department

$$\frac{£2,400}{£340,000} = £0.007 \text{ per £ direct material}$$

Note. The question states that space costs (rent and rates, buildings insurance and heat and light) are not to be included in the ABC analysis.

(c)

> **Helping hand**
>
> The ABC process tested in parts (b) and (c) of this question was explained and illustrated in an article in the ACCA *Technician Bulletin* in August 2000. Make sure that you review the relevant journals for articles by the examiner and take note of what he has to say.

PRODUCT X
PRODUCTION OVERHEAD COST

	Machining £	*Per 1,000 units* Assembly £	Total £
Indirect labour			
Set-up costs (W1)	843		843
Inspection costs (W2)	389	829	1,218
Component handling costs (W3)		952	952
Maintenance (W4)	656	610	1,266
Other indirect materials (W5)	100	26	126
	1,988	2,417	4,405

Workings

1 **Indirect labour set-up costs**

   Machining

   £60.20 × 14 set-ups   = £842.80
                              = £843 (to the nearest £)

2 **Indirect labour – inspection costs**

   Machining

   £6.48 × 60 inspection hours = £388.80
                              = £389 (to the nearest £)

   Assembly

   £82.9 × 10 batches   = £829 (to the nearest £)

3 **Indirect labour – component handling costs**

   Assembly

   £95.20 × 10 batches   = £952 (to the nearest £)

4 **Maintenance**

   Machining

   £8.74 × 75 machine hours   = £655.50
                              = £656 (to the nearest £)

   Assembly

   £12.20 × 50 machine hours = £610

5 **Other indirect materials**

   Machining

   £0.027 × £3,700   = £99.9
                              = £100 (per £ direct materials)

Assembly

£0.007 × £3,700   = £25.90

= £26 (per £ direct materials)

Examiner's marking scheme			**Marks**	
(a)	Limitations of traditional approach		2	
	Increased significance of overheads		2	
				4
(b)	Apportionment of maintenance labour & power		2	
	Absorption rates:	indirect labour, machining	3	
		indirect labour, assembly	3	
		other indirect materials	1	
		maintenance	2	
				11
(c)	Product overhead cost:	indirect labour	2	
		other indirect materials	1	
		maintenance etc	1	
		total	1	
				5
				20

5   QUESTION WITH HELP: MARGINAL COSTING AND ABSORPTION COSTING

Your firm manufactures and sells a single product - Product Delta.

	Product Delta per unit
Selling price	£30
Direct costs	£8

Details for the months of September and October are as follows.

	September	*October*
Production of Delta	750 units	1,000 units
Sales of Delta	600 units	1,150 units
Fixed production overheads	£4,500	£4,500

The normal level of activity for both sales and production is 900 units per month. Fixed production overheads are budgeted as £4,500 per month and are absorbed on a unit basis. There are no opening stocks.

Required

As accounts assistant, you have been asked to do the following.

(a)   Prepare for September and October profit statements showing stock valuations, based on the following principles.

    (i)   Absorption costing
    (ii)   Marginal costing   (12 marks)

(b)   Briefly comment on your results.   (4 marks)

(c)   State and explain three business situations where the use of marginal costing may be beneficial to management in making a decision.   (4 marks)

                                                                                                             (20 marks)

If you are stuck, look at the next page for detailed help as to how you should tackle this question.

APPROACHING THE ANSWER

Step 1. *Draw up proforma profit statements*

Profit statements using absorption costing

	September		October	
	£	£	£	£
Sales revenue				
Cost of goods sold				
Opening stock				
Direct cost				
Fixed production overhead				
Less closing stock				
Under-/(over-) absorbed prod o/h				
Profit				

Profit statements using marginal costing

	September		October	
	£	£	£	£
Sales revenue				
Variable cost of goods sold				
Opening stock				
Direct costs				
Less closing stock				
Contribution				
Fixed production overhead				
Profit				

Step 2. *Calculate the fixed overhead absorption rate.*
This is calculated as fixed production overheads ÷ *normal* level of activity

Step 3. *Calculate the absorption costing stock valuation.*
Units of product Delta are valued at full cost (direct cost per unit plus fixed production overhead absorbed per unit (from step 2)) = £   + £   = £
Use this figure to value each month's opening and closing stock.

Step 4. *Calculate the fixed production overhead absorbed each month*
This is calculated as the number of units produced in the month multiplied by the fixed production overhead absorption rate per unit (from Step 2).

Step 5. *Calculate the under-/over-absorbed overhead each month*
This is the difference between overhead incurred and overhead absorbed. If overhead incurred is greater than overhead absorbed we have under-absorbed overhead and the difference is deducted from profit. We have done September's calculation for you: overhead incurred - overhead absorbed = £4,500 - £3,750 = £750 under-absorbed overhead.

Step 6. *Calculate the marginal costing stock valuation.*
Units of product Omega are valued at variable cost (ie direct cost).Use this figure to value each month's opening and closing stock.

Step 7. *Deal with fixed production overheads in the marginal costing profit statement*
Overheads *incurred* are deducted from contribution.

Step 8. Your commentary in part (b) should explain why the monthly profits using the two methods are different.

Step 9. For part (c) think about some of the decision-making scenarios covered in the chapter on decision making in the BPP Interactive Text.

5   ANSWER TO QUESTION WITH HELP: MARGINAL COSTING AND ABSORPTION COSTING

(a) (i)   **Profit statements using absorption costing**

	September		October	
	£	£	£	£
Sales revenue		18,000		34,500
Cost of goods sold				
Opening stock	-		1,950	
Direct cost	6,000		8,000	
Fixed production overhead (W3)	3,750		5,000	
	9,750		14,950	
Less closing stock (W2)	1,950		-	
	7,800		14,950	
Under-/(over-) absorbed production o/h	750		(500)	
		8,550		14,450
Profit		9,450		20,050

Workings

(1) Fixed overhead absorption rate $= \dfrac{£4,500}{900 \text{ units}} = £5$ per unit

(2) September closing stocks $= (750 - 600) \times (£5 + £8) = £1,950$

(3) Fixed production overhead = September $750 \times £5 = £3,750$
       October $1,000 \times £5 = £5,000$

(ii)   **Profit statements using marginal costing**

	September		October	
	£	£	£	£
Sales revenue		18,000		34,500
Variable cost of goods sold				
Opening stock	-		1,200	
Direct costs	6,000		8,000	
	6,000		9,200	
Less closing stock (150 × £8)	1,200		-	
		4,800		9,200
Contribution		13,200		25,300
Fixed production overhead		4,500		4,500
Profit		8,700		20,800

(b) Since opening and closing stocks are both zero, the total profit over the two months is the same under both methods.

In September the **profit was £750 higher when the absorption costing method was used**. This is **because of the fixed production overhead carried forward in the September closing stock** = 150 units × £5. This cost is charged to October when the units are actually sold and the comparative profit position is then reversed.

(c) Three business **situations where the use of marginal costing may be beneficial** to management **in making a decision** are as follows.

(i)   Deciding whether to **buy components from an external manufacturer or to manufacture them internally.** Very often it is only the variable costs which are relevant to the decision, since fixed cost may be incurred anyway.

(ii)   Deciding **whether to discontinue a product** which is apparently unprofitable. As long as a product is making a contribution it may be worth continuing it, even though it is not covering its fair 'share' of fixed overheads. These fixed overheads would not be saved if the product was discontinued, but the contribution would be lost.

(iii) Deciding **which products to manufacture in order to optimise the use of a limited resource**. The general decision rule is to allocate the resource to those products which earn the highest contribution per unit of the limiting factor.

6   ZBD (6/99)   *36 mins*

ZBD has two production departments, cutting and assembly, that are supported by a further two service departments, stores and maintenance. Both of the service departments undertake work for each other as well as for the production departments. The costs of the service departments are recharged as follows.

	Cutting %	Assembly %	Stores %	Maintenance %
Stores charged to	40	30	-	30
Maintenance charged to	70	20	10	-

Cost information for period seven was as follows.

	Cutting £	Assembly £	Stores £	Maintenance £
Actual overhead	77,000	99,000	125,000	50,000

	Cutting (Machine hours)	Assembly (Direct labour hours)
Budgeted overhead*	£180,000	£156,000
Budgeted activity	7,200 hours	48,000 hours
Actual activity	7,030 hours	52,580 hours

★ After recharges

Required

(a) Calculate the total actual overhead for both the cutting and the assembly departments in period seven, after apportionment of the two service departments using the repeated distribution method (show workings to the nearest £). (6 marks)

(b) Calculate the predetermined absorption rates for the cutting and assembly departments. (2 marks)

(c) Prepare the overhead (control) accounts for the cutting and the assembly departments for period seven, showing any under or over absorption of overhead.

Show all your workings. (6 marks)

(d) The managing director has recently attended a conference at which a speaker suggested that when activity levels are fluctuating it is better to use a marginal costing system.

Briefly explain *three* benefits of continuing to use an absorption costing system.

(6 marks)

(20 marks)

Helping hand

This is a fairly **straightforward** question.

Note in part (a) that you need to show **working to the nearest £**. The examiner has noted in his report that candidates often lose marks because they don't present their answers correctly.

You will have used control accounts (part (c)) in your earlier studies. Remember that you can check if you've prepared them correctly if **both sides of the account balance.**

Part (d) asks for **three benefits**. Not two. Not four. Three.

---

6   ANSWER: ZBD

> **What the examiner said**
>
> Most candidates achieved full marks in part (a). In part (c), however, there was much confusion over the entries for work in progress. Many candidates debited the accounts with the budgeted overheads rather than the actual overhead incurred and calculation of the amount of under-/over-absorbed overhead caused problems.
>
> Many candidates struggled with part (d) despite the fact that a key part of the syllabus requires candidates to be able to appreciate the appropriateness of various costing methods in different situations.

(a)

> **Helping hand**
>
> In order to calculate the total actual overhead for the two production departments, we need to apportion the stores and maintenance costs to the other departments, **taking account of the reciprocal servicing**. We are told to use the **repeated distribution method** to do this. It **does not matter which service department you apportion first**. The final result should be the same.

	Cutting	Assembly	Stores	Maintenance
	£	£	£	£
Actual overhead	77,000	99,000	125,000	50,000
Apportion stores costs	50,000	37,500	(125,000)	37,500
			0	87,500
Apportion maintenance costs	61,250	17,500	8,750	(87,500)
			8,750	0
Apportion stores costs	3,500	2,625	(8,750)	2,625
			0	2,625
Apportion maintenance costs	1,838	525	262	(2,625)
			262	0
Apportion stores costs	104	79	(262)	79
			0	79
Apportion maintenance costs	55	16	8	(79)
			8	0
Apportion stores costs	3	3	(8)	2
			0	2
Apportion maintenance costs	1	1	0	(2)
Total actual overhead	193,751	157,249		

> **Helping hand**
>
> You will notice that some of our figures were approximated in order to arrive at the correct total overhead with each apportionment. **Your decision on roundings may have been different** and hence you might have a slightly different (but perfectly acceptable) final answer.

(b)

> **Helping hand**
>
> Remember that **predetermined overhead absorption rates** are **always based on budgeted data**, never on actual data.

$$\text{Predetermined overhead absorption rate} = \frac{\text{budgeted overhead}}{\text{budgeted activity}}$$

	Cutting		*Assembly*
Overhead absorption rate	$= \dfrac{£180,000}{7,200 \text{ hours}}$		$= \dfrac{£156,000}{48,000 \text{ hours}}$
	$= £25$ per machine hour		$= £3.25$ per direct labour hour

(c)

> **Helping hand**
>
> The **overhead control accounts** act as a sort of 'collecting place' for the **actual overheads incurred**, which are **debited** to the account. The **overheads absorbed** are then **transferred out to work in progress based on actual activity.** The balance on the account is then the overhead under or over absorbed in the period. A **debit balance** indicates **over absorption** (more overhead absorbed than incurred), a **credit balance** indicates **under absorption**. The first thing to calculate is the overhead absorbed in each department.

Cutting department overhead absorbed	$= 7,030$ machine hours $\times £25$
	$= £175,750$

Assembly department overhead absorbed	$= 52,580$ labour hours $\times £3.25$
	$= £170,885$

CUTTING DEPARTMENT OVERHEAD CONTROL ACCOUNT

	£		£
Actual overhead	193,751	Work in progress	175,750
		Under-absorbed overhead	18,001
	193,751		193,751

ASSEMBLY DEPARTMENT OVERHEAD CONTROL ACCOUNT

	£		£
Actual overhead	157,249	Work in progress	170,885
Over-absorbed overhead	13,636		
	170,885		170,885

(d) Three **benefits of continuing to use an absorption costing system** are as follows.

(i) In order to **comply with SSAP 9 for external profit reporting,** stocks must be valued at full production cost and absorption costing must therefore be used. Although compliance with accounting standards is not a requirement for internal reporting, the use of absorption costing for internal reporting as well as for external reporting can avoid the potential confusion that could arise from the existence of two different profit reporting systems.

(ii) Selling prices based on marginal costing might enable the organisation to earn a contribution on each unit of product or service, but the total contribution earned might be insufficient to cover all fixed costs. With absorption costing, the use of full cost ensures that **managers are aware of the total unit cost when determining selling prices.**

(iii) **Fixed costs** are a **significant** part of total costs, particularly in the modern manufacturing environment. In order to carry out the manufacturing process they must be incurred. They should therefore logically be **included in stock valuations** because marginal costing may imply that fixed costs are not a relevant part of production cost.

Examiner's marking scheme

			Marks
(a)	Apportionment of overheads		
	Application of repeated distribution methodology		to 2
	Correct treatment of service departments (× 1 mark each)		to 2
	Correct totals for production departments (× 1 mark each)		to 2
			6
(b)	Calculation of predetermined rates (2 depts × 1 mark each)		2
(c)	Preparation of two overhead accounts (× 3 marks as follows)		
	Overhead incurred	- 1 mark	to 2
	Work in progress	- 1 mark	to 2
	Under-/over-absorbed overhead	- 1 mark	to 2
			6
(d)	Three reasons for using absorption costing (× 2 marks each)		6
			20

7   WALK-TALK (12/99)   *36 mins*

Walk-talk manufactures a cordless telephone system. At the beginning of the financial year ending 30 November 20X9, the firm planned to make and sell 50,000 units of its only product, the Nova, at a selling price of £30.00 per unit. Information on standard costs used in the preparation of the budget is as follows.

	£
Direct materials	4.00 per unit
Direct labour	6.00 per unit

Fixed production overheads for the year were estimated at £800,000, to be absorbed on the basis of the number of units produced. There are no variable overheads.

Fixed selling and administration expenses were estimated at £100,000, to be absorbed on the basis of the number of units sold.

At the beginning of the year (1 December 20X8) there were no units in stock and no units were budgeted to be in stock at the end of the year (30 November 20X9).

Situation as at 1 December 20X9

The market for cordless telephones has changed rapidly over the course of the past year. In response to competitive pressures, Walk-talk has had to make a number of changes both to the operating programmes within the Nova model and the range of colours available. There are now three different versions of the Nova available in a choice of eight different colours.

During the year the cost of materials and direct labour per unit has been incurred in line with standard costs, although production overheads incurred during the year have risen to £830,000, due to a higher than expected rent review for the factory. Selling and administration costs were as budget. Production exceeded budget with 52,000 units being made. However, despite the changes in product specification, sales have only reached 45,000 units with 7,000 units of finished systems remaining in stock on 30 November 20X9. There was no stock of work in progress at the year end.

Stocks of finished goods are to be valued on the basis of the standard cost of production.

Required

(a) Prepare a budgeted profit and loss account for Walk-talk for the year ending 30 November 20X9, using an absorption costing basis.   (3 marks)

(b) Prepare the actual profit and loss account for the year ended 30 November 20X9, using the following two methods.

    (i)   Absorption costing   (4 marks)
    (ii)   Marginal costing   (4 marks)

(c) Compare the budgeted profit with the actual profit and explain the reasons for any differences occurring. Your answer should include reference to the effect of sales and overhead variances on the difference between the following.

    (i)   The budget and the actual profits on the absorption basis   (3 marks)
    (ii)   The budget and the actual profits on the marginal costing basis   (3 marks)

(d) State any concerns you may have about valuing the finished stock of telephones at the year end (30 November 20X9).   (3 marks)

(20 marks)

Helping hand

Read the requirements carefully.

- Part (a) asks for a **budgeted P & L account** for year ending 30/11/X9 using **absorption costing.**

- Part (b) asks for an **actual P & L account** for year ending 30/11/X9 using **marginal and absorption costing.**

Try to think how budgeted and actual P & L accounts might differ using absorption costing. Here's a **hint**: think about the **difference between sales and production.**

For part (d) think about the fact that actual **sales** have fallen way **short of budget** yet there has been **an increase in production.**

7   ANSWER: WALK-TALK

> **What the examiner said**
>
> There was a wide range of marks achieved on this question. Many candidates were able to work through the three versions of the P & L statements but few were able to suggest that a cautious approach should be taken to stock valuation in (d).

(a)

> **Helping hand**
>
> Because budgeted sales equals budgeted production, there is **no under- or over-absorbed overhead** and absorption costing profit equals marginal costing profit.

**BUDGETED PROFIT AND LOSS ACCOUNT
YEAR ENDING 30 NOVEMBER 20X9**

	£'000	£'000
Sales (50,000 × £30)		1,500
Cost of goods sold		
Direct materials (50,000 × £4)	200	
Direct labour (50,000 × £6)	300	
Fixed production overheads	800	
		1,300
Gross profit		200
Selling and administration expenses		100
Net profit		100

(b)   (i)

> **Helping hand**
>
> Notice that **selling and administration expenses are absorbed on the basis of units sold**.

**PROFIT AND LOSS ACCOUNT (ABSORPTION COSTING)
YEAR ENDED 30 NOVEMBER 20X9**

	£'000	£'000
Sales (45,000 × £30)		1,350
Cost of goods sold		
Opening stock	-	
Direct materials (52,000 × £4)	208	
Direct labour (52,000 × £6)	312	
Fixed production overheads absorbed		
(52,000 × £16 (W1))	832	
	1,352	
Less closing stock (7,000 × £26 (W2))	(182)	
	1,170	
Over-absorbed fixed production overhead (W3)	(2)	
		1,168
Gross profit		182
Selling and admin expenses absorbed (45,000 × £2 (W4))	90	
Under-absorbed selling and admin expenses (W5)	10	
		100
Net profit		82

Workings

1   Fixed production overhead absorption rate per unit = £800,000/50,000 = £16

2   *Standard cost of production per unit*

	£
Direct materials	4
Direct labour	6
Fixed production overhead (W1)	16
	26

3   *Fixed production overhead*

	£
Overhead absorbed (see profit and loss account)	832,000
Over-absorbed overhead	2,000

4   Fixed selling and administration expenses absorption rate per unit = £100,000/50,000 = £2.

5   *Selling and admin expenses*

	£
Overhead absorbed (see profit and loss account)	90,000
Overhead incurred	100,000
Under-absorbed overhead	10,000

(ii)

> **Helping hand**
>
> A marginal costing profit and loss account should show clearly the **variable cost of goods sold, contribution earned** and **fixed costs**. There is **no under- or over-absorption** of overhead.

PROFIT AND LOSS ACCOUNT (MARGINAL COSTING)
YEAR ENDED 30 NOVEMBER 20X9

	£'000	£'000
Sales (45,000 × £30)		1,350
Variable cost of goods sold		
Opening stock	-	
Direct materials (52,000 × £4)	208	
Direct labour (52,000 × £6)	312	
	520	
Less closing stock (7,000 × £(4 + 6))	(70)	
		450
Contribution		900
Fixed production overhead		(830)
Gross profit		70
Fixed selling and administration expenses		100
Net loss		(30)

(c)

> **Helping hand**
>
> To determine the reasons for the differences between the profit figures you need to **compare all budgeted costs and volumes** with **all actual costs and volumes** and then **determine the variances** which will arise as a result of the differences. A difference between budgeted and actual material cost per unit, for example, would have led to a material variance. The question gives you a big hint, however, in asking you to refer to **sales** and **overhead** variances.

(i)   **Difference between budget and actual profits on an absorption basis**

There are a number of reasons why there is a difference in the two profit figures.

(1) The **actual sales volume** was **5,000 units less than budgeted**. This will cause an adverse sales volume variance of £20,000 (indicating a loss of profit of £2 per unit and an under absorption of selling and admin costs of £2 per unit for each of the 5,000 units).

Sales volume variance

Budgeted sales volume	50,000	units
Actual sales volume	45,000	units
Variance in units	5,000	units (A)
× standard margin per unit		
(£(30 – 26 (from (b)(i) (W2)))	× £4	
	£20,000	(A)

(2) The **actual production volume** was **2,000 units greater than budgeted**. This will cause a favourable fixed production overhead volume variance (indicating that £32,000 of overheads have been carried forward in the value of stock).

Fixed production overhead volume variance

Budgeted volume	50,000	units
Actual volume	52,000	units
	2,000	units (F)
× absorption rate per unit (from (b)(i) (W1))	× £16	
	£32,000	(F)

(3) The **actual fixed production overhead** incurred was **£30,000 greater than budgeted** (increase in factory rent). This will cause an adverse fixed production overhead expenditure variance.

Fixed production overhead expenditure variance

	£
Budgeted expenditure	800,000
Actual expenditure	830,000
	30,000 (A)

Reconciliation between budgeted and actual absorption costing profits

	£'000		£'000
Budgeted profit			100
Variances			
Sales volume	20	(A)	
Overhead volume	32	(F)	
Overhead expenditure	30	(A)	
			18 (A)
Actual profit			82

(ii)

Helping hand

Remember to **value the sales volume variance at standard variable cost margin**. There are **no overhead volume variances** in a marginal costing system.

Difference between budget and actual profits on a marginal basis

(1) The **actual sales volume** was **5,000 units less than budgeted**. This will cause an adverse sales volume variance, this time of £100,000 due to the fact that a contribution of £20 per unit is lost on each of the 5,000 units.

Sales volume variance

Variance in units (from (c)(i))	5,000 units	(A)
× standard margin per unit (£30 – (4 + 6))	× £20	
	£100,000	(A)

(2) The **actual fixed production overhead incurred** was **£30,000 greater than budgeted** (due to the increase in factory rent).

Fixed production overhead expenditure variance

As (c)(i)	£30,000	(A)

Reconciliation between budgeted and actual marginal costing profits

	£'000		£'000
Budgeted profit			100
Variances			
Sales volume	100	(A)	
Overhead expenditure	30	(A)	
			130 (A)
Actual loss			(30)

(d)

Helping hand

You have not yet needed to rely on or refer to the **information about the market for cordless telephones** and so, unless the examiner has planted a red herring, you probably need to consider it in this part of the question.

There are a number of problems associated with the valuation of the finished stock of telephones at the year end.

(1)   **Obsolescence.** The cordless telephone market is changing rapidly and there is no guarantee that there will be consumer demand for the version/colour of units in stock. They may need to be sold at less than the current price of £30 or may even have to be scrapped.

(2)   **Appropriate valuation.** The valuation of the units (standard cost) does not reflect the actual production costs during the year, given that fixed production costs were higher than anticipated. If there is demand for the units, they have been undervalued.

(3)   **Different versions.** It may be inappropriate to give the same value to each version/colour of phone. If closing stock is made up of version 1 of the Nova, these may only have a scrap value. Version 3 in colour 4 may have a value in excess of standard cost.

(4)   **Absorption costing v marginal costing.** It may be more appropriate to value the stock at marginal cost given the potential obsolescence problem.

Examiner's marking scheme

					Marks
(a)		Budgeted profit and loss account			
		- prime cost			to 1
		- total cost			to 1
		- sales and profit (½ mark each)			to 1
					3
(b)	(i)	Actual profit and loss account – absorption costing			
		- production cost			to 1
		- overheads			to 1
		- sales			to 1
		- profit			to 1
					4
	(ii)	Actual profit and loss account – marginal costing			
		- variable costs			to 1
		- contribution			to 1
		- selling and administration expenses			to 1
		- profit			to 1
					4
(c)		Reconciliation and comment			
	(i)	Budget and absorption costing	- reconciliation		to 2
			- comment		to 1
	(ii)	Budget and marginal costing	- reconciliation		to 2
			- comment		to 1
					6
(d)		Concerns regarding finished stock			3
					20

8   RANGE OF PRODUCTS (12/01)

A company which manufactures a range of products, has decided to introduce a product costing system.

Required

(a) Compare and contrast, the use of absorption and marginal costing methods to establish product costs and profit.   (7 marks)

The following data is available for the previous four periods.

	Period 1	Period 2	Period 3	Period 4
Total costs (£)	190,760	224,020	236,100	255,600
Total output (units)	64,200	79,350	80,170	85,620
Period inflation		5%	4%	3%

Required

(b) Adjust the total cost in each period to Period 4 prices.   (3 marks)

(c) Using the high-low method, applied to the adjusted costs in answer to part (b), establish a linear function of the form:

y = a + bx

to represent the total costs.   (5 marks)

(d) Plot the adjusted costs for the four periods (ie at Period 4 prices) on a scattergraph and draw the linear cost function, established in part (c), on the graph.   (6 marks)

(e) Use the linear function to forecast costs in the following period (Period 5) when output is expected to be 87,500 units and period inflation is forecast at 2%.   (3 marks)

(f) Outline limitations of the analysis carried out in answer to parts (b) to (e).   (3 marks)

(g) An analysis of the costs incurred in the last period (Period 4) has been carried out as a basis for setting up the product costing system. Initially, costs and profit are being established for Product X only. The following data has been obtained relating to Period 4:

Sales of product X   16,720 units (at £4.00 per unit)
Production of Product X   17,160 units

Production is a two-stage process with each stage carried out in a separate department (Department A and Department B). The following estimates have been made of direct materials and direct labour costs incurred in Period 4 on Product X:

Direct materials	- Department A	£14,130
	- Department B	£2,660
Direct labour	- Department A	£11,200 (1,400 direct labour hours)
	- Department B	£9,570 (1,595 direct labour hours)

Other costs incurred in Period 4, within manufacturing as a whole on all products, were as follows.

Indirect labour costs   £29,320
Space costs   £40,300

The key driver of the indirect labour costs is the labour costs that can be directly related to products. Direct labour costs on all products totalled £88,640 in Period 4. Space costs are to be shared between the two production departments (A and B) in the ratio 40:60. Space costs are to be absorbed into product costs on the basis of direct labour hours. A total of 6,525 direct labour hours were worked in Department A in Period 4 and 6,095 in Department B.

Non-manufacturing costs totalled £33,640 in Period 4. These are to be related to products on the basis of sales value. Company sales in Period 4 totalled £290,000.

Required:

Determine the unit costs and unit profit of Product X in Period 4 (to four decimal places of £) using absorption costing. (13 marks)

(40 marks)

8   ANSWER: RANGE OF PRODUCTS

What the examiner said

According to the examiner, part (a) was well answered by well-prepared candidates but many candidates were unable to compare and contrast absorption and marginal costing. It was apparent (in part (c)) that many candidates knew nothing or very little of the high-low method.

In part (d) many candidates failed to use the graph paper provided and presentation was rarely good.

Parts (e) and (f) were frequently not attempted, and in part (g), many candidates failed to follow the rounding instructions.

Helping hand

In part (b) note that, starting from period 1 as index number 100, the inflation for each period occurs **in addition** to the inflation for the previous periods. Therefore the price level index for period 3 is 100 × 1.05 × 1.04, and so on. In part (d) you need to select a large scale for the scattergraph, otherwise your plotted points will be so close together that it will be difficult to draw the linear cost function.

(a)   The difference between the marginal and absorption costing methods of establishing product costs and profit arises in their **treatment of fixed production overheads**.

In marginal costing

(i)   Closing stocks are valued at **variable or marginal production cost**.

(ii)   **Contribution** is highlighted as the difference between the sales value and the variable cost of sales.

(iii)   Fixed costs are treated as **period costs** and are **charged in full** against the contribution of the period in which they are incurred.

In absorption costing

(i)   Closing stocks are valued at **full production cost** and unit product costs **include a share of fixed production overheads**.

(ii)   It is **not necessary to distinguish variable costs from fixed costs**.

If there is a change in the volume of stock during a period the two methods result in different reported profits. For example if stocks increase, absorption costing will report a higher profit figure than marginal costing. This is because some of the fixed overhead incurred in the period will be carried forward with absorption costing in the higher valuation of the units in stock. The reverse will happen if stocks decrease.

If stock levels **do not change** during the period there is **no difference in the profits reported** under the two costing systems.

(b)   Let the price level index for period 1 be 100. Index numbers for periods 2 to 4 are therefore:

Period		Price level index
2	100 × 1.05	105.0
3	105 × 1.04	109.2
4	109.2 × 1.03	112.476

Adjusting the total costs in each period to period 4 prices:

Period	Actual cost		Cost at period 4 prices
	£		£
1	190,760	× 112.476/100	214,559
2	224,020	× 112.476/105.0	239,970
3	236,100	× 112.476/109.2	243,183
4			255,600

(c)

	Units	£
High output	85,620	255,600
Low output	64,200	214,559
	21,420	41,041

Variable cost per unit (b) = £41,041/21,420 = £1.92

Substituting in high output:

	£
Total cost	255,600
Variable cost (£1.92 × 85,620)	164,390
Fixed cost (a)	91,210

The required linear function to represent total costs is:

y = 91,210 + 1.92x

(d)

Scattergraph of total cost data for periods 1 to 4

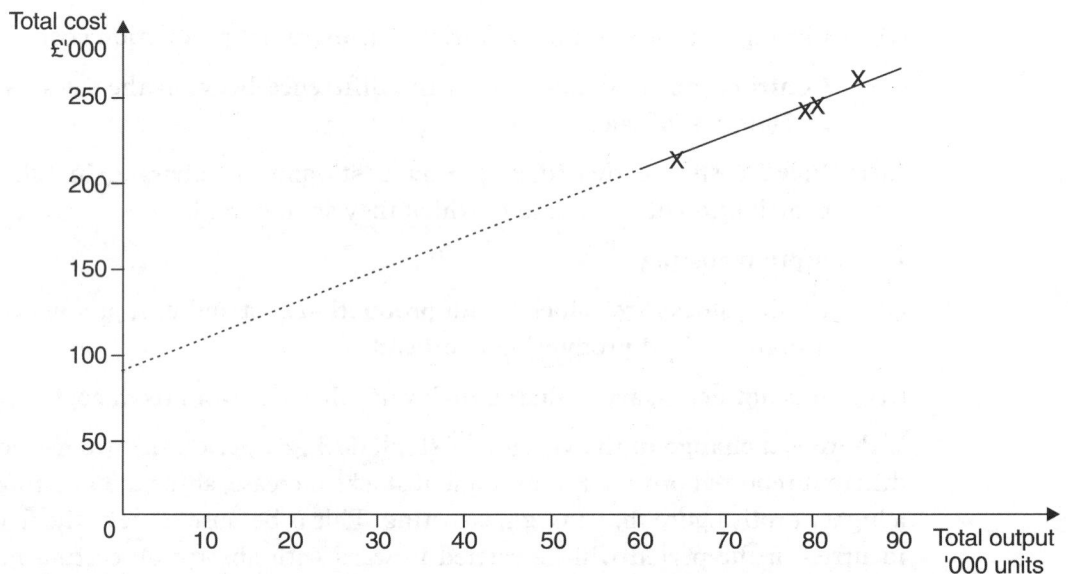

(e)   The linear function is y = 91,210 + 1.92x

Period 5 costs at period 4 prices   = 91,210 + (1.92 × 87,500)
                                     = £259,210

Period 5 costs at period 5 prices   = £259,210 × 1.02
                                     = £264,394

(f)   There are a number of limitations to the techniques used in the above analysis.

Adjustments of costs to period 4 prices (part (b))

The accuracy of this analysis depends on the ability to identify those cost changes which are caused by inflation and those which are caused by other factors.

The high-low method (part (c))

- **Only two pairs of data are used.** Unless the cost behaviour pattern is perfectly linear, these may not be representative data

- Once the effects of inflation have been removed, it is assumed that the level of activity is the **only factor affecting cost**

- The resulting linear function can only be assumed to apply within the **relevant range** of recorded data

The scattergraph technique (part (d))

- The cost line is drawn by visual judgement and so is a **subjective approximation** of the linear cost function

Using the linear function to forecast costs (part (e))

- The relationship which existed between costs and activity in the past is **assumed to continue into the future**

- In this situation, the linear function is being used to predict costs for a level of activity which is **outside the range of recorded data**

- It is **difficult to predict accurately** the rate of cost inflation for the forthcoming period

(g) **Calculation of overhead absorption rate for indirect labour cost**

Indirect labour as a percentage of direct labour cost $= \dfrac{£29,320}{£88,640} \times 100\%$

$$= 33.0776\%$$

Calculation of overhead absorption rates for space costs

	Dept A	Dept B	Total
Apportioned space costs (40:60)	£16,120	£24,180	£40,300
Direct labour hours	6,525	6,095	
Space cost per direct labour hour	£2.4705	£3.9672	

Calculation of overhead absorption rate for non-manufacturing costs

Non-manufacturing costs as a percentage of company sales value $= \dfrac{£33,640}{£290,000} \times 100\%$

$$= 11.6\%$$

Unit costs and unit profit of product X in period 4

Production output: 17,160 units

	£	£	£ per unit
Direct materials - department A	14,130		
Direct materials - department B	2,660		
		16,790	0.9784
Direct labour - department A	11,200		
Direct labour - department B	9,570		
		20,770	1.2104
Total direct cost		37,560	2.1888
Indirect labour cost (20,770 × 33.0776%)		6,870	0.4004
Space cost			
- department A (£2.4705 × 1,400 hr)	3,459		
- department B (£3.9672 × 1,595 hr)	6,328		
		9,787	0.5703
Total production cost		54,217	3.1595
Non-manufacturing costs (11.6% × £4)			0.4640
Total unit cost			3.6235
Unit profit *			0.3765
Unit sales price			4.0000

* Unit sales price - total unit cost = unit profit

Examiner's marking scheme		**Marks**
(a)	Comparison	1
	Contrast - general	2
	- specific: absorption costing	2
	- specific: marginal costing	2
		7
(b)	Inflation adjustment to Periods 1–3	2
	Period 4 unchanged	1
		3
(c)	Variable cost per unit	2
	Fixed cost	2
	Cost function	1
		5
(d)	Labelling/scaling/heading/general presentation	2
	Plotting of adjusted costs	2
	Drawing of linear cost function	2
		6
(e)	Variable cost	1
	Fixed cost	1
	Inflation adjustment	1
		3
(f)	Limitations (1½ for each)	max 3
(g)	Direct materials and labour (1 for each)	2
	Indirect labour	2
	Space costs (2 for each department)	4
	Non-manufacturing costs	2
	Total cost, selling price, profit (1 for each)	3
		13
		40

BPP PROFESSIONAL EDUCATION

DO YOU KNOW? – COSTING METHODS

- *Check that you can fill in the blanks in the statements below before you attempt any questions. If in doubt, you should go back to your BPP Interactive Text and revise first.*

- Job costing is the costing method used if each cost unit is separately identifiable. The work is undertaken to customers' special requirements, it is of comparatively .... duration and moves through processes as a continuously identifiable unit.

- Batch costing is similar to job costing in that each .... of similar articles is separately identifiable.

- .... is a form of job costing which applies if the job is on a large scale and for a long duration.

- .... is used if there is a continuous flow of identical units.

- Losses may occur in process. If a certain level of loss is expected, this is known as .... If losses are greater than expected, the extra loss is .... If losses are less than expected, the difference is known as .... A normal loss is given no value. Abnormal losses and gains never affect the cost of good units of production and are valued at ....

- When units are partly completed at the beginning and end of a period (and hence there is opening and closing work in progress), it is necessary to calculate the .... in order to determine the cost of a completed unit.

- Account can be taken of opening work in progress using either the FIFO method or the weighted average cost method.

   ° The basic assumption of the .... is that the first units completed in any period are the units of opening stock held at the beginning of the period.

   ° In the ...., no distinction is made between units of opening stock and new units introduced to the process during the period. The cost of opening stock is added to costs incurred during the period, and units of opening stock are each given a value of one full equivalent unit of production.

- There is a four-step framework to completing process costing questions.

   Step 1. Determine output and losses (may involve drawing up a statement of ....).

   Step 2. Calculate cost per unit of output, losses and WIP (may involve drawing up a statement of ....).

   Step 3. Calculate total cost of output, losses and WIP (may involve drawing up a statement of ....).

   Step 4. Prepare accounts.

- .... are two or more products separated in a process, each of which has a significant value compared to the other. A .... is an incidental product from a process which has an insignificant value compared to the main product.

- The point at which joint and by-products become separately identifiable is known as the .... or .... Costs incurred up to this point are called common costs or joint costs.

- There are four methods of apportioning joint costs, each of which can produce significantly different results. These methods are as follows.

   ° ....   ° ....
   ° ....   ° ....

- The most common method of accounting for by-products is to ....

TRY QUESTIONS 9 – 13

- *Possible pitfalls*

Write down the mistakes you know you should avoid.

DID YOU KNOW? – COSTING METHODS

- *Could you fill in the blanks? The answers are in bold. Use this page for revision purposes as you approach the exam.*

- Job costing is the costing method used if each cost unit is separately identifiable. The work is undertaken to customers' special requirements, it is of comparatively **short** duration and moves through processes as a continuously identifiable unit.

- Batch costing is similar to job costing in that each **batch** of similar articles is separately identifiable.

- **Contract costing** is a form of job costing which applies if the job is on a large scale and for a long duration.

- **Process costing** is used if there is a continuous flow of identical units.

- Losses may occur in process. If a certain level of loss is expected, this is known as **normal loss**. If losses are greater than expected, the extra loss is **abnormal loss**. If losses are less than expected, the difference is known as **abnormal gain**. A normal loss is given no value. Abnormal losses and gains never affect the cost of good units of production and are valued at **the same unit cost as good units.**

- When units are partly completed at the beginning and end of a period (and hence there is opening and closing work in progress), it is necessary to calculate the **equivalent units of production** in order to determine the cost of a completed unit.

- Account can be taken of opening work in progress using either the FIFO method or the weighted average cost method.
    - The basic assumption of the **FIFO method** is that the first units completed in any period are the units of opening stock held at the beginning of the period.
    - In the **weighted average method**, no distinction is made between units of opening stock and new units introduced to the process during the period. The cost of opening stock is added to costs incurred during the period, and units of opening stock are each given a value of one full equivalent unit of production.

- There is a four-step framework to completing process costing questions.
    Step 1. Determine output and losses (may involve drawing up a statement of **equivalent units**).
    Step 2. Calculate cost per unit of output, losses and WIP (may involve drawing up a statement of **cost per equivalent unit**).
    Step 3. Calculate total cost of output, losses and WIP (may involve drawing up a statement of **evaluation**).
    Step 4. Prepare accounts.

- **Joint products** are two or more products separated in a process, each of which has a significant value compared to the other. A **by-product** is an incidental product from a process which has an insignificant value compared to the main product.

- The point at which joint and by-products become separately identifiable is known as the **split-off point** or **separation point**. Costs incurred up to this point are called common costs or joint costs.

- There are four methods of apportioning joint costs, each of which can produce significantly different results. These methods are as follows.
    - **Physical measurement**
    - **Weighting**
    - **Sales value at split-off point**
    - **Sales value of end product less further processing costs after split-off point**

- The most common method of accounting for by-products is to **deduct the net realisable value of the by-product from the cost of the main products.**

TRY QUESTIONS 9 – 13

- *Possible pitfalls*
    - **Valuing normal loss in the process account**
    - **Using the FIFO method when the weighted average method would be most appropriate and vice versa**
    - **Failing to follow our four-step approach to process costing questions and producing a muddled and confused answer**

9   AEROPARTS LTD

Aeroparts Ltd manufactures precision high value components to customer specification. A job costing system is operated in which direct production costs are allocated to cost centres. Indirect costs are then apportioned to cost centres on what is considered to be an equitable basis.

Individual machine hour rates are then calculated and used for purposes of costing individual jobs. A profit margin of 12% is added to establish the customer's selling price. At the end of the last financial year however, the company discovered that a profit margin of only 3% had been achieved.

You work for a consultancy firm which has been called in to offer Aeroparts Ltd some advice.

Required

Write a report to the directors of the company explaining possible reasons for the poor result. Recommend any changes to the costing system which you feel would improve the present unsatisfactory situation.

(20 marks)

Helping hand

Don't forget that you have to write the report from the point of view of an outsider to the company. Make sure that you **understand the system** that is currently in use and make this clear to the examiner by **incorporating a summary of the details in the question** actually in your report. Remember that the company manufactures to customer specification so don't talk about demand.

---

9   ANSWER: AEROPARTS LTD

> **Helping hand**
>
> We have begun our report by **summarising the current system** at Aeroparts Ltd. This gives the examiner a clear indication of your understanding of the costing method used by the organisation and will help you to come up with possible reasons for the poor result and make recommendations.

REPORT

To: The board of directors, Aeroparts Ltd
From: Management consultant
Date: 1.1.X7
Subject: Costing system and pricing policy

This report examines the costing system currently used by Aeroparts Ltd, looks at reasons for the last financial year's poor result and sets out changes to the costing system that might improve the current situation.

Current system

From the information provided the current costing system appears to operate as follows.

(a) **Costs are ascertained for each cost centre in the organisation**

	£
Cost centre 1	
Total direct production costs	A
Share of indirect costs	$\underline{\text{B}}$
	$\underline{\underline{\text{C}}}$
Total machine hours, cost centre 1	$\underline{\text{D}}$
Machine hour rate, cost centre 1	$\underline{\underline{\text{C/D}}}$

(b) **Individual jobs are then costed and priced on a 'full cost plus' basis**

	£
Job 1	
Hours in cost centre 1 × C/D	X
Hours in cost centre 2 × rate for cost centre 2	X
Etc	$\underline{\text{X}}$
Full cost	$\underline{\text{X}}$
Profit margin (full cost + 12%)	$\underline{\text{X}}$
Selling price	$\underline{\underline{\text{X}}}$

Possible reasons for poor result

Results for the last financial year reveal a profit margin of 3% rather than the 12% desired. In other words the **costing system does not account for all of the costs that are incurred**.

The **problem** lies in the **use of a machine hour rate as the basis of attributing all costs to individual jobs.** This will only achieve an accurate allocation of costs which really do vary according to the number of machine hours.

Clearly materials costs do not vary in this way and yet a job using high value materials and taking 2 hours in cost centre A would be costed at the same price as a job using low value materials but also taking 2 hours. The cost of the former job would be understated and that of the latter overstated. This would not in itself erode the margin, but it would probably make many of the **prices charged uncompetitive**.

There are a number of **further considerations**, all of which will affect margins.

(a) When preparing estimates, **are current production costs used?** If material prices are subject to frequent fluctuation or if labour has been awarded a pay rise, the most up to date rates should be used in the calculations.

(b) **Are all production costs taken into account?** For example the cost of cleaning materials or oil for machinery may have been ignored, or the calculations may not have reckoned with the need for overtime working due to the demands on labour from other jobs.

(c) Are adjustments made for differences between the amount of indirect costs apportioned to jobs and the amount actually incurred? **Under absorption of overheads** is the single most likely explanation for the erosion of the profit margin.

Improved system

The **usual approach to job costing** is as follows.

(a) Each job should be given a number to distinguish it from other jobs.

(b) Costs for each job should be collected on a job cost sheet or job card.

(c) Materials costs for each job should be determined from material requisition notes.

(d) Labour times on each job should be recorded on a job ticket which can then be costed and recorded on the job cost sheet. Some labour costs, for example overtime premium or the cost of rectifying sub-standard output might be charged either directly to a job or else as an overhead cost, depending on the circumstances in which the costs have arisen.

(e) Overhead is absorbed into the cost of jobs using predetermined overhead absorption rates. Overheads should be apportioned on a 'fair' basis, and separate departmental absorption rates should be used, as appropriate. There should not be an excessive amount of under- or over-absorbed overhead at the end of the period. If there is a dramatic increase in overhead costs (for example a large rise in office or factory rent) the rates should be revised.

(f) The desired profit margin should then be added to the 'full cost' as established above, but with an eye to prices charged by competitors and the possibility of obtaining repeat orders.

Such a system should help to improve the organisation's performance.

I hope this information is useful but if I can be of any further assistance please do not hesitate to contact me.

10   BATCH 106 (12/99)   *36 mins*

The following information relates to batch 106.

1   **Materials**

Two materials, Ogar and Troy, are used in the manufacture of batch 106. Material movement tickets provide the following data.

		Ogar	**Troy**
Issued to batch 106	4 November	600 kgs	50 metres
Issued to batch 108	16 November	120 kgs	nil
Issued to batch 106	17 November	270 kgs	nil
Transferred from batch 106 to 107	24 November	nil	10 metres
Returned from batch 106	28 November	nil	4 metres

On 1 November, 700 kgs of material Ogar were in stock at a price of £2.15 per kg. On 10 November there was a delivery into stores of 200 kgs of Ogar at a price of £2.20 per kg. A further delivery of 150 kgs of Ogar was received on 13 November at a price of £2.22 per kg.

On 1 November, 1,000 metres of material Troy were held in stock at a price of £10.00 per metre. No further deliveries of Troy were received during the period.

The company uses a LIFO (Last In, First Out) system to value stock issues.

2   **Labour**

		Dept A	**Dept B**
Direct labour	Skilled	180 hours	106 hours
	Unskilled	205 hours	78 hours
Direct labour rates	Skilled	£5 per hour	£6 per hour
	Unskilled	£3 per hour	£3 per hour

3   Production overhead is recovered on the cost of materials and direct labour as follows.

Total materials cost	10%
Total labour cost	120%

4   Administration overhead is charged at 20% of the total batch production cost.

5   Selling and distribution expenses are levied at a rate of £600 per batch.

6   The selling price for batch 106 has previously been set by the estimating department at £11,000, based on the estimated cost, plus a 25% mark-up on **total cost** to provide for profit.

Required

(a) Prepare a cost schedule for batch 106 showing the following components.

    (i)   Prime cost   (6 marks)

    (ii)   Production cost   (3 marks)

    (iii) Total cost   (2 marks)

    (iv) Profit   (1 mark)

Note. Remember to show all workings. Show all figures to the nearest £1.

(b) Compare the actual batch profit with the estimated profit and state the amount of any difference.   (2 marks)

(c) Explain briefly what actions you might take as production accountant if batches of work were consistently showing lower profits than the estimating department had predicted when quoting for the work.   (6 marks)

                                                                      (20 marks)

Helping hand

Note in part (a) that you need to show all **figures to the nearest £.** You will need to rely on knowledge from **Paper B2** in (a) when you come to price the issues of material to batch 106.

Don't simply list every type of cost that might contribute to cost overruns in part (c). Think about **wider issues** such as stock valuation methods and estimating procedures.

10   ANSWER: BATCH 106

> **What the examiner said**
>
> Some good marks were scored on this question but many candidates were not prepared to deal with a subject that had been covered in an earlier paper, valuing stock issues on a LIFO basis.
>
> Few candidates were able to calculate a profit mark-up on cost.

(a)

> **Helping hand**
>
> Begin by **drawing up a proforma cost schedule** and then **do your workings** and **fill in the missing figures**. You may find it useful to **draw up a stock card** to help you to calculate the cost of Ogar used in the batch.

Cost schedule for batch 106

		£
	Direct materials (W1)	2,243
	Direct labour (W2)	2,385
(i)	**Prime cost**	4,628
	Production overhead (W3)	3,086
(ii)	**Production cost**	7,714
	Administration overhead (W4)	1,543
	Selling and administration expenses	600
(iii)	**Total cost**	9,857
(iv)	**Profit** (W5)	1,143
	Selling price	11,000

Workings

1   **Calculation of value of Ogar issued to batch 106**

We begin by drawing up a stock card for Ogar.

Ogar

Date	Receipts		Issues			Balance	
	kgs	£/kg	kgs	£/kg	£	kgs	£/kg
1/11						700	2.15
4/11			600	2.15	1,290.00	100	2.15
10/11	200	2.20				100	2.15
						200	2.20
						300	
13/11	150	2.22				100	2.15
						200	2.20
						150	2.22
						450	
16/11			120	2.22	266.40	100	2.15
						200	2.20
						30	2.22
						330	
17/11			30	2.22	66.60		
			200	2.20	440.00		
			40	2.15	86.00		
			270		592.60	60	2.15

Cost of Ogar used in batch 106

		£
Issue 4/11	600 × £2.15	1,290.00
Issue 17/11	30 × £2.22	66.60
	200 × £2.20	440.00
	40 × £2.15	86.00
		1,882.60

Calculation of value of Troy held

		£
1/11	Stock value of Troy (1,000m × £10)	10,000
4/11	Issued to batch 106 (50m × £10)	(500)
	Stock value (950m × £10)	9,500
28/11	Return from batch 106 (4 × £10)	40
30/11	Stock value (954 × £10)	9,540

Cost of Troy used in batch 106

	£
Issue 4/11	500
Transfer 24/11 (10 × £10)	(100)
Return 28/11	(40)
Value ((50 − 10 − 4) × £10)	360

Total cost of direct materials used in batch 106 (to nearest £1)

	£
Ogar	1,883
Troy	360
	2,243

2 Cost of direct labour

		£
Skilled:	Dept A (180 hrs × £5)	900
	Dept B (106 hrs × £6)	636
Unskilled:	Dept A (205 hrs × £3)	615
	Dept B (78 hrs × £3)	234
		2,385

3 Production overhead

$= (10\% \times \text{total materials cost}) + (120\% \times \text{total labour cost})$

$= (10\% \times £2,243) + (120\% \times £2,385) = \underline{£3,086.3}$

$= £3,086$ to nearest £1

4 Administration overhead

$= 20\% \times \text{total batch production cost}$

$= 20\% \times £7,714 = \underline{£1,542.8}$

$= £1,543$ to nearest £1

5 Profit

$= \text{selling price} - \text{total cost} = £(11,000 - 9,857) = £1,143$

(b)

Helping hand

In (a) the profit calculation was straightforward, being simply £11,000 minus total cost. Here, however, we know that **£11,000 = total cost plus 25% of total cost = 125% × total cost**. We can therefore write **£11,000/125% = total cost**, and so **total cost = £8,800**. Profit is therefore calculated as 25% × £8,800 = £2,200.

	£
Actual batch profit (from (a))	1,143
Estimated profit (£11,000 × (0.25/1.25))	2,200
Difference	1,057

(c)

Helping hand

Work through each of the components of total cost and comment on how the estimated and actual costs could differ.

If batches of work were consistently showing **lower profits than the estimating department had predicted** when quoting for the work, the following action could be taken.

(i)   Ensure that the estimating department is **using an appropriate unit valuation** for direct materials. They could be using the wrong valuation method (FIFO valuations are likely to be lower than LIFO valuations) or they could be using current cost (which could well be lower than the LIFO valuation when the work is carried out, especially if prices are increasing and/or there are numerous material movements). If raw material prices are particularly volatile, standard cost could be used. Alternatively, the estimating department may be basing the estimates on out-of-date standard costs.

(ii)   Check that the estimating department is **incorporating the current quantity of materials** into the cost estimate. They may not be taking into consideration scrap and/or waste that is part of the normal production process. Alternatively, actual scrap and wastage levels may be much higher than anticipated, a factor which should be investigated by the production manager.

(iii)   Investigate to see whether the **wage rates** used in the estimate are **correct**. There may have been a pay increase of which the estimating department are unaware. If overtime is a normal occurrence, the premium may be included in the direct labour rates, unbeknown to the estimating department.

(iv)   Determine the basis for the **labour hours content** of the estimate. The estimating department may not be incorporating standard allowances for reworking, for example. On the other hand, the workforce may be working inefficiently, taking longer than the standard time for particular tasks. Labour efficiency levels may require investigation by the production manager.

(v)   Check that the estimating department is using the correct overhead **recovery bases** and expense rates.

(vi)   Use **variance analysis** and determine where estimated and actual costs are differing.

Examiner's marking scheme

			Marks
(a)	*Cost schedule*		
	Calculation of material issues - Ogar	to 2	
	- Troy	to 1	
	Transfer to Ogar to batch 108	to 1	
	Prime cost - summary of materials	to 1	
	- direct labour	to 1	
	Production cost	to 3	
	Total cost	to 2	
	Profit	to 1	
			12
(b)	Comparison of estimated and actual profit		2
(c)	Actions to remedy reduced batch profitability (three actions × 2 marks each)		6
			20

11   EQUIVALENT UNITS AND PROCESS LOSSES

You work in the head office management accounting department of a large multinational manufacturing organisation. You have been asked to provide information about two of your organisation's divisions.

(a)   Division A operates expensive process plant to produce a single product from one process. At the beginning of October, 3,400 completed units were still in the processing plant, awaiting transfer to finished stock. They were valued as follows.

	£	
Direct material	25,500	
Direct wages	10,200	
Production overhead	20,400	(200% of direct wages)

During October, 37,000 further units were put into process and the following costs charged to the process.

	£
Direct materials	276,340
Direct wages	112,000
Production overhead	224,000

36,000 units were transferred to finished stock and 3,200 units remained in work in progress at the end of October which were complete as to material and half-complete as to labour and production overhead. A loss of 1,200 units, being normal, occurred during the process.

Required

Prepare the process account for the month of October.   (10 marks)

(b)   Division B manufactures a single product which passes through two processes, the output of process 1 becoming the input to process 2.

The following information relates to the month of October.

Raw material issued to process 1 was 3,000 units at a cost of £5 per unit.

There was no opening or closing work in progress but opening and closing stocks of finished goods were £20,000 and £23,000 respectively.

	Process 1	*Process 2*
Normal loss as a percentage of input	10%	5%
Output in units	2,800	2,600
Additional components	£400	£80
Direct wages incurred	£4,000	£6,000
Direct expenses incurred	£10,000	£14,000
Production overhead as a percentage of direct wages	75%	125%

Required

Present the accounts for Process 1 and Process 2.   (10 marks)

                                                                    (20 marks)

Helping hand

Part (a) of this question tests your ability to manipulate equivalent units, one tricky area of process costing. Part (b) tests the second tricky area of process costing, that of losses.

As with all process costing questions, you need to adopt the four-step approach which we looked at in the Interactive Text. In case you need a reminder, here is a brief summary of the four steps.

Step 1. Determine output and losses. (This involves drawing up a **statement of equivalent units** if equivalent units are a factor in the question.)

Step 2. Calculate the cost per unit of output, losses and WIP. (This involves drawing up a **statement of cost per equivalent unit** if equivalent units are a factor in the question.)

Step 3. Calculate the total cost of output, losses and WIP. (This involves drawing up a **statement of evaluation** if equivalent units are a factor in the question.)

Step 4. Complete the **accounts** required by the question.

In part (a) you also need to think about the method of dealing with opening WIP that you should use.

11   ANSWER: EQUIVALENT UNITS AND PROCESS LOSSES

(a)

> **Helping hand**
>
> You need to begin by drawing up a **statement of equivalent units** (step 1) which shows opening stock, fully worked units, output to finished goods, normal loss and closing stock, the total equivalent units and the equivalent units for material, labour and overhead. Don't forget that **equivalent units for normal loss** for materials, labour and overhead **are zero**. The number of fully worked units is the difference between the units transferred to finished stock and the units in opening stock.

Statement of equivalent units

	Total units	Direct materials	Direct wages	Production overhead
Opening stock	3,400	3,400	3,400	3,400
Fully worked units	32,600	32,600	32,600	32,600
Output to finished goods	36,000	36,000	36,000	36,000
Normal loss	1,200	-	-	-
Closing stock	3,200	3,200	1,600	1,600
	40,400	39,200	37,600	37,600

> **Helping hand**
>
> Now you need to prepare a **statement of cost per equivalent unit** (step 2). You should have realised that, because you are given the value of each cost element in opening stock but not its degree of completion, **weighted average costing should be used**. The calculation of the costs per equivalent unit must therefore include the costs brought forward in opening stock. If the FIFO method had been used, brought forward costs would not be included in the calculations.

Statement of cost per equivalent unit

Costs	Total	Direct materials	Direct labour	Production overhead
	£	£	£	£
Opening stock	56,100	25,500	10,200	20,400
Charged to process	612,340	276,340	112,000	224,000
	668,440	301,840	122,200	244,400
Equivalent units	40,400	39,200	37,600	37,600
Cost per equivalent unit	£17.45	£7.70	£3.25	£6.50

> **Helping hand**
>
> Step 3 in the four-step approach requires you to draw up a **statement of evaluation**. Don't forget that you do not need to account for opening stock separately because we are using the average cost method.

Statement of evaluation

	Total	Direct materials	Direct labour	Production overhead
	£	£	£	£
Finished stock transfer	628,200	277,200	117,000	234,000
Closing work in progress	40,240	24,640	5,200	10,400

> **Helping hand**
>
> You are now ready to draw up the **process account** (step 4). Of course, opening stock must now be separately identified, as must normal loss (which has no value in the process account). You don't need to perform any further calculations. All the entries for the account have either been provided in the question or calculated in the steps above.

PROCESS ACCOUNT

	Units	£		Units	£
Opening stock	3,400	56,100	Finished goods	36,000	628,200
Added to process	37,000	612,340	Normal loss	1,200	-
			Closing stock	3,200	40,240
	40,400	668,440		40,400	668,440

(b)

> **Helping hand**
>
> Again, you need to follow the four-step approach. You need to complete the steps for Process 1 before attempting them for Process 2 because the input costs to Process 2 include the cost of output from Process 1 (which is determined from the Process 1 account).

(i) **Process 1**

Step 1. **Determine output and losses**

Normal output is 90% of 3,000 units = 2,700 units. There is therefore an abnormal gain of 100 units.

Step 2. **Determine cost per unit of output, losses and WIP**

Cost per unit = costs ÷ expected output =

$$\frac{(3,000 \times £5) + £400 + £4,000 + £10,000 + (75\% \times £4,000)}{2,700 \text{ units}}$$

= £32,400 ÷ 2,700 units = £12 per unit

> **Helping hand**
>
> **Normal loss** is given **no value** but units of **abnormal gain** are **valued at the full cost per unit**.

Step 3. **Calculate total cost of output and losses**

	£
Cost of actual output (2,800 × £12)	33,600
Normal loss (given no cost) (300 × £0)	-
Abnormal gain (100 × £12)	(1,200)
	32,400

> **Helping hand**
>
> Note that the **total cost calculated in Step 3 equals the cost calculated in Step 2.**

Step 4.   **Complete accounts**

PROCESS 1

	Units		£		Units		£
Raw material	3,000		15,000	Process 1	2,800	(× £12)	33,600
Additional comp.			400	Normal loss			
Direct wages			4,000	(10% × 3,000)	300		-
Direct expenses			10,000				
Production o/head			3,000				
Abnormal gain	100	(× £12)	1,200				
	3,100		33,600		3,100		33,600

(ii)   **Process 2**

Step 1.   Normal output is 95% of 2,800 units = 2,660 units. There is therefore an abnormal loss of 60 units.

Helping hand

Don't forget to include the cost of output from Process 1 as a cost of input to Process 2.

Step 2.   Cost per unit = (£33,600 (from Process 1) + £80 + £6,000 + £14,000 + (125% × £6,000))/2,660 units

= £61,180/2,660 units = £23 per unit

Step 3.   Total cost of output and losses

	£
Cost of actual output (2,600 × £23)	59,800
Normal loss (140 × £0)	-
Abnormal loss (60 × £23)	1,380
	61,180

Step 4.

PROCESS 2

	Units	£		Units		£
Process 1	2,800	33,600	Finished goods	2,600	(× £23)	59,800
Additional components		80	Normal loss			
Direct wages		6,000	(5% × 2,800)	140		-
Direct expenses		14,000	Abnormal loss	60	(× £23)	1,380
Production o/head		7,500				
	2,800	61,180		2,800		61,180

69

BPP
PROFESSIONAL EDUCATION

12   QUESTION WITH HELP: PROCESS COSTING

Your company manufactures a product that goes through two processes. You are given the following cost information about the processes for the month of November.

	Process 1	Process 2
Units input	15,000	-
Finished units input from Process 1	-	10,000
Finished units output to Process 2	10,000	-
Finished units output from Process 2	-	9,500
Opening WIP - units	-	2,000
- value	-	£26,200
Input - materials	£26,740	
- labour	£36,150	£40,000
- overhead	£40,635	£59,700
Closing WIP - units	4,400	1,800

You are told the following.

- The closing WIP in Process 1 was 80% complete for material, 50% complete for labour and 40% complete for overhead.

- The opening WIP in Process 2 was 40% complete for labour and 50% complete for overhead. It had a labour value of £3,200 and an overhead value of £6,000 for work done in Process 1.

- The closing WIP in Process 2 was two thirds complete for labour and 75% complete for overhead.

- No further material needed to be added to the units transferred from Process 1.

- Normal loss is budgeted at 5% of total input in Process 1 and Process 2. Total input is to be inclusive of any opening WIP.

- Abnormal losses have no sales value.

- It is company policy to value opening WIP in a process using weighted average costing.

Required

Prepare accounts for Process 1 and Process 2.

(20 marks)

> *If you are stuck, look at the next page for detailed help as to how you should tackle this question.*

APPROACHING THE ANSWER

In question 11 we looked at how to deal with equivalent units in process costing questions and then at how to deal with losses. This question incorporates both. If you follow our step-by-step approach, however, you will have no difficulty in dealing with any process costing question you encounter, even this one!

We'll begin with Process 1.

Step 1.   *Determine output and losses*

This involves drawing up a statement of equivalent units. A proforma is provided below. Try and fill it in. We have given you a few of the entries.

	Total units	Process 1 material	Labour	Overheads
Opening stock			-	
Fully worked units	10,000	_____	_____	
Output to process 2				10,000
Normal loss (5% of input)		-		
Abnormal loss/(gain)			(150)	
Closing stock	_____	3,520 *	_____	_____

* (80% × 4,400)

Step 2.   *Calculate the cost per unit of output, losses and WIP*

This involves drawing up a statement of cost per equivalent unit. Again, you should fill in the proforma we have provided below.

	Material	Labour	Overhead
Cost		£36,150	
Equivalent units (from Step 1)	13,370		
Cost per equivalent unit			

Step 3.   *Calculate the total cost of output, losses and WIP*

This involves drawing up a statement of evaluation. Try to complete the proforma we have provided.

	Material £	Labour £	Overhead £	Total £
Output to process 2		30,000*		
Abnormal gain				1,275
Closing stock			6,160**	

* 10,000 units × £3
** 1,760 units × £3.50

Step 4.   *Complete process 1 account*

You can complete the account below using information from the question and from your workings above.

PROCESS 1 ACCOUNT

	Units	£		Units	£
Material			To process 2		
Labour			Normal loss		
Overhead			Closing stock		
Abnormal gain	_____	_____	Abnormal loss	_____	_____

Having given you lots of help for Process 1 you should be able to go through the steps for Process 2 yourself. But watch out!

- When using weighted average costing, opening stock counts as a full equivalent unit.

- You need to include the costs of opening stock in your cost per equivalent unit calculations.

- Work to 2 decimal places.

- You will have a difference of £30 in your process account due to rounding.

12   ANSWER TO QUESTION WITH HELP: PROCESS COSTING

PROCESS 1

STATEMENT OF EQUIVALENT UNITS

	Total units		Material		Labour		Over-heads
Opening stock	-		-		-		-
Fully worked units	10,000		10,000		10,000		10,000
Output to process 2	10,000		10,000		10,000		10,000
Normal loss	750		-		-		-
Abnormal loss/(gain)	(150)		(150)		(150)		(150)
Closing stock	4,400	(× 80%)	3,520	(×50%)	2,200	(× 40%)	1,760
	15,000		13,370		12,050		11,610

STATEMENT OF COST PER EQUIVALENT UNIT

	Material	Labour	Overhead
Cost	£26,740	£36,150	£40,635
Equivalent units	13,370	12,050	11,610
Cost per equivalent unit	£2.00	£3.00	£3.50

STATEMENT OF EVALUATION

	Material £	Labour £	Overhead £	Total £
Output to process 2*	20,000	30,000	35,000	85,000
Abnormal gain**	300	450	525	1,275
Closing stock***	7,040	6,600	6,160	19,800

★   10,000 × appropriate cost per equivalent unit

★★   150 × appropriate cost per equivalent unit

★★★   3,520/2,200/1,760 × appropriate cost per equivalent unit

PROCESS 1 ACCOUNT

	Units	£		Units	£
Material	15,000	26,740	To Process 2	10,000	85,000
Labour		36,150	Normal loss	750	-
Overhead		40,635	Closing stock	4,400	19,800
Abnormal gain	150	1,275			
	15,150	104,800		15,150	104,800

PROCESS 2

STATEMENT OF EQUIVALENT UNITS

	Total units		Process 1 material		Labour		Overheads
Opening stock	2,000	(× 100%)	2,000	(× 100%)	2,000	(× 100%)	2,000
Fully worked units	7,500		7,500		7,500		7,500
Output to finished goods	9,500		9,500		9,500		9,500
Normal loss	600		-		-		-
Abnormal loss/(gain)	100		100		100		100
Closing stock	1,800	(× 100%)	1,800	(× 2/3)	1,200	(× 75%)	1,350
	12,000		11,400		10,800		10,950

STATEMENT OF COST PER EQUIVALENT UNIT

	Process 1 material £	Labour £	Overhead £
Opening stock	17,000*	3,200	6,000
Added in period	85,000	40,000	59,700
	102,000	43,200	65,700
Equivalent units	11,400	10,800	10,950
Cost per equivalent unit	£8.95	£4.00	£6.00

* £(26,200 – 3,200 – 6,000)

STATEMENT OF EVALUATION

	Process 1 material £	Labour £	Overhead £	Total £
Output to finished goods*	85,025	38,000	57,000	180,025
Abnormal loss**	895	400	600	1,895
Closing stock	16,110	4,800	8,100	29,010

*   9,500 × appropriate cost per equivalent unit

**   100 × appropriate cost per equivalent unit

*** 1,800/1,200/1,350 × appropriate cost per equivalent unit

PROCESS 2 ACCOUNT

	Units	£		Units	£
From Process 1	10,000	85,000	To finished goods	9,500	180,025
Opening stock	2,000	26,200	Closing stock	1,800	29,010
Labour	-	40,000	Normal loss	600	-
Overheads		59,700	Abnormal loss	100	1,895
			Rounding	-	(30)
	12,000	210,900		12,000	210,910

13   **CONTRACT 733 (12/00)**   *36 mins*

The following information relates to contract 733, which ended on 30 November 20X0.

	£
Materials issued to site less returns	183,000
Direct labour (32,000 hours × £4.00 per hour)	128,000
Loose tools – issued at commencement of contract 4 January 20X0	23,000
– returned at end of contract	11,000

Overheads are recovered at a rate of £5.25 per direct labour hour.

The company submitted a binding tender to undertake this contract for £580,000 based on estimated costs of £530,000.

The company owns three specialist cranes, one of which is rather old. All three were used on contract 733 as follows.

Crane time booked to site for contract 733

Crane No 1 – 44 working days
Crane No 2 – 150 working days
Crane No 3 – 196 working days*

* During this period Crane 3 was transferred to contract 740 for 50 working days. None of the cranes were used on any other contract.

The cranes are the company's most significant items of equipment and are charged out to contracts at a notional rent of £200 per working day. Depreciation is charged on a straight line basis at an annual rate of 20%.

A crane recharge control account is used for the purpose of recharging the notional charges to individual contracts. Any surplus after charging the depreciation for the year is written off to the general profit and loss account.

Extract from the balance sheet as at 1 December 20W9

Fixed assets	*Cost*	*Dep'n*	*WDV*
	£'000	£'000	£'000
Crane No 1	100	90	10
Crane No 2	90	54	36
Crane No 3	120	24	96
Total	310	168	142

Required

(a) Complete the crane recharge control account for the year ended 30 November 20X0.

(4 marks)

(b) Draw up a profit and loss statement for contract 733.   (4 marks)

(c) Explain briefly the benefits and drawbacks to a business of using notional charges.

(6 marks)

(d) Explain briefly what actions you might take as company accountant if contracts were consistently showing lower profits than the estimating department had predicted when quoting for the work.   (6 marks)

(20 marks)

13   ANSWER: CONTRACT 733

> **What the examiner said**
>
> Common errors included the following.
>
> - Not appearing to understand double entry bookkeeping
>
> - Taking the overall under recovery into the accounts of contract 733 instead of writing it off to the overall company profit and loss account
>
> - Not appearing to be familiar with the topic of notional costs

(a)   **Crane recharge control account**

> **Helping hand**
>
> Crane No 1 was almost fully depreciated. A full year's charge would have been £20,000.

Date		DR £	CR £
30.11.X0	Crane No 1-contract 733, 44 days		8,800
30.11.X0	Crane No 2-contract 733, 150 days		30,000
30.11.X0	Crane No 3-contract 733, 146 days		29,200
30.11.X0	Crane No 3-contract 740, 50 days		10,000
30.11.X0	Depreciation – crane No 1	10,000	
30.11.X0	Depreciation – crane No 2	18,000	
30.11.X0	Depreciation – crane No 3	24,000	
30.11.X0	Profit and loss account	26,000	
		78,000	78,000

(b)

> **Helping hand**
>
> The crane recharge figure should not include the cost of crane no 3 being used on contract 740.

Profit and loss account for contract 733

	£	£
Revenue		580,000
Costs:		
Materials used	183,000	
Direct labour	128,000	
Loose tools consumed (£(23,000 – 11,000))	12,000	
Crane recharges (£(8,800 + 30,000 + 29,200))	68,000	
Overheads recovered (32,000 direct hours @ £5.25)	168,000	
Total costs		559,000
Profit		21,000

(c)   **Benefits achieved by using notional charges for the use of an asset**

(i)   A more realistic picture of what something (a product, contract, department) costs is obtained, as for contract 733 above.

(ii)   An understanding of the way in which an asset has been used is obtained (see the crane recharge control account above).

(iii)   It encourages a more effective deployment of the asset as users cannot regard it as having no cost of use.

Drawbacks of using notional charges

(i)   It can be difficult to decide on a realistic charging rate if there is no market rate available.

(ii)   The notional charge may discourage managers from using idle assets. (Crane numbers 1 and 2 were not fully utilised during the year).

(d)

Helping hand

Note that this is very similar to part of a question in the December 1999 exam.

It should be noted that the **profitability of contracts** is the **responsibility of the sales, estimating and contract management**. The accountant is responsible for providing information which management can use for decision making, planning, control and appraisal.

Actions that could be taken by a company accountant if contracts are consistently showing lower profits than the estimating department has predicted

(i)   Compare in detail the actual cost of past contracts with calculations used to build up the estimated cost. This will identify any regular under-estimates of cost elements. Labour efficiency may be over-estimated on a regular basis, for example.

(ii)   Prepare regular progress reports on contracts, including expected costs to completion. This will give an early warning of cost overruns and may allow remedial action to be taken.

(iii)   Check the rates (for wages, overheads and so on) used by the estimating department to establish whether they are up to date and realistic. The estimating department may be using an inappropriate valuation method for direct materials. FIFO valuations are likely to be lower than LIFO valuations for example. If material prices are particularly volatile, standard cost could be used.

(iv)   Check that the estimating department is incorporating the correct quality of materials into the estimates. They may not be taking into consideration normal levels of scrap and/or waste.

(v)   Determine the basis for the labour hours content of the estimate. The estimating department may not be incorporating standard allowances for reworks, for example.

(vi)   Check all estimates before quotes are prepared to ascertain whether they are complete and arithmetically accurate. Estimating procedures may need to be revised.

Examiner's marking scheme

		Marks
(a) Recharge control account		
- depreciation	to 2	
- recharges	to 1	
- balance to P & L	to 1	
		4
(b) Profit and loss account		
- direct costs	to 1	
- crane recharge	to 1	
- profit	to 1	
- format	to 1	
		4
(c) Notional costs		
- benefits	to 3	
- drawbacks	to 3	
		6
(d) Actions to remedy reduced profitability (3 actions × 2 marks)		6
		20

BPP
PROFESSIONAL EDUCATION

DO YOU KNOW? - BUDGETS

- *Check that you can fill in the blanks in the statements below before you attempt any questions. If in doubt, you should go back to your BPP Interactive Text and revise first.*

- The planning and control cycle has seven steps.

  - ° *Step 1.......................*
  - ° *Step 2.......................*
  - ° *Step 3.......................*
  - ° *Step 4.......................*
  - ° *Step 5.......................*
  - ° *Step 6.......................*
  - ° *Step 7.......................*

- Responsibility centres can be divided into three types: cost centres, ... and ....

- Budgets have a number of very important functions in an organisation.

  - ° ....
  - ° ....
  - ° ....
  - ° ....
  - ° ....
  - ° ....
  - ° ....

- The budget preparation timetable involves eight basic steps.

  - ° *Step 1.......................*
  - ° *Step 2.......................*
  - ° *Step 3.......................*
  - ° *Step 4.......................*
  - ° *Step 5.......................*
  - ° *Step 6.......................*
  - ° *Step 7.......................*
  - ° *Step 8.......................*

- When all of the functional budgets have been prepared, they are summarised and consolidated into a master budget which consists of the ...., ... and ....

- Costs can be forecast using the ....

- Time series analysis involves finding the trend (using moving averages) and seasonal variations by applying the .... model. Forecasts can then be made by inspection or using a common sense 'rule-of-thumb' approach.

- .... remain unchanged regardless of the level of activity; .... are designed to flex with the level of activity. Budgetary control is based on the comparison of a .... with .... The differences are known as ....

- .... budgeting aims to eliminate slack and wasteful spending from budgets.

- .... budgets are continuously updated by adding a further period and deducting the earliest period.

- Budgets can be set from the top down (.............................), from the .... (participative) or a negotiated style can be adopted.

TRY QUESTIONS 14-19

- *Possible pitfalls*

Write down the mistakes you know you should avoid.

BPP
PROFESSIONAL EDUCATION

DID YOU KNOW? - BUDGETS

- *Could you fill in the blanks? The answers are in bold. Use this page for revision purposes as you approach the exam.*

- The planning and control cycle has seven steps.

  - *Step 1.* **Identify objectives**
  - *Step 2.* **Identify potential strategies**
  - *Step 3.* **Evaluate strategies**
  - *Step 4.* **Choose alternative courses of action**
  - *Step 5.* **Implement the long-term plan**
  - *Step 6.* **Measure results and compare with plan**
  - *Step 7* **Respond to divergences from plan**

- Responsibility centres can be divided into three types: cost centres, **profit centres** and **investment centres.**

- Budgets have a number of very important functions in an organisation.

  - **Ensure the achievement of the organisation's objectives**
  - **Communicate ideas and plans**
  - **Provide a framework for responsibility accounting**
  - **Compel planning**
  - **Co-ordinate activities**
  - **Establish a system of control**
  - **Motivate employees to improve their performance**

- The budget preparation timetable involves eight basic steps.

  - *Step 1.* **Communicate details of budget and budget guidelines**
  - *Step 2.* **Determine factor that restricts output (principal/key/limiting budget factor)**
  - *Step 3.* **Prepare the sales budget (if sales is the key budget factor)**
  - *Step 4.* **Initial preparation of budgets**
  - *Step 5.* **Negotiate budgets with superiors**
  - *Step 6.* **Co-ordinate budgets**
  - *Step 7.* **Final acceptance of the budget**
  - *Step 8.* **Budget review**

- When all of the functional budgets have been prepared, they are summarised and consolidated into a master budget which consists of the **budgeted profit and loss account**, **budgeted balance sheet** and **cash budget.**

- Costs can be forecast using the **scattergraph method**.

- Time series analysis involves finding the trend (using moving averages) and seasonal variations by applying the **additive** model. Forecasts can then be made by inspection or using a common sense 'rule-of-thumb' approach.

- **Fixed budgets** remain unchanged regardless of the level of activity; **flexible budgets** are designed to flex with the level of activity. Budgetary control is based on the comparison of a **flexed budget** with **actual results**. The differences are known as **variances.**

- **Zero based** budgeting aims to eliminate slack and wasteful spending from budgets.

- **Rolling or continuous** budgets are continuously updated by adding a further period and deducting the earliest period.

- Budgets can be set from the top down (**imposed**), from the **bottom up** (participative) or a negotiated style can be adopted.

  TRY QUESTIONS 14-19

- *Possible pitfalls*

  - **Failing to take account of mixed costs when preparing flexible budgets**

  - **Preparing a cash budget on an accruals basis and/or a budgeted profit and loss account on a cash received/paid basis**

  - **Taking a moving average over an inappropriate period, such as over a week when a month would be better**

14 TDF (12/98)   *36 mins*

TDF manufactures high quality curtain fabric which is sold to retailers for sale to the public. The turnover for the present year is expected to be £20 million. The business has performed well in recent years although TDF, in common with the rest of the curtain industry, is beset with uncertainty caused by the effect of economic cycles, together with shortages and price volatility with regard to raw materials. Natural fibres such as wool are particularly prone to the forces of supply and demand.

Over the years the company has developed a number of ways of working around such problems. For example, man-made fibres can be substituted for wool, but this has processing and cost implications in the weaving and dyeing departments. Depressed trading conditions in the home market can be compensated to some extent by increasing export sales, although the marketing department has to change the style and emphasis of their marketing campaigns and different designs are often required in local markets.

The company is about to prepare next year's budget. Unfortunately since the last budget preparation cycle, the accountant has left and his files cannot be found. As the new accountant you have the responsibility of preparing next year's budget. The new financial year will start in four months' time. The managing director has promised you the full support of all the departmental managers in this task. He has suggested that you come to the next management meeting to talk through the process of budget preparation: all managers should know what is expected from them, and how their individual departments will fit into the overall plan.

Required

(a) With reference to the information above, prepare notes for circulation at the meeting on how you propose to undertake the budget preparation process at TDF. Your answer should include a reference to the following.

   (i)   A brief summary of the steps in the budgetary control process (which you should illustrate with a diagram)   (5 marks)

   (ii)   The term 'principal budget factor'   (3 marks)

   (iii)   The purpose and content of the budget manual   (3 marks)

   (iv)   Departmental and master budgets   (3 marks)

(b) Explain how computers might assist in the preparation of budgets.   (6 marks)

                                                                           (20 marks)

Helping hand

In **part (a)** you are writing notes for circulation at a meeting for managers of all functions (not just from finance) and so you must be careful to **keep technical language to a minimum.** Make sure that you **refer to the four areas** requested. You may like to include references to (ii), (iii) and (iv) within your summary of the steps.

Part (b) is also standard textbook material. Use your own practical experience of computers if possible.

---

14   ANSWER: TDF

What the examiner said

This question was not popular with candidates and there were a number of weak answers. Many candidates made little reference to the circumstances of TDF. It was disappointing to see that many candidates were unaware of the role that computers might play in supporting the overall process of budgeting.

(a)

Helping hand

It is important to utilise the **specific situation** described in the question when you are explaining the budgetary process. You are asked to prepare **notes on the budget preparation process**, which includes the preparation of the master budget. The requested **diagram** should show the **budgetary control process**, however, which also includes the recording of actual results and reporting of variances.

The **steps in the budgetary process** are shown in the following diagram. Further explanations of each of the steps follow at the end of the diagram.

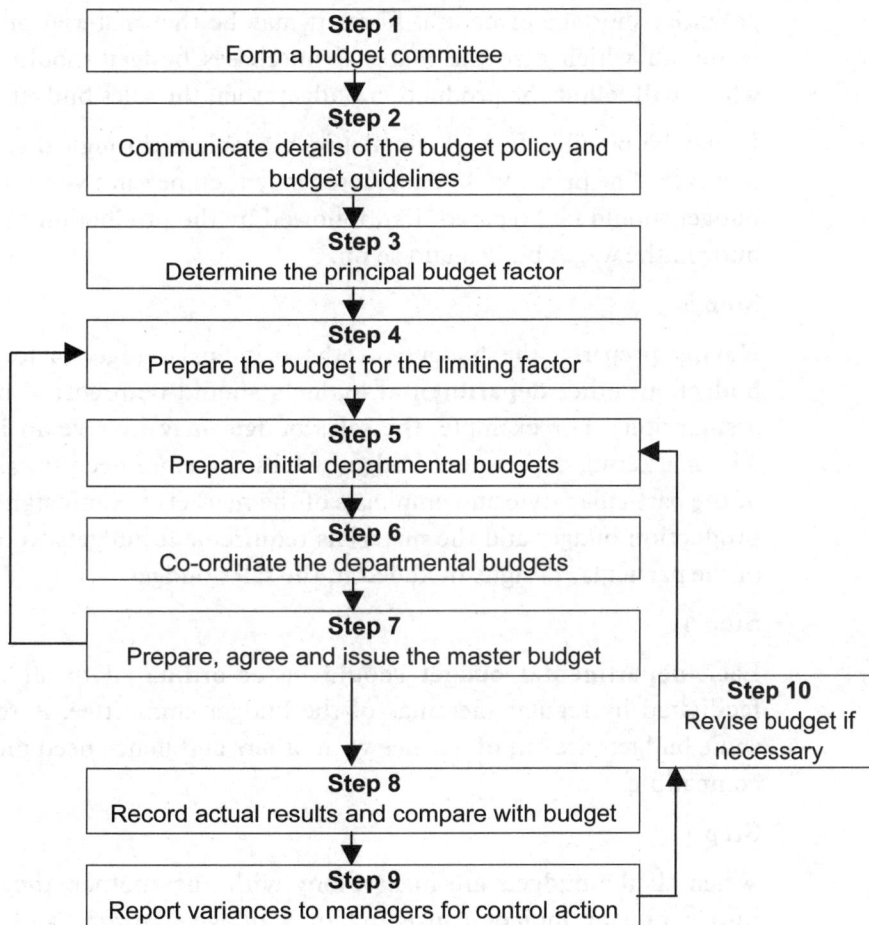

Step 1
Form a budget committee

Step 2
Communicate details of the budget policy and budget guidelines

Step 3
Determine the principal budget factor

Step 4
Prepare the budget for the limiting factor

Step 5
Prepare initial departmental budgets

Step 6
Co-ordinate the departmental budgets

Step 7
Prepare, agree and issue the master budget

Step 8
Record actual results and compare with budget

Step 9
Report variances to managers for control action

Step 10
Revise budget if necessary

Step 1

The **budget committee** acts as the **co-ordinating body** throughout the planning process. Every part of the organisation should be represented on the committee; there should therefore be a representative from sales, production, marketing and so on. The committee should meet regularly to maintain communication between departments and to ensure a co-ordinated approach to the preparation of budgets.

Step 2

The company's **long-term plan** should provide the **framework for the annual budget**. The budget should be seen as one step towards the achievement of the long-term plan. For example, if the long-term plan calls for an increase in export sales, this will need to be taken into account in the preparation of the annual budget. Such policies and guidelines should be contained within the **budget manual**. This is a collection of instructions governing the responsibilities of the people involved in the preparation of the budgets, and the records relating to the preparation and use of budgetary data. The budget manual should also contain information such as an organisation chart, a list of budget holders, the timetable for the preparation of budgets, important guidelines for wage rate increases, productivity assumptions and so on and a chart of accounts. The budget manual provides a source of information that everyone can refer to for guidance throughout the budget preparation process.

Steps 3 and 4

The **principal budget factor,** or limiting or key factor, is the factor that limits the company's performance for the forthcoming budget period. The budget for this factor must be prepared first and then all other budgets co-ordinated with it. In view of the potential shortage of natural fibres it may be that material purchases are the limiting factor, in which case the material purchases budget should be prepared first, from which will follow the production budget, then the sales budget and so on.

It may be possible to alleviate a supply problem through the use of man-made fibres, however. The principal budget factor may then be sales volume, in which case the sales budget should be prepared first, followed by the production budget, then the materials budget, the wages budget and so on.

Step 5

Having prepared the budget for the principal budget factor, for example the sales budget, all other **departmental budgets** should be prepared based on the same basic assumptions. For example, the sales budget may involve an increase in export sales. The marketing department budget would therefore need to take into account the cost of the particular style and emphasis of the marketing campaigns required. Similarly the production budget and the materials requirement budgets would need to take account of the particular designs included in the sales budget.

Step 6

Each **departmental budget** should be **co-ordinated** to all others, a task which is facilitated by regular meetings of the budget committee. A review may indicate that some budgets are out of balance with others and hence need modifying so that they are compatible.

Step 7

When all the budgets are in harmony with one another, they should be summarised into a **master budget** consisting of a budgeted profit and loss account, budgeted balance sheet and cash budget. This budget should be agreed by managers and by the board of directors as an acceptable plan for the forthcoming year. If the plan is not acceptable then it may be necessary to return to step 4 to carry out adjustments until a master budget is finally agreed and accepted.

(b)

> **Helping hand**
>
> Again, you will gain extra marks if you refer to TDF. Don't forget that there is more to computers than just spreadsheet packages.

The preparation of a budget involves the manipulation of a large volume of data, and numerous detailed calculations. When adjustments are required the revision of one budget may lead to the need to revise all other budgets. **Computers** can assist in the **manipulation of data**, however, leaving managers free to undertake the real planning process.

A major advantage of computerised budget models is their ability to **evaluate different options** and carry out 'what if' analysis. By changing the value of certain variables, for example changing the sales forecast, managers are able to assess the effect of potential changes in the environment. This would be particularly useful for TDF because of the uncertainty they face, together with the price volatility in their industry. Furthermore, because of the potential shortages, TDF could be assisted by the computerised optimisation models that are available, to ensure that the best use is made of limited resources.

The most common package used in the preparation of budgets is a **spreadsheet**. A major advantage of a spreadsheet is that once the basic model has been constructed, containing the inter-relationships of all the budgets, the model will **ensure that the departmental budgets and master budget are co-ordinated**. Data and information from the departmental budgets will be automatically fed through to the master budget model, ensuring that the master budget is a true reflection of all the subsidiary budgets.

Examiner's marking scheme		**Marks**
(a)	Overview of budgetary control process	
	- process	to 3
	- diagram (or equivalent description)	to 2
	- principal budget factor	to 3
	- departmental budget	to 1
	- master budget	to 2
	- budget manual	to 3
		14
(b)	Role of computers in budgeting	
	- mechanise accounting process - spreadsheets	to 3
	- computer modelling	to 3
		6
		20

15   **LUX LTD (6/99)**   *72 mins*

You are employed by a firm of certified accountants. One of your clients, David Brown, is about to start a business, Lux Ltd, making and selling decorative candles. He anticipates that he will need a bank overdraft facility. Candle sales tend to be seasonal in the UK, most sales occurring in the autumn months. He hopes, however, that once the business is established he will be able to export some candles throughout the year. The bank manager has asked for a budgeted income statement and a cash flow forecast for the six months ending 31 December 20X9. At your request, David has drawn up estimates of the likely sales and costs for the first six months of trading, commencing on 1 July 20X9.

The production process is relatively straightforward. David intends to employ one full-time member of staff and use a number of part-time workers as necessary. He plans to spend his own time on selling and administration.

He has provided the following information.

1   Premises suitable for production have been acquired and these will be occupied from 1 July 20X9. Rent of £600 is payable quarterly, on the first day of each quarter.

2   Production equipment costing £20,000, payable two months after delivery, will be installed in the first week of July.

3   David's estimates for sales and stock levels are as follows.

	Stock at month end	Sales
	Candles	Candles
July	2,000	-
August	6,000	-
September	10,000	4,400
October	6,000	9,000
November	4,000	6,800
December	3,000	3,000

4   The cost of raw materials for each candle is £0.60. No stocks of raw material will be kept. Purchases are to be paid in the month following delivery.

5   All workers will be paid £0.50 per candle produced, paid in the same month as production. David has no plans to draw a salary from the business at present.

6   Cash expenses are estimated at £400 per month - £250 for production expenses and £150 for administration and distribution expenses.

7   The selling price will be £1.65 per candle. All sales will be made to retail shops. Customers will be allowed two months credit, as is customary practice in this trade.

8   David will invest £25,000 of his own savings as share capital in the business. A friend will lend the business another £10,000, but requires interest to be paid each month equivalent to a rate of 15% per annum. Both amounts will be paid into the business on 1 July 20X9.

9   Depreciation should be provided on the production equipment using a straight-line basis at an annual rate of 20%.

10   For the purpose of budgeting, interest payable or receivable on bank balances should be ignored at this stage (only interest arising on the loan in note 8 should be provided).

11   You have suggested to David that for the purpose of producing management accounts a marginal costing system is used. The stock of finished candles at 31 December 20X9 is to be valued on the basis of prime cost only.

Required

(a) Prepare the following budgets for the six months ending 31 December 20X9.

    (i)   A production budget for each of the six months   (4 marks)

    (ii)   A production cost budget for the six month period   (6 marks)

    (iii)   A budgeted profit and loss account for the period   (8 marks)

(b) Prepare a cash flow forecast for each month of the business until 31 December 20X9.

                                                  (16 marks)

(c) Bearing in mind that this is a new business with *no previous trading record*, suggest two ways by which David might reduce the extent of the overdraft required.   (6 marks)

                                                    (40 marks)

Helping hand

Before you rush in and start preparing your budgets, take a **few moments to think about layout**. The examiner has stressed the emphasis given to the presentation of answers in a manner which **facilitates management understanding**. Neat presentation also helps you to **work systematically** through the information provided, thus reducing the risk of leaving out something important.

---

15 **ANSWER: LUX LTD**

What the examiner said

Part (c) was not answered particularly well.

(a) (i)

Helping hand

A **production budget** shows the **number of candles** to be produced each month. No costs are shown in this budget, only quantities. Remember that the **closing stock** for each month **becomes the opening stock** for the next month.

Production budget for July to December 20X9

	July Candles	*August* Candles	*September* Candles	*October* Candles	*November* Candles	*December* Candles	*Total* Candles
Sales	-	-	4,400	9,000	6,800	3,000	
Closing stock	2,000	6,000	10,000	6,000	4,000	3,000	
	2,000	6,000	14,400	15,000	10,800	6,000	
Less opening stock	-	2,000	6,000	10,000	6,000	4,000	
Production required	2,000	4,000	8,400	5,000	4,800	2,000	26,200

(ii)

Helping hand

You are asked to prepare a **production cost budget**, which shows the production cost of producing the number of units indicated in your production budget in (i). Production costs will **include depreciation** on the production equipment and rent for the production premises. **Good presentation** requires you to show a subtotal for prime cost. Note that the budget is for the six-month period, not for each of the six months as in (i).

Production cost budget for six months ending 31 December 20X9

Production volume	26,200 candles	
	£	£
Raw materials (26,200 × £0.60)		15,720
Direct labour (26,200 × £0.50)		13,100
Prime cost		28,820
Production expenses (£250 × 6 months)	1,500	
Depreciation on production equipment (£20,000 × 20% × 6/12)	2,000	
Rent on production premises (£600 × 2 quarters)	1,200	
Production overhead		4,700
Total production cost		33,520

(iii)

Helping hand

You are asked to use a **marginal costing system** to produce the management accounts. You therefore need to highlight **contribution** by separating the fixed and variable costs. The variable cost of production is labelled as prime cost in the production cost budget (£28,820). The question tells you to **value stock** on the basis of **prime cost** only.

Budgeted profit and loss account for six months ending 31 December 20X9

	£	£
Sales revenue (23,200 candles × £1.65)		38,280
Less variable cost of goods sold:		
variable cost of production	28,820	
less closing stock (3,000 candles × £(0.60 + 0.50))	3,300	
		25,520
Contribution		12,760
Less fixed costs:		
production overhead (from (a)(ii))	4,700	
administration and distribution expenses (£150 × 6)	900	
loan interest (£10,000 × 15% × 6/12)	750	
		6,350
Net profit		6,410

(b)

Helping hand

Clear presentation and a **systematic approach** are particularly important when preparing **cash flow forecasts**. The examiner will expect to see **separate totals for receipts and payments**, not a jumbled list of inflows and outflows mixed together. You should also show the net cash flow for each month and the **closing balance at the month end**. Remember that depreciation is not a cash flow and does not appear in the cash forecast.

Initial workings

	July	*August*	*September*	*October*	*November*	*December*
Sales income (at £1.65 per candle)			£7,260	£14,850	£11,220	£4,950
Income actually received after two months			-	-	£7,260	£14,850
Monthly production (units)	2,000	4,000	8,400	5,000	4,800	2,000
Materials at £0.60 per unit, paid one month later		£1,200	£2,400	£5,040	£3,000	£2,880
Labour at £0.50 per unit, paid in same month	£1,000	£2,000	£4,200	£2,500	£2,400	£1,000

Cash flow forecast for July to December 20X9

	July £	*August* £	*September* £	*October* £	*November* £	*December* £
Receipts						
Sales income					7,260	14,850
Share capital	25,000					
Loan	10,000					
	35,000	-	-	-	7,260	14,850
Payments						
Rent	600			600		
Production equipment			20,000			
Raw materials		1,200	2,400	5,040	3,000	2,880
Direct labour	1,000	2,000	4,200	2,500	2,400	1,000
Cash expenses	400	400	400	400	400	400
Loan interest	125	125	125	125	125	125
	2,125	3,725	27,125	8,665	5,925	4,405
Net cash flow	32,875	(3,725)	(27,125)	(8,665)	1,335	10,445
Opening cash balance	0	32,875	29,150	2,025	(6,640)	(5,305)
Closing cash balance	32,875	29,150	2,025	(6,640)	(5,305)	5,140

(c)

> **Helping hand**
>
> Although only two suggestions were required, we have listed more so that you can see the range of possible answers. In an examination, do not waste time by providing more suggestions than the number requested.

Since this is a **new business** with **no previous trading record,** it may **not be possible to obtain longer credit facilities** than have already been assumed in the budgets. Other possible **ways of reducing the required overdraft include the following.**

- Increase the amount of initial share capital or loan.
- Commence sales earlier.
- Encourage customers to pay earlier by offering early settlement discounts.
- Reduce the level of stock held at each month end.
- Lease or rent the equipment instead of buying it outright.

Examiner's marking scheme

				Marks
(a)	Budgets for the six months ended 31 December 20X9			
	(i)	Production budget	to 4	
	(ii)	Production cost budget		
		Prime costs	to 2	
		Overheads	to 3	
		Total	to 1	
				10
	(iii)	Budgeted profit and loss account		
		Sales	to 2	
		Stock	to 2	
		Cost of sales	to 1	
		Other overheads	to 2	
		Net profit	to 1	
				8
(b)	Cash flow forecast			
	Receipts		to 4	
	Payments		to 7	
	Net inflow/outflow and balances		to 3	
	Presentation		to 2	
				16
(c)	Finance suggestions (2 suggestions × 3 marks each)			6
				40

16   MASTER BUDGET

As finance assistant, you are part of the team responsible for preparing your organisation's master budget for the six months ending 31 December 20X2.

You have been provided with the following information.

- *Estimated balance sheet for year ended 30 June 20X2*

	Cost £	Depreciation provision £	Net book value £
Fixed assets	140,000	14,000	126,000
Current assets			
Stock	25,000		
Trade debtors	24,600		
Bank	3,000		
Net current liabilities		52,600	
Creditors: Amounts falling due within one year			
Trade creditors	25,000		
Other creditors	9,000		
		34,000	
Net current assets			18,600
Total assets less current liabilities			144,600
Capital and reserves			
Share capital			100,000
Profit and loss account			44,600
			144,600

- *Trading forecasts for the six months ending 31 December 20X2*

	Sales in units	Purchases £	Wages and salaries £	O/hds excluding depreciation £	Purchase of fixed assets £	Issue of 20,000 £1 shares £	Divi-dends £
May	4,000	12,000	8,000	7,000			
June	4,200	13,000	8,000	7,000			
July	4,500	14,000	8,000	7,000			
August	4,600	18,000	10,000	7,000			
Sept	4,800	16,000	10,000	7,000		20,000	
October	5,000	14,000	10,000	8,000			10,000
Nov	3,800	12,000	12,000	8,000	30,000		
Dec	3,000	12,000	12,000	8,000			

- The selling price of your organisation's product in May 20X2 was £6 per unit and this is to be increased to £8 per unit in October. 50% of sales are for cash and 50% are on credit, to be paid two months later.

- Purchases are to be paid for two months after purchase.

- Wages and salaries are to be paid 75% in the month incurred and 25% in the following month.

- Overheads are to be paid in the month after they are incurred.

- The fixed assets are to be paid for in three equal instalments in the three months following purchase.

- Dividends are to be paid three months after they are declared and the receipts from the share issue are budgeted to be received in the month of issue.

- Fixed assets are depreciated 10% per annum on a straight line basis on those assets owned at 31 December 20X2.

- Closing stock, at the beginning of the period under review was equal to the previous two months' purchases. At 31 December 20X2 it was equal to three months' purchases.

Required

(a) Prepare the following budgets for the six months ended 31 December 20X2.

   (i)   Cash budget
   (ii)   Budgeted profit and loss account
   (iii) Budgeted balance sheet   (32 marks)

(b) Comment upon the results, highlighting those areas that you wish to draw to the attention of the budget committee.   (8 marks)

(40 marks)

Helping hand

Cash budgets are so much easier to prepare if you **keep all of your workings off of the face of the budget** and do them (neatly) on a separate piece of paper. Make sure that you reference your workings to the cash budget.

Don't forget that a **profit and loss account and balance sheet** must be **prepared on an accruals basis** rather than a receipts and payments basis.

---

16   ANSWER: MASTER BUDGET

> **Helping hand**
>
> The forecasts of sales units, purchases and so on provided in the question are **trading forecasts** and not payments/receipts forecasts.

(a) (i)   **CASH BUDGET** JULY TO DECEMBER 20X2

	July £	August £	Sept £	Oct £	Nov £	Dec £
Receipts						
From sales (W1)	25,500	26,400	27,900	33,800	29,600	32,000
Share issue	-	-	20,000	-	-	-
	25,500	26,400	47,900	33,800	29,600	32,000
Payments						
Purchases (W2)	12,000	13,000	14,000	18,000	16,000	14,000
Wages and						
salaries (W3)	8,000	9,500	10,000	10,000	11,500	12,000
Overheads	7,000	7,000	7,000	7,000	8,000	8,000
Fixed assets (W5)	-	-	-	-	-	10,000
	27,000	29,500	31,000	35,000	35,500	44,000
Excess of receipts						
over payments	(1,500)	(3,100)	16,900	(1,200)	(5,900)	(12,000)
Balance b/f	3,000	1,500	(1,600)	15,300	14,100	8,200
Balance c/f	1,500	(1,600)	15,300	14,100	8,200	(3,800)

(ii)   **BUDGETED PROFIT AND LOSS ACCOUNT**
      JULY TO DECEMBER 20X2

	£	£
Sales (W7)		177,800
Less cost of sales		
Opening stock	25,000	
Purchases	86,000	
Closing stock	(38,000)	
		(73,000)
Gross profit		104,800
Less expenses		
Wages and salaries	62,000	
Overheads	45,000	
Depreciation (W8)	8,500	
		(115,500)
Net loss		(10,700)
Profit and loss account balance b/f		44,600
Profits available for appropriation		33,900
Less dividends		(10,000)
Profit and loss account balance c/f		23,900

(iii)   **BUDGETED BALANCE SHEET**
AS AT 31 DECEMBER 20X2

	Cost £	Prov for dep'n £	Net book value £
Fixed assets	170,000	22,500	147,500
Current assets			
Stock	38,000		
Trade debtors (W1)	27,200		
		65,200	
Current liabilities			
Bank overdraft	3,800		
Trade creditors (W2)	24,000		
Other creditors (W9)	41,000		
		(68,800)	
Net current assets			(3,600)
Total assets less current liabilities			143,900
Capital and reserves			
Share capital			120,000
Profit and loss account			23,900
			143,900

Helping hand

If your balance sheet doesn't balance you know you've made a mistake somewhere! In an **exam** you **shouldn't waste time looking for your error**, however. Go back to the question at the end of the exam if you have a spare few minutes.

Workings

1   *Receipts from sales*

Helping hand

The **debtors** figure for the balance sheet is made up of the **November and December credit sales**.

	May £'000	June £'000	July £'000	August £'000	Sept £'000	Oct £'000	Nov £'000	Dec £'000	Debtors £'000
Total	24.0	25.2	27.0	27.6	28.8	40.0	30.4	24.0	NA
Cash	12.0	12.6	13.5	13.8	14.4	20.0	15.2	12.0	NA
Credit	NA	NA	12.0	12.6	13.5	13.8	14.4	20.0	27.2★
Receipts	NA	NA	25.5	26.4	27.9	33.8	29.6	32.0	

★(£15,200 + £12,000)

2   *Purchases*

Helping hand

The **creditors** figure for the balance sheet is made up of the **November and December purchases**.

	May £'000	June £'000	July £'000	August £'000	Sept £'000	Oct £'000	Nov £'000	Dec £'000	Creditors £'000
Purchases	12	13	14	18	16	14	12	12	NA
Payment	NA	NA	12	13	14	18	16	14	24★

★(£12,000 + £12,000)

3 *Wages and salaries*

	June £'000	July £'000	August £'000	Sept £'000	Oct £'000	Nov £'000	Dec £'000	Creditors £'000
Total incurred	8	8	10	10	10	12	12	NA
75%	NA	6	7.5	7.5	7.5	9.0	9	NA
25%	NA	2	2.0	2.5	2.5	2.5	3	3
		8	9.5	10.0	10.0	11.5	12	

4 *Overheads*

Creditor at December of £8,000.

5 *Fixed assets*

	November £'000	December £'000	Creditor £'000
Purchase	30		
Payment		10	
Creditor			20

6 *Dividends*

Dividends - declared October and therefore paid in January
         - creditor at December of £10,000

7 *Sales*

> **Helping hand**
>
> The **sales figure in the cash budget** (receipts) is **not the same as the sales figure required for the P&L account**.

	£
$(4{,}500 + 4{,}600 + 4{,}800) \times £6 =$	83,400
$(5{,}000 + 3{,}800 + 3{,}000) \times £8 =$	94,400
	177,800

8 *Depreciation*

> **Helping hand**
>
> **Depreciation** is based on assets owned at 31 December 20X2. The **charge is for six months** only.

	£
Assets owned at 30 June 2092	140,000
Additions	30,000
	170,000

Depreciation = $£170{,}000 \times 10\% \times 0.5 =$	£8,500

9 *Other creditors*

> **Helping hand**
>
> It would have been very easy to forget one of these other creditors. **Neat and sensible workings**, such as the inclusion of creditors columns in workings 3 and 5, help.

	£
Wages and salaries (W3)	3
Overheads (W4)	8
Fixed assets (W5)	20
Dividend (W6)	10
	41

(b)

> **Helping hand**
>
> There is little point in simply telling the budget committee that there will be an overdraft at the end of August. Try to **offer advice**.

(i)   The cash budget shows that there will be an **overdraft** at the end of August and at the end of December, despite the share issue in September. Payments in January and February 20X3 for the fixed asset and the payment of the dividend in January will only increase the overdraft. Sufficient **overdraft facilities must therefore be arranged or other action**, such as a reversal of the decision to purchase the fixed asset, should be considered.

(ii)   A reduction in sales quantities in November and December results in a **net loss** of £10,700. If such a reduction is not part of a plan then ways of either **cutting costs** or **increasing sales** must be considered.

(iii)   Stock at the end of the period represents three months' purchases whereas stock at the beginning of the period represents two months' purchases. If this is due to the reduction in sales quantities then it may be advisable to **reduce purchases if the drop in sales is unavoidable.**

17   PERSONAL REASONS

(a)   Your organisation's sales analyst had made some progress in preparing the sales forecasts for year 5 when she unexpectedly needed to take a holiday for personal reasons.

She has left you the following memo.

MEMORANDUM

To:	Assistant Management Accountant
From:	Sales analyst
Date:	12 December 20X4
Subject:	Sales forecasts for year 5

In preparing the sales volume forecasts for year 5, I have got as far as establishing the following trend figures and average seasonal variations.

	Quarter 1 Units	*Quarter 2* Units	*Quarter 3* Units	*Quarter 4* Units
Year 3 - trend figures	3,270	3,313	3,358	3,407
Year 4 - trend figures	3,452	3,496	3,541	3,587
Average seasonal variation	−50	+22	+60	−32

As a basis for extrapolating the trend line, I forecast that the trend will continue to increase in year 5 at the same average amount per quarter as during year 4.

Sorry to leave with this unfinished job, but it should be possible to prepare an outline forecast for year 5 with this data.

Required

(i)   Briefly explain what is meant by the following.

(1)   Seasonal variations
(2)   Extrapolating a trend line

Use the data from the memorandum to illustrate your explanations.   (5 marks)

(ii)   Prepare a forecast of sales volumes for each of the four quarters of year 5, based on the data contained in the analyst's memo.   (6 marks)

(b)   After preparing the sales forecasts, you are asked to draw up some information for the budget manual.

Required

(i)   Explain the role of managers and the budget committee in the budget preparation process.

(ii)   Explain how the use of spreadsheets may improve the efficiency of the budget preparation process.   (9 marks)

(20 marks)

Helping hand

We suggest that you use the **common sense 'rule-of-thumb' approach to forecast the sales volumes**. Drawing the trend line by eye on a graph is far more time consuming.

It would be very easy, in part (b), to simply apply common sense rather than knowledge. Waffle does *not* earn marks.

---

17   ANSWER: PERSONAL REASONS

(a)

> **Helping hand**
>
> Don't forget to **illustrate** your explanations with data from the question.

(i) (1) **Seasonal variations** are **regular patterns of fluctuations** which occur over the year. For example, the seasonal variation for quarter 1 is minus 50 units. This indicates that the sales volume for quarter 1 is on average 50 units below the general trend in sales. Similarly the sales volume for quarter 2 is generally 22 units above the general trend.

(2) A **trend line** is the **underlying direction in which a time series is moving**. The **trend is determined by removing the effect of seasonal variations from data**, usually by **using the technique of moving averages**.

In the data provided, the monthly sales volume appears to be increasing by an average of 45 units in each quarter, after eliminating the seasonal variations. This is the underlying trend in the data, which the analyst suggests should be used to project the sales data into the future. This is known as **extrapolating the trend,** that is, continuing its general direction as a basis for the sales forecast.

(ii)

> **Helping hand**
>
> Remember that the seasonal adjustment shows whether the **forecast should be lower than the trend (a negative seasonal adjustment) or above the trend (a positive seasonal adjustment)**.

Working

Calculating the average quarterly increase in the trend.

Year	Quarter	Trend	Increase in trend
		Units	Units
3	4	3,407	
4	1	3,452	45
	2	3,496	44
	3	3,541	45
	4	3,587	46
			180 **Average = 180/4 = 45 units**

Sales volume forecast for year 5

Quarter	1	2	3	4
	Units	Units	Units	Units
Trend	3,632	3,677	3,722	3,767
Seasonal adjustment	−50	+22	+60	−32
Forecast	3,582	3,699	3,782	3,735

(b)

> **Helping hand**
>
> If you have any **practical experience** of the value of computers in budgeting you should include it.

(i)   **Role of managers**

The **responsibility for preparing the budgets should**, ideally, **lie with the managers who are responsible for implementing them**. Thus the preparation might be allocated as follows.

(1) The sales manager should draft the sales budget and the selling overhead cost centre budgets.

(2) The purchasing manager should draft the material purchases budget.

(3) The production manager should draft the direct production cost budgets.

Role of budget committee

The **whole process is usually overseen by a budget committee**, which should, ideally comprise **representatives from every part of the organisation**. A budget committee might be **responsible** for the following.

(1) **Co-ordinating and allocating responsibility** for the preparation of budgets.

(2) **Timetabling.**

(3) **Providing information** to assist in the preparation of budgets.

(4) **Monitoring the budgeting and planning process** by comparing actual and budgeted results.

(ii)   **Spreadsheets** have the basic advantages of computerisation, that computers can **process a larger volume of data more rapidly** (and **often more accurately**) than a manual system.

A spreadsheet also is a convenient financial model of the relationships between the different variables in a budget.

In real life, preparing budgets may be complex; **budgets may need to go through several drafts. Spreadsheets aid this process in that one or two figures can be changed and then the computer will automatically make all the consequential changes to the other figures.**

Budgets on spreadsheets can also be **amended easily during the year** if a major change in circumstances means the original budget was based on out-of-date assumptions.

Similarly management may well wish to evaluate different options by **'what if' analysis**. One or a number of variables can be changed on spreadsheets, and as an automatic result, management will be able to see the consequences of the decisions they take or possible future events such as increased demand.

Once budgets have been set up on spreadsheets, the **same model can be used year after year** by changing the values of the variables.

Spreadsheets can also **incorporate actual as well as budgeted figures. Comparisons** between budgeted and actual information are vital **for control purposes**, and can also help budgetary preparation in future years by highlighting the actual figures that were not in line with expectations.

18 QUESTION WITH HELP: FLEXIBLE BUDGETS

Excelsior Manufacturing Company produces a single product on an assembly line. As Budget Officer you have prepared the following production budgets from the best information available, to represent the extremes of high and low volume of production likely to be encountered by the company over a three-month period.

	Production of 4,000 units £	Production of 8,000 units £
Direct materials	80,000	160,000
Indirect materials	12,000	20,000
Direct labour	50,000	100,000
Power	18,000	24,000
Repairs	20,000	30,000
Supervision	20,000	36,000
Rent, insurance and rates	9,000	9,000

Supervision is a 'step function'. One supervisor is employed for all production levels up to and including 5,000 units. For higher levels of production an assistant supervisor (£16,000) is also required. For power, a minimum charge is payable on all production up to and including 6,000 units. For production above this level there is an additional variable charge based on the power consumed. Other variable and semi-variable costs are incurred evenly over the production range.

Required

(a) Prepare a set of flexible budgets for presentation to the production manager to cover the following levels of production over a period of three months:

   4,000; 5,000; 6,000; 7,000; 8,000 units   (10 marks)

(b) During the three months July to September (covering most of the summer holiday period) 5,000 units were produced. Costs incurred during the three-month period were as follows.

	£
Direct materials	110,000
Indirect materials	14,000
Direct labour	70,000
Power	18,000
Repairs	30,000
Supervision	20,000
Rent, insurance and rates	8,000

Present the above figures as a budget report for presentation to the Production Manager. Write a brief note against each significant variance suggesting any further investigations which might be required.   (10 marks)

(20 marks)

> *If you are stuck, look at the next page for detailed help as to how you should tackle this question.*

APPROACHING THE ANSWER

The wrong approach to part (a) is to determine costs for 4,000 units and then to multiply the costs by 1.25 to get costs for 5,000 units, 1.5 for 6,000 units and so on. Such an approach assumes all costs are variable and takes no account of fixed and mixed costs. The correct approach is to work out whether a cost is variable, mixed or fixed and then to work out the budget allowances given the cost's behaviour.

Step 1. *Examine each cost classification*
Does doubling the production level lead to double the costs?
Yes. This means it is a variable cost - go to Step 2.
No, there is no change. This means that it is a fixed cost - go to Step 3.
No, the costs change but do not double. This means it is a mixed cost - go to Step 4.
No, but you are given extra information about the cost's behaviour in the question - go to Step 5.

Step 2. *Deal with variable costs*
Work out the cost per unit by dividing total cost at a particular production level by the number of units. Calculate the budget cost allowance at each production level by multiplying the cost per unit by the relevant number of units.
Example: direct labour - cost per unit = £50,000/4,000 = £.........
budget for 6,000 units = 6,000 x cost per unit

Step 3. *Deal with fixed costs*
Fixed costs will be the same at all levels of production.

Step 4. *Deal with mixed costs*
Separate the fixed and variable components of the mixed cost using the high-low method.

Example: repairs

Production Units	Cost £
8,000	30,000
4,000	20,000
4,000	10,000

Variable cost per unit = £10,000/4,000 = £2.50
Fixed cost (using production of 4,000 units) = £20,000 − (4,000 × £2.50) = £10,000
Example: budget for 6,000 units = £10,000 + £(6,000 × £2.50) = £25,000

Step 5. *Deal with other costs*

Example: power
If the minimum charge is payable on all production up to and including 6,000 units then it is paid on production of 4,000 units and is £18,000. This represents a fixed cost at all levels of production. On production over 6,000 units there is a variable charge based on power consumed. Production of 8,000 units will have incurred the variable charge on 2,000 units. This variable charge for 2,000 units = £(24,000 − 18,000) = £6,000. The charge per unit = £6,000/2,000 = £3.
For production up to 6,000 units, the budget is £18,000. For production over 6,000 units, the budget is £18,000 plus £3 per unit over 6,000 units.
Example: budget for 7,000 units = £18,000 + ((7,000 − 6,000) × £3) = £21,000

Let's now turn our attention to part (b).

Step 1. Head up your report with 'To:', 'From:', 'Date:', and 'Subject:'.

Step 2. Divide it into sections headed Introduction, Findings and Conclusion.

Step 3. In the Introduction explain the purpose of the report and the work carried out.

Step 4. Compare the budgeted costs at output of 5,000 units (calculated in part (a)) with the actual costs and determine variances (the difference between the budgeted and actual costs). Indicate whether the variances are adverse or favourable.

Step 5. In the Findings, make a note of those variances that need investigating and suggest reasons why the variances may have occurred and/or what the variance could indicate.

Step 6. In the Conclusion summarise your findings and suggest suitable management action.

Step 7. Always end with a phrase such as 'If you require further information then please do not hesitate to contact me'.

18   ANSWER TO QUESTION WITH HELP: FLEXIBLE BUDGETS

(a)   *Budgets at different levels of activity*

	4,000 units	5,000 units	6,000 units	7,000 units	8,000 units
	£	£	£	£	£
Direct materials (W1)	80,000	100,000	120,000	140,000	160,000
Indirect materials (W2)	12,000	14,000	16,000	18,000	20,000
Direct labour (W3)	50,000	62,500	75,000	87,500	100,000
Power (W4)	18,000	18,000	18,000	21,000	24,000
Repairs (W5)	20,000	22,500	25,000	27,500	30,000
Supervision (W6)	20,000	20,000	36,000	36,000	36,000
Rent, insurance and rates (W7)	9,000	9,000	9,000	9,000	9,000
Total	209,000	246,000	299,000	339,000	379,000

Workings

1   *Direct materials*

4,000 units cost £80,000 and 8,000 units cost £160,000. A doubling of units leads to a doubling of cost. Direct materials is therefore a **variable cost**.

Cost per unit = £80,000/4,000 = £20.

Example: budget for 6,000 units = 6,000 × £20 = £120,000.

2   *Indirect materials*

A doubling of production does not result in a doubling of cost. Indirect materials is therefore a **mixed cost**. We can separate the fixed and variable components of the cost using the **high-low technique**.

	Production Units	Cost £
	8,000	20,000
	4,000	12,000
Difference	4,000	8,000

The variable cost of 4,000 units is therefore £8,000 and thus the variable cost per unit = £8,000/4,000 = £2.

Consider the total cost of 4,000 units.

	£
Variable cost (4,000 × £2)	8,000
Total cost	12,000
Fixed cost	4,000

The total cost of indirect materials is therefore based on a **fixed cost of £4,000 plus a variable cost of £2 per unit**.

Example: budget for 6,000 units = £4,000 + £(6,000 × 2) = £16,000.

3   *Direct labour*

See 'Approaching the answer'.

4   *Power*

See 'Approaching the answer'.

BPP
PROFESSIONAL EDUCATION

5 *Repairs*

See 'Approaching the answer'.

6 *Supervision*

We are told supervision is a **step cost**. For 4,000 and 5,000 units the budget will be £20,000. Over 5,000 units the budget will be £20,000 + £16,000 = £36,000.

Example: budget for 6,000 units = £36,000.

7 *Rent, insurance and rates*

The cost does not change despite a doubling of production and hence it is a **fixed cost**.

Example: budget for 6,000 units = £9,000.

(b)

REPORT

To: Production Manager
From: N Accountant
Date: XX October 20X7
Subject: Operating costs - July to September

1 INTRODUCTION

This report provides a **review of operating costs** incurred during the three-month period from July to September. Actual costs incurred during the period have been compared with budgeted results and differences highlighted. The budgeted results are those costs which should have been expected at the actual level of activity during the three-month period (that is, at output of 5,000 units).

Suggestions for those variances (differences between actual and budgeted results) which may require investigation have been made as necessary.

(A) denotes an adverse variance and (F) a favourable variance.

2 FINDINGS

Cost	Budgeted cost at output of 5,000 units £	Actual cost £	Variance £
Direct materials	100,000	110,000	10,000 (A)
Indirect materials	14,000	14,000	-
Direct labour	62,500	70,000	7,500 (A)
Power	18,000	18,000	-
Repairs	22,500	30,000	7,500 (A)
Supervision	20,000	20,000	-
Rent, insurance and rates	9,000	8,000	1,000 (F)
	246,000	270,000	24,000 (A)

Direct materials variance

An investigation is needed to determine whether this is a price or a usage variance and when this has been ascertained, the cause of the variance needs investigating. It may have arisen because of price increases, careless purchasing or a change in the material standard (if a **price variance**) or because of defective material, excessive waste, theft or stricter quality control (if a **usage variance**).

Direct labour variance

Again an investigation is required to determine what type of variance this is, a **rate variance** or an **efficiency variance**. If it is a rate variance an investigation may discover that it is due to a wage rate increase or because excessive overtime has been worked, although this is unlikely since production levels were fairly low. If the variance is a labour efficiency variance an investigation may reveal it being due to a cause such as machine breakdown, non-availability of material or excessive lost time.

Repairs variance

This variance should be investigated since it may indicate that capital equipment needs replacing. If so, the equipment should be replaced as soon as possible so as to avoid a total stoppage of production. On the other hand, it could indicate that the original budget was incorrect.

Rent, insurance and rates variance

This should be a fixed cost and so the variance is more than likely an **expenditure variance**. An investigation should reveal that either the original budget was incorrect or that a one-off exceptional payment has not been necessary.

3   CONCLUSION

The findings laid out in the previous section indicate that **actual results** for the three-month period from July to September **were not as good as expected,** costs being £24,000 higher than anticipated. The **variances** highlighted by the budget statement **should therefore be investigated and their cause determined so as to ascertain whether original budgets and standards were incorrect or whether cost control needs tightening.**

If you require any further information then please do not hesitate to contact me.

19   WHOLESALER (12/01)

A wholesaler buys and sells a range of goods. A cash budget has been prepared for the first three months of the next financial year as follows.

	Month 1 £'000	Month 2 £'000	Month 3 £'000
Receipts from:			
Credit sales	162.0	208.0	206.0
Issue of shares	500.0	-	-
	662.0	208.0	206.0
Payments for:			
Goods	140.4	106.8	112.8
Overheads	59.0	50.0	52.0
Buildings and fittings	-	245.0	-
Redemption of debentures	-	-	300.0
Interest on debentures (6 months)	-	12.0	-
Taxation	-	-	29.0
Final dividend	-	20.0	-
	199.4	433.8	493.8
Net cash flow	462.6	(225.8)	(287.8)
Opening balance	78.9	541.5	315.7
Closing balance	541.5	315.7	27.9

Notes

(i)   All sales are on credit. 50% of payments are made by customers in the month after sale, with the remaining 50% one month later. Sales in Month 12 of the financial year just ending are expected to total £182,000. Cash receipts from customers in Month 4 of the next financial year are estimated to be £183,000.

(ii)   Purchases of goods are budgeted so that the stock of goods at the end of a month is sufficient to meet expected sales demand in the month following. Goods are paid for in the month after purchase. Payments made in Month 12 of the financial year just ending are expected to total £109,200, and in Month 4 of the next financial year are estimated to be £117,600.

(iii) Overheads are paid for in the month in which they are incurred.

(iv)   Depreciation is £16,000 per month.

Required

(a)   Calculate the value of sales for each of the three months (months 1 to 3).   (4 marks)

(b)   Prepare a single budget statement for months 1 to 3 in total (ie figures for individual months are not required in the statement) showing:

    (i)   sales, costs, gross profit and operating profit (ie before interest and tax) in £'000;

    (ii)   gross profit and operating profit percentage margins.   (6 marks)

(c)   Explain in general terms, and also with specific reference to the budgets in the question, why the operating profit and the net cash flow for a period may be significantly different.   (10 marks)

(20 marks)

19   ANSWER: WHOLESALER

What the examiner said

'In parts (a) and (b) many candidates had difficulty working from given cashflows to establish sales and cost of sales. In part (b) many candidates simply copied the cash budget given in the question and thus included many irrelevant items in the statement of operating profit (eg buildings and fittings expenditure, redemption of debentures and interest, tax and dividends). ... Many good answers were provided to part (c) but it was also clear that many other candidates did not understand the difference between cashflow and operating profit.'

Helping hand

Notice that half of the available marks for this question are awarded for the discussion in part (c). This demonstrates the importance of continuing to the end of the question until you have used all the allotted time according to the marks available. Never abandon a question part way through, perhaps because you have got into a muddle with the figurework.

(a) Cash receivable in month 2 in respect of month 12 sales $= £182,000 \times 50\%$
                                                                     $= £91,000$

∴ Cash receivable in month 2 in respect of month 1 sales $= £(208,000 - 91,000)$
                                                                     $= £117,000$

∴ Sales value for month 1 $= £117,000 \times 2$ $= \underline{£234,000}$

Cash receivable in month 3 in respect of month 1 sales $= £117,000$
∴ Cash receivable in month 3 in respect of month 2 sales $= £(206,000 - 117,000)$
                                                                     $= £89,000$

∴ Sales value for month 2 $= £89,000 \times 2$ $= \underline{£178,000}$

Cash receivable in month 4 in respect of month 2 sales $= £89,000$
∴ Cash receivable in month 4 in respect of month 3 sales $= £(183,000 - 89,000)$
                                                                     $= £94,000$

∴ Sales value for month 3 $= £94,000 \times 2$ $= \underline{£188,000}$

(b) Budgeted profit statement for months 1 to 3

	£'000	%
Sales value (W1)	600	
Cost of goods sold (W2)	360	
Gross profit	240	40
Overheads (W3)	209	
Operating profit	31	5.2

Workings

1   **Sales value** (from part (a))

Period	Sales value
	£'000
1	234
2	178
3	188
	600

2   **Cost of goods sold**

> **Assumption**. Opening stock is sold in the month and purchases for the month are carried forward in closing stock and sold in the following month. Therefore the purchases in a month = the cost of sales for the following month.

Month	Purchases	
	£'000	
12	140.4	= month 1 cost of sales
1	106.8	= month 2 cost of sales
2	112.8	= month 3 cost of sales
3	117.6	

$\therefore$ Months 1-3 cost of sales = £140,400 + £106,800 + £112,800
= £360,000

3   **Overheads**

	£'000
Cash payments for overheads (59 + 50 + 52)	161
Depreciation (£16,000 × 3 months)	48
	209

(c)   There are a number of reasons why the operating profit and the net cash flow for a period may be significantly different.

(i)   **Timing differences arise.** For example the sales value for month 3 is included in the operating profit figure but the cash from these sales will be received in months 4 and 5.

(ii)   Operating profit is stated **after charging depreciation** for the period, but depreciation does not represent a cash flow. For example in months 1 to 3 a total of £48,000 is charged against profit in respect of depreciation, but no cash flow arises as a result.

(iii) **Stock levels may alter.** For example if stocks increase the cash outflow to pay for the stocks will be greater than the charge to cost of sales for the cost of the goods actually sold.

(iv)   **Capital expenditure may increase cash outflow.** Capital expenditure results in an outflow of cash but it is not immediately charged against the operating profit for the period. Instead the expenditure is capitalised and charged against the profits of a number of accounting periods in the form of a depreciation charge. For example the wholesaler has budgeted a cash outflow of £245,000 for buildings and fittings in month 2, but this amount is not charged against the operating profit for the period.

(v)   **Financing operations affect cash flow but do not affect operating profit.** For example the wholesaler has budgeted for £500,000 inflow from the issue of shares and £300,000 outflow for the redemption of debentures. These items do not affect the operating profit for the period.

(vi)   **Interest, taxation and dividend payments increase cash outflow but do not affect operating profit.** The wholesaler has budgeted for a total outflow of £61,000 in respect of these items in months 1 to 3.

Examiner's marking scheme

				Marks
(a)	Sales			4
(b)	(i)	Cost of sales		2
		Overheads		2
	(ii)	Gross profit margin		1
		Operating profit margin		<u>1</u>
				6
(c)	General (1½ for each)			
	Detail (1½ for each)			max <u>10</u>
				<u><u>20</u></u>

DO YOU KNOW? – VARIANCE ANALYSIS AND MANAGEMENT CONTROL

- *Check that you can fill in the blanks in the statements below before you attempt any questions. If in doubt, you should go back to your BPP Interactive Text and revise first.*

- If an organisation uses standard marginal costing instead of standard absorption costing, there will be no .... variance and the ..../............./............./.............. variances will be valued at the standard contribution per unit (as opposed to standard profit per unit).

- There are many possible reasons for variances arising including efficiencies and inefficiencies of operations, errors in standard setting and changes in exchange rates.

- Individual variances should not be looked at in isolation. They might be interdependent/ interrelated. One may be .... and one ....

- An .... provides a reconciliation between budgeted and actual profit.

- ...., ... and .... should be considered before a decision about whether or not to investigate a variance is taken. One way of deciding whether or not to investigate a variance is to investigate only those variances which exceed pre-set tolerance limits.

- Control limits may be illustrated on a control chart. A .... shows the cumulative sum of variances over a period of time.

- A variance should only be investigated if the expected value of .... from investigation and any control action exceed the .... of investigation.

- If the cause of a variance is controllable, action can be taken to bring the system back under control in future. If the variance is uncontrollable, but not simply due to chance, it will be necessary to review forecasts of expected results, and perhaps to revise the budget.

- Cost .... is about regulating the costs of operating a business and keeping costs within acceptable limits.

- Cost .... is a planned and positive approach to reducing expenditure.

- .... is a planned, scientific approach to cost reduction, which reviews a product's material composition and design so that modifications and improvements can be made which do not reduce the value of the product to the customer or user.

- Value analysis considers four aspects of value.
  - ....   ○ ....
  - ....   ○ ....

- .... is the application of similar techniques to new products.

- .... is the process of applying a zero defect philosophy to the management of all resources and relationships within an organisation as a means of developing and sustaining a culture of continuous improvement which focuses on meeting customer expectations.

- The costs of quality failure can be divided into .... costs and .... costs. .... costs represent the cost of any action taken to investigate, prevent or reduce defects and failures. .... costs are the costs of assessing quality achieved.

- A .... compares anything with anything if it is meaningful to do so.

- .... show how a particular variable has changed relative to a base date.

- Performance of non-profit making organisations (NPMOs) can be measured as follows.
  - ....   ○ ....
  - ....

- Possible management performance measures include the following.
  - ....   ○ ....
  - ....   ○ ....

TRY QUESTIONS 20-32

- *Possible pitfalls*
  Write down the mistakes you know you should avoid.

DID YOU KNOW? – VARIANCE ANALYSIS AND MANAGEMENT CONTROL

- *Could you fill in the blanks? The answers are in bold. Use this page for revision purposes as you approach the exam.*

- If an organisation uses standard marginal costing instead of standard absorption costing, there will be no **fixed overhead volume** variance and the **sales volume/quantity/mix** variances will be valued at the standard contribution per unit (as opposed to standard profit per unit).

- There are many possible reasons for variances arising including efficiencies and inefficiencies of operations, errors in standard setting and changes in exchange rates.

- Individual variances should not be looked at in isolation. They might be interdependent/ interrelated. One may be **adverse** and one **favourable**.

- An **operating statement** provides a reconciliation between budgeted and actual profit.

- **Materiality**, **controllability** and **variance trend** should be considered before a decision about whether or not to investigate a variance is taken. One way of deciding whether or not to investigate a variance is to investigate only those variances which exceed pre-set tolerance limits.

- Control limits may be illustrated on a control chart. A **cusum chart** shows the cumulative sum of variances over a period of time.

- A variance should only be investigated if the expected value of **benefits** from investigation and any control action exceed the **costs** of investigation.

- If the cause of a variance is controllable, action can be taken to bring the system back under control in future. If the variance is uncontrollable, but not simply due to chance, it will be necessary to review forecasts of expected results, and perhaps to revise the budget.

- Cost **control** is about regulating the costs of operating a business and keeping costs within acceptable limits.

- Cost **reduction** is a planned and positive approach to reducing expenditure.

- **Value analysis** is a planned, scientific approach to cost reduction, which reviews a product's material composition and design so that modifications and improvements can be made which do not reduce the value of the product to the customer or user.

- Value analysis considers four aspects of value.
  - **Cost value**
  - **Exchange value**
  - **Use value**
  - **Esteem value**

- **Value engineering** is the application of similar techniques to new products.

- **Total quality management (TQM)** is the process of applying a zero defect philosophy to the management of all resources and relationships within an organisation as a means of developing and sustaining a culture of continuous improvement which focuses on meeting customer expectations.

- The costs of quality failure can be divided into **internal failure** costs and **external failure** costs. **Prevention** costs represent the cost of any action taken to investigate, prevent or reduce defects and failures. **Appraisal** costs are the costs of assessing quality achieved.

- A **non-financial indicator (NFI)** compares anything with anything if it is meaningful to do so.

- **Indices** show how a particular variable has changed relative to a base date.

- Performance of non-profit making organisations (NPMOs) can be measured as follows.
  - **In terms of inputs and outputs**
  - **By judgement**
  - **By comparison**

- Possible management performance measures include the following.
  - **Subjective measures**
  - **Judgement of outsiders**
  - **Upward appraisal**
  - **Accounting measures**

  TRY QUESTIONS 20-32

- *Possible pitfalls*
  - **Confusing adverse and favourable fixed overhead volume capacity variances (if actual hours worked are *greater* than budgeted, the variance is favourable)**
  - **Confusing cost reduction with cost control**
  - **Suggesting the performance of NPMOs be measured in terms of profit**

20   STANDARD COSTING SYSTEM

(a) As a member of your organisation's management accounting team, you are asked to plan the installation and operation of a standard costing system. Describe how you would install this system. Indicate what problems are likely to be encountered and how they could be overcome.   (14 marks)

(b) A member of your management accounting team believes that past performance is the best guide to ascertaining standard costs. Discuss this point of view.   (6 marks)

(20 marks)

Helping hand

This question will **test your understanding of standard costing in general** before we look at variance calculations in detail. If you are able to recommend how to install a standard costing system then it is likely that you understand what standard costing is and why it is used.

Begin part (a) of your solution by setting out what you need to know about the organisation and its products before a standard costing system can be implemented. Next consider the type of performance standard to be used. Then explain how standards for materials, labour and overhead would be set. Conclude with any examples you might have on the possible behavioural implications of setting standards.

In part (b) you need to consider the value of measuring performance against out of date standards and the motivational implications.

---

20   **ANSWER: STANDARD COSTING SYSTEM**

(a)

Helping hand

Before installing a standard costing system it is vital to have an understanding of the **structure of the organisation**, and knowledge of the **manufacturing processes** in use and **how other operations are carried out**.

Before attempting to install a standard costing system it would be **essential to be familiar with a number of aspects of the organisation and its products**. In particular the following aspects would be important.

(i)   A full understanding of the **structure of the organisation**: the cost centres in operation, the identity and ability of each cost centre manager, the reports and feedback information already available.

(ii)   The **manufacturing processes** in use: how operations are carried out, the extent to which they can be standardised and monitored, and so on.

(iii)   **How other operations are carried out**: the ordering and storage procedures for materials, any bonus schemes in operation for the payment of labour and so on.

Helping hand

Current and basic standards are generally **unhelpful** and so we have just considered attainable and ideal standards.

Establishing a standard costing system involves calculating predetermined units costs for each cost element of each product. A decision must be taken as to **which type of performance standard** is to be used. For example an **ideal standard would not include any allowances for inefficiencies, breakdowns, losses and so on**. An **attainable standard** would allow an efficient level of breakdowns, losses and so on and this type of standard is **likely to have a more favourable motivational impact**. Motivation problems could arise if an ideal standard is used, since such a standard almost always results in adverse variances which can be demotivating.

Setting standards

(i)   **Direct material costs**

It will be necessary to **establish a standard for material usage and for material price.** Standard material usage would take account of any allowances for breakages and losses and would be based on careful monitoring and observation of the production processes used. Standard material price would take account of a number of factors including desired quality, the availability of bulk discounts and any anticipated price inflation.

(ii)   **Direct labour costs**

Standards must be established for labour times and for hourly rates of pay. The former would require the assistance of a work study specialist, who would investigate the method used and establish an efficient standard time. Employees may be suspicious of the reasons for which they are being observed and timed as they are doing their work. This problem can be overcome by involving them fully in the task of establishing standard times. They should understand that the standard times are to be used for cost control purposes and not as a device to reduce or affect their remuneration or job security. The personnel department would assist in establishing standard rates of pay, taking account of the skill levels required and the likely results of any future negotiations with trade unions.

(iii) **Production overhead**

The cost centre structure would be used to **allocate and apportion overheads to obtain cost centre totals for forecast overheads**. There may be a problem in identifying the most **appropriate basis for overhead absorption** but it is likely to be some form of time based method. An hourly rate could be determined for production overhead and this rate would be applied to the standard times identified in the work study exercise.

Helping hand

It is important to **answer the question set**. You were asked to indicate problems that could arise and how they could be overcome. Look at how we have done this in the next paragraph, for example.

Once the standards have been established it will be necessary to install a system for collecting the actual costs for the purposes of monitoring and controlling costs. Once again there may be resistance from employees if they do not understand the reasons for the monitoring. For example they may not be willing to co-operate in completing the necessary documentation for the analysis of labour times. It will be important to educate and communicate with all employees involved in the monitoring of actual costs, to ensure the smooth and efficient installation and operation of the system.

(b)

Helping hand

Although you may not agree with the view that past performance is the best guide to ascertaining standard costs, try to **give a balanced and reasoned argument**.

Past performance is **one possible guide to the ascertainment of standard costs but it is not necessarily the best guide**. For example, if it is known at the time when standards are being set that a new labour rate has been agreed, that new more efficient working methods are to be introduced, that materials prices are going to rise or that the materials specification of products is going to change then the standard should be revised accordingly. There is no point in measuring performance against out-of-date standards.

The point should also be made that **standards can be used as a psychological incentive** by giving employees a realistic but challenging target of efficiency. Standards based on past performance will not have any motivational impact.

The most that can be said, therefore, is that past performance may offer a starting point for ascertaining standard costs, but only in the absence of change will it provide the best available basis for doing so.

21   QUESTION WITH HELP: VARIANCES

You have been asked to examine the performance of a subsidiary company for May 20X1. The subsidiary supplies kitchen units to the building industry. The standard cost of one unit for May was as follows.

		£
Direct material	5 kilos at £4 per kilo	20
Direct labour	4 hours at £6 per hour	24
Direct expense		10
Variable overheads (based upon an overhead absorption rate of £2 per labour hour)		8
Fixed overheads (based upon an overhead absorption rate of £4 per labour hour)		16
		78

Budgeted output in May was 1,200 units.

The actual results were as follows.

- 1,300 units were made.
- Direct material used was 6,600 kilos at a total cost of £25,080.
- Direct labour was 5,330 hours at a cost of £32,513.
- Actual direct expenses totalled £12,500.
- Actual variable overheads were £13,325.
- Actual fixed overheads were £22,000.

Required

Calculate the following.

(a) (i)   Material total variance
     (ii)   Material price variance
     (iii)   Material usage variance
     (iv)   Labour total variance
     (v)   Labour rate variance
     (vi)   Labour efficiency variance
     (vii)   Expense variance
     (viii) Variable overhead total variance ‐
     (ix)   Variable overhead expenditure variance
     (x)   Variable overhead efficiency variance
     (xi)   Fixed overhead total variance ‐
     (xii)   Fixed overhead expenditure variance
     (xiii) Fixed overhead volume variance
     (xiv)   Fixed overhead volume efficiency variance
     (xv)   Fixed overhead volume capacity variance

(14 marks)

(b) Prepare a variance report for management for May 20X1 reconciling the standard costs for actual production with actual costs, clearly showing the sub-variances for each element of cost.   (6 marks)

(20 marks)

> *If you are stuck, look at the next page for detailed help as to how you should tackle this question.*

APPROACHING THE ANSWER

Step 1. *Calculate the material variances*

The *material total variance* is the difference between what the actual output should have cost in terms of material (actual number of units x standard material cost per unit) and what it did cost. The *material price variance* is the difference between what the actual material used should have cost (actual quantity used x standard price per kilo) and what it did cost. The *material usage variance* is the difference between how much material should have been used for the actual number of units (actual number of units x standard material usage per unit) and how much material was used. Value this variance in £ by multiplying by the standard price per kilo.

Step 2. *Calculate the labour variances*

The *labour total variance* is the difference between what the output have cost in terms of labour (actual number of units x standard labour cost per unit) and what it did cost. The *labour rate variance* is the difference between what the actual labour hours should have cost (actual hours worked x standard rate per hour) and what they did cost. The *labour efficiency variance* is the difference between the number of labour hours that should have been worked for the actual number of units (actual number of units x standard labour hours per unit) and how many hours were worked. Value this variance in £ by multiplying by the standard rate per hour.

Step 3. *Calculate the expense variance*

The *expense variance* is the difference between what the expense should have been for the actual number of units (actual number of units x standard expense per unit) and what it was.

Step 4. *Calculate the variable overhead variances*

The *variable overhead total variance* is the difference between what the actual number of units should have cost in terms of variable overhead (actual number of units x standard variable overhead cost per unit) and what they did cost. The *variable overhead expenditure variance* is the difference between the amount of variable overhead that should have been incurred in the hours worked (hours worked x standard rate per hour) and the actual amount of variable overhead incurred. The *variable overhead efficiency variance* is the difference between the number of hours that should have been worked for the actual number of units (actual number of units x standard hours per unit) and how many hours were worked. Value this variance in £ by multiplying by the standard rate per hour.

Step 5. *Calculate the fixed overhead variances*

The *fixed overhead total variance* is the difference between fixed overhead incurred and fixed overhead absorbed (actual number of units x standard absorption rate per unit). The *fixed overhead expenditure variance* is the difference between budgeted expenditure (budgeted number of units x standard absorption rate per unit) and actual expenditure. The *fixed overhead volume variance* is the difference between actual and budgeted production volume multiplied by the standard absorption rate per unit. The *fixed overhead volume efficiency variance* is the difference between the number of hours that actual production should have taken (actual number of units x standard labour hours per unit) and the number of hours actually taken. Value this variance in £ by multiplying by the standard rate per hour. The *fixed overhead volume capacity variance* is the difference between budgeted hours of work (budgeted number of units x standard labour hours per unit) and actual hours of work. Value this variance in £ by multiplying by the standard rate per hour.

Step 6. *Prepare the reconciliation*

Begin by calculating the standard cost of actual production (standard cost per unit x actual number of units). List the sub-variances (not the total variances otherwise you will be duplicating) and put their values in a column for adverse variances or a column for favourable variances and calculate a net total (either adverse or favourable). Deduct a positive variance from/add an adverse variance to the standard cost of actual production to give the actual cost of production. You can check you reconciliation by calculating the actual cost of production from the information in the question. It should be the same as the standard cost of actual production adjusted by the net total of the variances.

21   ANSWER TO QUESTION WITH HELP: VARIANCES

(a) (i)

		£
1,300 units should have cost (× £20)		26,000
but did cost		25,080
Material total variance		920 (F)

(ii)

	£
6,600 kg of materials should cost (× £4)	26,400
but did cost	25,080
Material price variance	1,320 (F)

(iii)

1,300 units should use (× 5 kg)	6,500 kgs
but did use	6,600 kgs
Material usage variance (kg)	100 kgs (A)
× standard price per kg	× £4
Material usage variance (£)	£400 (A)

(iv)

	£
1,300 units should have cost (× £24)	31,200
but did cost	32,513
Labour total variance	1,313 (A)

(v)

	£
5,330 hours should cost (× £6)	31,980
but did cost	32,513
Labour rate variance	533 (A)

(vi)

1,300 units should take (× 4 hours)	5,200 hrs
but did take	5,330 hrs
Labour efficiency variance (hrs)	130 hrs (A)
× standard rate per hour	× £6
Labour efficiency variance (£)	£780 (A)

(vii)

	£
Expense for 1,300 units should have been (× £10)	13,000
but was	12,500
Expense variance	500 (F)

(viii)

	£
1,300 units should have cost (× £8)	10,400
but did cost	13,325
Variable overhead total variance	2,925 (A)

(ix)

	£
5,330 hours should have cost (× £2)	10,660
but did cost	13,325
Variable overhead expenditure variance	2,665 (A)

			£
(x)	1,300 units should have taken (× 4 hrs)		5,200 hrs
	but did take		5,330 hrs
	Variable overhead efficiency variance (hrs)		130 hrs (A)
	× standard rate per hour		× £2
	Variable overhead efficiency variance (£)		£260 (A)

		£
(xi)	Fixed overhead incurred	22,000
	Fixed overhead absorbed (1,300 units × £16)	20,800
	Fixed overhead total variance	1,200 (A)

		£
(xii)	Budgeted overheads (1,200 × £16)	19,200
	Actual overheads	22,000
	Fixed overhead expenditure variance	2,800 (A)

(xiii)	Actual production volume	1,300 units
	Budgeted production volume	1,200 units
	Fixed overhead volume variance (units)	100 units (A)
	× standard rate per unit	× £16
	Fixed overhead volume variance (£)	£1,600 (F)

(xiv)	1,300 units should have taken (× 4 hrs)	5,200 hrs
	but did take	5,330 hrs
	Fixed overhead volume efficiency variance (hrs)	130 hrs (A)
	× standard rate per hour	× £4
	Fixed overhead volume efficiency variance (£)	£520 (A)

(xv)	Budgeted hours of work (4 hrs × 1,200)	4,800 hrs
	Actual hours of work	5,330 hrs
	Fixed overhead volume capacity variance (hrs)	530 hrs (F)
	× standard absorption rate per hour	× £4
	Fixed overhead volume capacity variance (£)	£2,120 (F)

(b) **Variance report**: *May 20X1*

	£
Expected costs (W)	101,400

Variances

	Adverse £	Favourable £		
Material price		1,320		
Material usage	400			
Labour rate	533			
Labour efficiency	780			
Expense		500		
Variable overhead expenditure	2,665			
Variable overhead efficiency	260			
Fixed overhead expenditure	2,800			
Fixed overhead volume efficiency	520			
Fixed overhead volume capacity		2,120		
	7,958	3,940	4,018	(A)
Actual costs (see check below)			105,418	

Working

Expected costs	£
Material (1,300 × £20)	26,000
Labour (1,300 × £24)	31,200
Expense (1,300 × £10)	13,000
Variable overhead (1,300 × £8)	10,400
Fixed overhead (1,300 × £16)	20,800
	101,400

Check

Actual costs	£
Material	25,080
Labour	32,513
Expense	12,500
Variable overhead	13,325
Fixed overhead	22,000
	105,418

22   **QUALK LTD (12/00)**   *72 mins*

Qualk Ltd designs and assembles specialist personal computers (PCs) from components bought in through a single wholesaler – who buys all the individual parts from a variety of manufacturers. The industry is expanding and the specification of new models is changing rapidly, as technology and customer expectations increase. Qualk designs a new model every six months to go on sale from either January or July. Each model is sold through the company's web site for six months, at which point it is withdrawn and replaced by the next model.

During each model cycle, the purchase price of the components tends to fall significantly. Because some of the components are specific to Qualk's requirements, a single purchase order has to be placed before the start of the model cycle. It is then not possible to vary the quantity without significant penalties. The wholesaler makes up the components for delivery into minimum batches of at least 200 sets of computers. The component kits are assembled into computers in the month in which they are sold. At the end of each six-month cycle the surplus stock of PCs has to be sold quickly before the computers become totally obsolete.

Qualk is in the process of preparing its budget for the six months starting 1 January 20X1. The following information is available for the new model, the Turbo.

	Jan	*Feb*	*Mar*	*April*	*May*	*June*
Sales in units	150	170	150	130	90	70
Components purchased per set*	200	200	200	200	–	–
Purchase price per set £	400	350	350	320	–	–
Marketing expenditure £'000 ★★	50	40	30	15	7	6

★ A set consists of all the components to make one complete computer.

★★ Marketing expenses are paid in the month in which they are incurred and include the cost of maintaining the web site, advertising in trade magazines, shipping costs and sales administration.

Notes

1   Computers are dispatched within three days of an order being placed. Payment is by credit card through the web site, with cash being received from the credit card company two months after the month of sale. The selling price is £800 after credit card commission.

2   The sets of components are assembled as necessary to meet each month's sales. Any components remaining at the end of the six-month model cycle are assembled and sold to a local trader on the first day of the following month for a price of £400 – cash on delivery. Such stock is included in the half-year management accounts at its resale value. In the six months to 30 June 20X1, it is planned to assemble ten surplus sets of components in May and 30 surplus sets in June.

3   Payment for component purchases is made one month after receipt of goods. There were no purchases of components in December 20X0.

4   Qualk has a permanent direct labour force with total salaries of £9,000 per month. These workers assemble up to 100 units per month. In months when sales, and thus production, exceed 100 units, additional labour is employed from an agency at a rate of £130 per computer assembled. The total charge for the agency workers is payable in May, one month after all their work has been completed.

5   Estimated production expenses of £6,000 per month will be paid in cash. This includes indirect labour consisting of a team of technicians who monitor the quality of

production and test the completed machines. The technicians also work on designing the next model as production reduces.

6   Depreciation is to be provided at the rate of 20% per annum of the cost of production equipment using a straight-line basis.

7   The taxation shown as a liability in the balance sheet is due for payment in March 20X1.

8   The balance sheet as at 31 December 20X0 is expected to be as follows.

Fixed assets	*Cost*	*Dep'n*	
	£'000	*£'000*	*£'000*
Premises*	100	–	100
Production equipment	200	160	40
	300	160	140
Current assets			
Stock of finished computers		20	
Debtors – November 20X0		110	
– Dec 20X0		90	
		220	
Current liabilities			
Taxation	50		
Bank overdraft	120		
	170		
Net current assets			50
Net assets			190
Represented by:			
Share capital			50
Retained profit			140
Total shareholders' funds			190

* It is the company's policy not to depreciate freehold premises.

Required

(a) (i)   Calculate the standard materials cost per computer over the six-month period.

(3 marks)

(ii) Calculate the standard cost per computer over the six-month period, showing prime cost and production cost. (4 marks)

(iii) Calculate the value of finished stock to be included in the accounts as at 30 June 20X1. (3 marks)

(b) Produce a budgeted profit and loss statement for the six months ended 30 June 20X1 showing production cost, cost of sales, gross profit and net profit. (6 marks)

Note. Show your answers to the nearest £'000.

(c) Produce a monthly cash budget for the six-month period commencing 1 January 20X1, in a suitable format for presentation to management. (10 marks)

Note. Show your answers to the nearest £'000.

(d) Briefly comment on the two statements produced in parts (b) and (c) above, explaining the significant elements of any difference between the profit and the net cash flow.

(8 marks)

(e) At the end of the last year the company's bank overdraft was uncomfortably high; the plans for the new year should lead to an improvement in the next six months. From the information supplied in the balance sheet at 31 December 20X0 and your answers to parts (c) and (d) above, identify TWO issues that may have a *significant effect* on Qualk's cash flow arising in the 12 months *after* the end of the cash budget to 30 June 20X1. (6 marks)

(40 marks)

22   **ANSWER: QUALK LTD**

> **What the examiner said**
>
> There were four marks (representing 10% of the total marks available) for presentation in this question. Many candidates did not take advantage of the opportunities to gain these relatively easy marks.

(a)

> **Helping hand**
>
> In parts (i) and (ii) you need to do some workings before you can calculate the standard costs. In part (iii) you need to apply the accounting rule that stock should be valued at the lower of cost and net realisable value.

(i)   **Calculation of purchases in the period**

Month	Component sets purchased	Purchase price per set £	Purchases £
Jan	200	400	80,000
Feb	200	350	70,000
Mar	200	350	70,000
Apr	200	320	64,000
Total	800		284,000

$$\text{Standard material cost per computer} = \frac{\text{cost of purchases}}{\text{sets purchased}}$$

$$= \frac{£284,000}{800} = £355 \text{ each}$$

(ii)   *Workings*

1   **Calculation of labour costs in period**

Month	Computers sold and assembled	Sets produced by permanent labour force	Sets produced by agency workers	Wages paid to permanent labour force £	Payment for agency workers £
Jan	150	100	50	9,000	–
Feb	170	100	70	9,000	–
Mar	150	100	50	9,000	–
Apr	130	100	30	9,000	–
May	100*	100	–	9,000	26,000
June	100*	100	–	9,000	–
Total	800	600	200	54,000	26,000

* Includes 10 surplus sets in May and 30 in June

$$\text{Standard labour cost per computer} = \frac{\text{wages paid} + \text{payments for agency workers}}{\text{computers assembled}}$$

$$= \frac{£(54,000 + 26,000)}{800} = £100$$

2   **Calculation of production overheads**

	£
Production expenses @ £6,000 per month	36,000
Depreciation (20% × £200,000) ÷ 2	20,000
	56,000

$$\text{Standard overhead cost per computer} = \frac{\text{overheads in period}}{\text{computers produced}}$$

$$= £56{,}000 \div 800$$
$$= \underline{£70}$$

	£
Materials (from (a) (i))	355
Labour	100
Prime cost	455
Production overheads	70
Production cost	525

(iii)   Value of finished stock at 30 June 20X1

(Assume computers assembled from surplus sets of components in May and June are not sold until 1st July 20X1.)

Computers assembled from surplus sets: 10 in May and 30 in June = 40

Standard product cost   = £525 each
Realisable value   = £400 each
∴ Value of stock   = £400 × 40 = £16,000

(b)

> **Helping hand**
>
> Don't forget to include the opening stock of finished computers. You can get the valuation from the balance sheet in the question.

Budgeted profit and loss account for six months ending 30 June 20X1

Sales	£	£
Finished computers in stock at 31.12.20X0		20,000
760 computers (at £800 each)		608,000
		628,000
Opening stock at valuation	20,000	
Production cost (800 × £525)	420,000	
	440,000	
Less closing stock (40 × £400)	16,000	
Cost of sales		424,000
Gross profit		204,000
Marketing expenditure		148,000
Net profit		56,000

(c)

> **Helping hand**
>
> Don't forget that the figure for January receipts needs to include the sale of stock of finished computers shown in the balance sheet.

Monthly cash budget Jan 20X1 to June 20X1

	Jan	*Feb*	*Mar*	*Apr*	*May*	*June*	*Total*
Receipts from debtors (W)	130	90	120	136	120	104	700
Payments:							
Purchases (from (a) (i))	–	80	70	70	64	–	284
Direct wages ,	9	9	9	9	9	9	54
Agency staff (from (a) (ii))	–	–	–	–	26	–	26
Production expenses	6	6	6	6	6	6	36
Marketing expenditure	50	40	30	15	7	6	148
Taxation	–	–	50	–	–	–	50
	65	135	165	100	112	21	598
Net cash flow	65	(45)	(45)	36	8	83	102
Opening balance	(120)	(55)	(100)	(145)	(109)	(101)	(120)
Closing balance	(55)	(100)	(145)	(109)	(101)	(18)	(18)

Working

January receipts are from November sales and from closing stock at December 20X0.

February receipts are from December sales.

March receipts are from January sales.

(d)

> **Helping hand**
>
> You may want to relate profit to the level of closing capital. Closing capital = opening capital of £190,000 + profit of £56,000 (as there were no dividends declared or share issues).

The profit and loss account shows that the business is budgeted to make a **profit** of £56,000 in the period ending 30 June 20X1. This represents 9% of sales of £628,000, 29% of opening capital of £190,000 or 23% of closing capital of £246,000. Gross profit is budgeted at 32.5% of sales.

The **budgeted net cash inflow** in the period is £102,000, resulting in a reduction in the overdraft from £120,000 to £18,000.

The £46,000 **difference between the budgeted net profit** of £56,000 **and the budgeted net cash inflow** of £102,000 can be analysed as follows.

	£
Depreciation charge (non-cash item)	20,000
Decrease in debtors (£200,000 – ((90 + 70) × £800))	72,000
Decrease in stock (£20,000 – (40 × £400))	4,000
Payment of tax	(50,000)
	46,000

(e)

> **Helping hand**
>
> You may have thought of completely different issues.

Issues which may have a significant effect on Qualk Ltd's cash flow in the period 1st July 20X1 to 30th June 20X2.

(i) **Replacement of production equipment** will probably be necessary - its written down value will be nil by 31.12. 20X1.

(ii)   A significant **tax liability** may arise in 20X1 (it was £50,000 in 20X0) and need to be discharged in March 20X2, which is in the trough of the six-month product cycle.

(iii)   No provision appears to have been made for the payment of **dividends** either at the end of 20X0 or in the first six months of 20X1.

(iv)   The personal computer industry is particularly volatile. If a new model of PC is uncompetitive and price discounts are necessary, the company could find itself with extreme **cash flow problems**. Although we are not provided with information about the overdraft limit, it is unlikely to be in excess of £100,000 (the cost of the company's premises).

Examiner's marking scheme

		Marks
(a) (i)	Standard materials cost - total	to 2
	- cost per unit	to 1
		3
(ii)	Standard cost	
	- labour	to 1
	- prime cost	to 1
	- production overheads	to 1
	- production cost	to 1
		4
(iii)	Value of finished stock	3
(b) Budgeted profit & loss		
-	production cost including labour and materials	to 1
-	cost of sales including stock adjustment	to 2
-	gross profit	to 1
-	marketing expenses and net profit	to 1
-	presentation	to 1
		6
(c) Cash budget		
-	format	to 3
-	inflows	to 1
-	materials	to 1
-	labour direct and agency	to 1
-	overheads; marketing and production expenses	to 1
-	taxation	to 1
-	balances	to 2
		10
(d) Comments		
-	profit	to 3
-	cash flow	to 2
-	reasons for difference	to 3
		8
(e) Cash flow concerns (2 significant factors × 3 marks)		6
		40

---

23   PERFORMANCE MANAGEMENT SYSTEM (12/01)

(a) Compare cost control and cost reduction   (6 marks)

(b) A company uses basic, attainable *and* ideal standards within its performance management system. Attainable standards are used, within each period, as the basis for monitoring and controlling short-term performance. Both basic and ideal standards are used to measure longer-term efficiency improvements.

The attainable standard time for one of the operations in the company's factory is currently set at 1.2 direct labour hours per hundred units of output. The basic and ideal standards for the operation, per direct labour hour are set at 75 units and 90 units of output respectively.

During the period just ended, 163,085 units were manufactured in 1,930 direct labour hours. The standard direct labour rate is £7.50 per hour.

Required

Calculate for the operation described above:

(i)   the direct labour efficiency variance (£) and the efficiency ratio (%) for the period   (7 marks)

(ii)   the % improvement achieved to date, based on the actual performance in the most recent period compared with the basic standard   (4 marks)

(iii) the further % improvement possible, based on a comparison of the ideal and the attainable standards.   (3 marks)

(20 marks)

23   **ANSWER: PERFORMANCE MANAGEMENT SYSTEM**

> **What the examiner said**
>
> 'In part (b)(i), the period variance was at times assumed to be actual versus the basic standard, or actual versus the ideal standard, despite the question stating that "attainable standards are used, within each period, as the basis for monitoring and controlling short-term performance". Some candidates were unable to convert 1.2 direct hours per hundred units of output into standard hours or units per hour. The efficiency ratio was reversed at times (ie actual hours ÷ standard hours).'

> **Helping hand**
>
> You need to be careful to use the correct standard times in part (b). The question states that attainable standards are used as the basis for monitoring and controlling short-term performance. Therefore the direct labour efficiency variance and the efficiency ratio in part (i) should be based on the **attainable standard**. The remainder of the question guides you as to which standard to use. However, you should take care to note that the basic and ideal standards are given in terms of the **output per hour**, whereas the attainable standard is quoted in terms of **the number of hours per hundred units of output**. Both of these forms of presentation can easily be converted to determine the **standard time that should be taken to produce 163,085 units.**

(a)   **Cost control** is concerned with **regulating costs** and keeping them within acceptable limits.

The limits will usually be the standard cost or target cost limits set out in the formal plan or budget for an organisation. If actual costs differ from planned costs then **control action** may be necessary.

Cost reduction, in contrast, **starts with an assumption that current cost levels,** or planned cost levels, are **too high,** even though cost control might be good and efficiency levels high. Cost reduction is a **planned and positive approach to reducing expenditure.**

Cost control action ought to lead to a **reduction in excessive spending.** A cost reduction programme, on the other hand, **aims to reduce expected cost levels** to below current budgeted or standard levels by **changing methods of working**.

In summary, cost control aims to reduce costs **to** budget or standard level, whereas cost reduction aims to reduce costs to **below** budget or standard level, as budgets and standards do not necessarily reflect the conditions which minimise costs.

(b)   The direct labour efficiency variance and the efficiency ratio are based on the attainable standard.

    (i)

163,085 units should take ($\times$ 1.2/100)	1,957.02	hours
but did take	1,930.00	hours
Labour efficiency variance in hours	27.02	hours (F)
$\times$ standard rate per hour	$\times$£7.50	
Direct labour efficiency variance	£202.65	(F)

$$\text{Efficiency ratio} = \frac{\text{standard hours produced}}{\text{actual hours worked}} \times 100\%$$

$$= \frac{1,957.02}{1,930.00} \times 100\%$$

$$= 101.4\%$$

(ii)

Basic standard time for 163,085 units (÷ 75 units per hour)	2,174.47	hours
Actual time taken	1,930.00	hours
Improvement achieved	244.47	hours

$$\% \text{ improvement achieved to date} = \frac{244.47}{2,174.47} \times 100\% = \quad 11.2\%$$

(iii)

Ideal standard time for 163,085 units (÷ 90 units per hour)	1,812.06	hours
Attainable standard time (from (i))	1,957.02	hours
Improvement possible	144.96	hours

$$\% \text{ improvement possible} = \frac{144.96}{1,957.02} \times 100\% = \quad 7.4\%$$

Examiner's marking scheme

			Marks
(a)	Cost control		2½
	Cost reduction		3½
			6
(b)	(i)	Efficiency variance (£)	3½
		Efficiency ratio (%)	3½
	(ii)	% improvement	4
	(iii)	% improvement	3
			14
			20

24   PLANTPOTS LTD (6/98)   *36 mins*

You work in a small accounting practice. One of your clients is Plantpots Ltd, a firm manufacturing and selling decorative garden pots. The managing director, Sally Miles, has asked you to have a look at the management accounts for the past year. She is having trouble understanding what has been happening. 'I know that we had a very bad year overall, but I cannot see how individual functions have performed. Each one of my managers tells me that they expect a bonus as they have done better than budget. Can you help me make sense of it?'

She provides you with the following information.

Budget for year ended 31 March 20X8

Sales	25,000 pots at £2.00 per pot
Variable costs	£1.20 per pot
Fixed costs	£12,000

Actual results for 12 months ended 31 March 20X8

Sales	20,000 pots at £2.10 per pot
Variable costs	£28,000
Fixed costs	£11,800

Plantpots Ltd uses a marginal costing system for its management accounts.

Required

(a)   Prepare a table showing: the original budget; the flexed budget for 20X7-X8; the actual results; and the total variances. Then produce an analysis of the sales variance.

(8 marks)

(b)   Prepare notes for a meeting with Sally Miles to discuss the likely reasons for the variances. You should also suggest how she might investigate further.   (12 marks)

(20 marks)

Helping hand

The first requirement of part (a) is simply asking you to prepare a **flexed budget statement**. Don't forget to denote your variances as either (F) or (A) and **explain what (F) and (A) mean**.

The analysis of the sales variance should show the **selling price** variance and the **sales volume** variance.

Remember, for part (b), that there are four basic reasons why variances occur.

- Measurement errors
- Out of date standards
- Efficient or inefficient operations
- Random or chance fluctuations

---

24   ANSWER: PLANTPOTS LTD

(a)

Helping hand

Remember that **fixed costs** are fixed - and so they **should not change when activity levels change**. The flexed budget value for fixed costs should therefore be the same as the original budget value.

The **selling price variance** is valued at **standard selling price** but the **sales volume variance** is valued at **standard contribution margin**.

Plantpots Ltd
Flexible budget and actual results for 20X7-8

	Original budget	Flexed budget		Actual results	Variance	
Sales (units)	25,000	20,000		20,000		
	£	£		£	£	
Sales revenue	50,000	40,000	(W1)	42,000	2,000	(F)
Variable costs	30,000	24,000	(W2)	28,000	4,000	(A)
Contribution	20,000	16,000		14,000	2,000	(A)
Fixed costs	12,000	12,000	(W3)	11,800	200	(F)
Profit	8,000	4,000		2,200	1,800	(A)

(F) denotes a favourable variance, (A) an adverse variance.

Workings

1   Actual number of units sold × budgeted selling price per unit
    = 20,000 × £2 = £40,000

2   Actual number of units sold × budgeted variable cost per unit
    = 20,000 × £1.20 = £24,000

3   Budgeted fixed costs (fixed costs not changing with changes in level of activity)

Analysis of sales variance

	£	
Revenue from selling 20,000 units should have been (× £2)	40,000	
but was (20,000 × £2.10)	42,000	
Selling price variance	2,000	(F)
Budgeted sales volume	25,000	pots
Actual sales volume	20,000	pots
Sales volume variance in units	5,000	pots (A)
× standard contribution per unit (× £(2 – 1.20))	× £0.80	
Sales volume variance in £	£4,000	(A)

The **total variance of £(8,000 – 2,200) = £5,800 between the original budget and the actual results can be reconciled as follows.**

	£		£	
Sales volume variance			4,000	(A)
Selling price variance	2,000	(F)		
Variable costs variance	4,000	(A)		
Fixed costs variance	200	(F)		
Variance between flexed budget and actual results			1,800	(A)
Total variance			5,800	(A)

(b)

Helping hand

Listing the four basic reasons why variances occur at the beginning of your answer may give you some ideas for explanations for the variances at Plantpots Ltd. Don't forget that you have been asked to suggest what **further investigation** might be needed.

NOTES FOR MEETING WITH SALLY MILES
LIKELY REASONS FOR THE VARIANCES

There are four basic reasons why variances occur.

(i)   **Measurement errors**. Scales may be misread, the pilfering or wastage of materials may go unrecorded, items may be wrongly classified or employees may make 'cosmetic' adjustments to the records to make their own performance look better.

(ii) **Out of date standards**. Inflation, learning curve effects and/or technological change may make standards out of date.

(iii) **Efficient or inefficient operations**. Spoilage, better quality material/more highly or lower skilled labour than standard are all likely to affect the efficiency of operations and hence cause variances.

(iv) **Random or chance fluctuations**. A standard is an average figure: really it represents the midpoint of a range of possible values and therefore actual results are likely to deviate unpredictably within a predictable range.

Variances at Plantpots Ltd - 20X7/8

(i)   **Sales volume variance**

The failure to achieve the budgeted level of sales has had a significant effect on the actual level of profit achieved, having caused a shortfall of £4,000. This may have been due to a number of factors beyond the company's control (such as the **effect of the weather** on the sales of gardening products). On the other hand it may have been due to **poor forecasting** by the sales department or a **response by customers to the increased selling price**. The 5% increase from £2 per pot to £2.10 per pot may have caused customers to take their business elsewhere. **Production difficulties** may have meant that it was only possible to manufacture 20,000 pots.

Sally Miles should consider investigating the situation further as follows.

(1) Review the **appropriateness and accuracy of the sales forecasting methods** adopted.

(2) **Assess whether production was limited** to 20,000 pots.

(ii) **Selling price variance**

The increase in the selling price led to a favourable variance of £2,000. There are a number of possible reasons for this increase. The sales department may have set the **budgeted price too low** or may have discovered that **competitors** were successfully charging more than £2 and raised the price in response.

Sally Miles should consider taking the following action.

(1) Commission **research** to assess the **sensitivity of customers** to changes in the selling price of the product.

(2) Commission **research** to determine the selling price charged by **competitors** and the extent of their success.

(iii) **Variable costs variance**

There is a significant variance of £4,000 between what the variable costs for 20,000 pots should have been and what they actually were. This was probably due to **inefficiency in production**. Material may have been of a lower standard than anticipated, there may have been theft or deterioration of the material or a new supplier may have been used. Supervision may have been poor, staff may have been badly trained, or there may have been low morale, equipment breakdowns, excessive idle time or poor working conditions.

Sally Miles needs to investigate the reasons for this variance. The **total variance should be broken down** into material price and usage variances, labour rate and efficiency variances and variable overhead expenditure and efficiency variances. The managers responsible can then be asked to provide reasons for significant variances.

(iv) **Fixed costs variance**

There was a small saving in fixed costs. This may have occurred because of **stringent cost control** or because of **budget padding** by the manager responsible for setting the budget. An **analysis of the overall expenditure** into various expense classifications is required in order to provide additional information.

Examiner's marking scheme

		Marks	
(a)	Original budget	to 1	
	Flexed budget	to 1	
	Actual results	to 1	
	Calculation of variances	to 2	
	Analysis of variances		
	- sales volume	to 2	
	- sales price	to 1	
			8
(b)	Advice to managing director with suggestions		
	for further investigation	to 2	
	Sales variances	to 4	
	Variable cost with reference to cost behaviour	to 4	
	Fixed cost with reference to budget setting	to 2	
			12
			20

---

25   **PQR MANUFACTURING (12/98)**   *36 mins*

PQR Manufacturing make a product with the following standard cost specification.

		£
Direct material	45 kgs at £8.20 per kilo	369
Direct labour	25 hrs at £6.00 per hour	150
Total standard variable cost		519
Fixed production overhead	£3.60 per direct labour hour	90
Total production standard cost		609

In period 7 there was a budget of 200 units. Actual production was 220 units with costs as follows.

Period 7 - Actual results

		£
Direct materials	10,390 kgs	82,704
Direct labour worked	5,700 hours × £5.90	33,630
Fixed overhead		18,912
Total costs		135,246

PQR operate a standard absorption costing system.

There were no stocks at the beginning or end of period 7.

Required

(a) Prepare a table showing the following.

    (i)   The standard absorption cost of actual production for period 7
    (ii)   The actual costs
    (iii) The total variance between standard and actual cost for each cost element

        (6 marks)

(b) Calculate the following cost variances.

    (i)   Direct materials; price and usage   (3 marks)
    (ii)   Direct labour; rate and efficiency   (3 marks)
    (iii) Fixed overhead; expenditure and volume   (3 marks)

(c) Comment briefly on the likely causes of the materials and labour variances.

        (5 marks)

        (20 marks)

Helping hand

You will be unable to analyse and interpret variances unless you know how to calculate them and so you are advised to **make sure that you are 100% competent at variance calculations** (required in part (b) above, for example) as well as variance interpretation. If you struggle with parts (a) and (b) you really need to do some revision.

---

25   ANSWER: PQR MANUFACTURING

> **What the examiner said**
>
> Overall this question was answered well. The vast majority of candidates were able to compute the required variances, although some candidates had difficulty in suggesting possible causes for those variances.

(a)

> **Helping hand**
>
> The table required could be laid out in a **variety of different ways**. As long as your table shows clearly all of the information required by the question, you will earn full marks.

Period 7 - Actual production 220 units

	Standard cost per unit £ per unit	Standard cost £	Actual cost £	Variance £	
Direct material	369	81,180	82,704	1,524	(A)
Direct labour	150	33,000	33,630	630	(A)
Total variable cost	519	114,180	116,334	2,154	(A)
Fixed production overhead	90	19,800	18,912	888	(F)
Total absorption cost	609	133,980	135,246	1,266	(A)

* Standard cost = standard cost per unit × 220

(b)

> **Helping hand**
>
> Notice the **check calculations** we have made between the total variances calculated in (a) and the sub-variances calculated below.

(i)   **Direct material price variance**

	£
10,390 kgs of material should have cost (× £8.20)	85,198
but did cost	82,704
Direct material price variance	2,494 (F)

Direct material usage variance

220 units should have used (× 45 kgs)	9,900	kgs
but did use	10,390	kgs
Usage variance in kgs	490	kgs (A)
× standard cost per kilogram	× £8.20	
Usage variance in £	£4,018	(A)

Check: £2,494 (F) + £4,018 (A) = £1,524 (A)

(ii)   **Direct labour rate variance**

	£
5,700 hours of labour should have cost (× £6.00)	34,200
but did cost	33,630
Direct labour rate variance	570 (F)

Direct labour efficiency variance

220 units should take (× 25 hrs)	5,500	hrs
but did take	5,700	hrs
Labour efficiency variance in hours	200	hrs (A)
× standard rate per hour	× £6	
Labour efficiency variance in £	£1,200	(A)

Check: £570 (F) + £1,200 (A) = £630 (A)

(iii) **Fixed production overhead expenditure variance**

	£	
Budgeted fixed production overhead expenditure (200 × £90)	18,000	
Actual fixed production overhead expenditure	18,912	
Fixed production overhead expenditure variance	912	(A)

Fixed production overhead volume variance

	£	
Actual production at standard rate (220 × £90)	19,800	
Budgeted production at standard rate (200 × £90)	18,000	
Fixed production overhead volume variance	1,800	(F)

Check: £912 (A) + £1,800 (F) = £888 (F)

(c)

> **Helping hand**
>
> Take note of whether the variances are **adverse or favourable** before making comment.

Direct material price variance

The **favourable variance** indicates that the price paid for materials was lower than the standard price. Possible causes are as follows.
(i)   Unforeseen discounts were received.
(ii)   Greater care was taken in purchasing.
(iii)   The material purchased was of a lower quality than standard.

Direct material usage variance

The **adverse variance** indicates that more materials were used to produce the output than allowed for in the standard. Possible causes are as follows.

(i)   Material purchased was of a lower quality (a possible cause of the favourable price variance), which led to higher levels of rejects and excessive waste.

(ii)   There was insufficient allowance for waste in the original standard.

(iii)   Materials may have been lost or stolen.

(iv)   Unskilled labour may have been used, leading to reworking and excessive waste.

Direct labour rate variance

The **favourable variance** indicates that the hourly rate paid for labour was lower than the standard rate. Possible causes are as follows.

(i)   Lower grade workers were used (a possible cause of the adverse material usage variance), who receive lower rates of pay.

(ii)   The original standard rate was set too high.

Direct labour efficiency variance

The **adverse variance** indicates that more labour hours were used to produce the output than allowed for in the standard. Possible causes are as follows.

(i)   If lower quality material was used, it may have been difficult to process.

(ii)   If lower grade employees were used, they may have worked at a slower rate than standard.

(iii)   Lost time was in excess of the standard allowance.

Examiner's marking scheme

		Marks	
(a)	Table		
	- standard absorption cost of production	to 2	
	- actual costs	to 2	
	- variances	to 2	
			6
(b)	Variance calculations		
	- variances (i) to (iii) - 3 marks for each cost heading		9
(c)	Comments on labour and materials variances		
	- rate/price	to 2	
	- efficiency/usage	to 3	
			5
			20

26   STANDARD HOURS (6/01)

A firm of accountants uses the standard hours worked by professional staff on client business as the basis for client charging, and for cost control. The standard hours for each client job are established in advance based on the expected amount of time required for each task. Some of the hours worked by professional staff are not on client business and are thus not chargeable.

Target control ratios are:

Activity	96.9%
Efficiency	102.0%
Capacity	95.0%

The activity ratio measures the standard hours of work, by professional staff on client business, as a proportion of the total hours worked by the professional staff. The efficiency ratio measures the relationship between the standard and the actual professional staff hours spent on client business. The capacity ratio measures the actual professional staff hours spent on client business as a proportion of their total hours worked.

During a period, the actual hours worked by professional staff totalled 3,630 of which 3,471 hours were spent on client business. The standard hours for the work totalled 3,502.

Required

(a) Calculate appropriate control ratios for the period (each to one decimal place of a per cent).   (6 marks)

(b) Prepare a brief report for the firm's senior partners that:

    (i)   interprets the control ratios calculated in (a) above;   (5 marks)

    (ii)   identifies possible causes of any variation from target.   (3 marks)

(c) Describe the factors that should be considered before a decision is made to investigate a variation from target.   (6 marks)

    (20 marks)

26 ANSWER: STANDARD HOURS

> **What the examiner said**
>
> This question on control ratios was not well answered. Despite clear instructions as to how each of the control ratios was to be calculated in part (a) candidates frequently confused ratios.

(a)

> **Helping hand**
>
> Use the information given to you in the question. The examiner tells you exactly how to calculate each of the required ratios.

$$\text{Activity ratio} = \frac{\text{Standard hours}}{\text{Total hours worked by professional staff}} \times 100\%$$

$$= \frac{3,502}{3,630} \times 100\%$$

$$= 96.5\%$$

$$\text{Efficiency ratio} = \frac{\text{Standard hours}}{\text{Professional hours spent on client business}} \times 100\%$$

$$= \frac{3,502}{3,471} \times 100\%$$

$$= 100.9\%$$

$$\text{Capacity ratio} = \frac{\text{Actual professional hours spent on client business}}{\text{Total hours worked by professional staff}} \times 100\%$$

$$= \frac{3,471}{3,630} \times 100\%$$

$$= 95.6\%$$

(b)

> **Helping hand**
>
> Remember the guidelines for preparing reports.
>
> - **To**: Who is the report to?
> - **From**: Who is the report from?
> - **Date**: What is the date of the report?
> - **Subject**: What is the subject of the report?

To: Senior Partners
From: Accounting Technician
Date: xx.xx.xx
Subject: Control ratios

The aim of this report is to identify the control ratios for the period under review and to interpret them and identify the possible causes of any variation from target.

Control ratios

Ratio	Target %	Actual %	Variance % points
Activity	96.9	96.5	0.4 (A)
Efficiency	102.0	100.9	1.1 (A)
Capacity	95.0	95.6	0.6 (F)

The control ratios are related as follows.

Efficiency	×	Capacity	=	Activity
100.9%	×	95.6%	=	96.5%

Activity ratio

This ratio measures the standard hours of work by professional staff on client business as a proportion of the total hours worked by the professional staff. This ratio was 0.4 percentage points below target this period.

Efficiency ratio

This is a measure of the relationship between the standard and actual professional hours spent on client business and in this period it was 1.1 percentage points below target. This means that the work achieved was not converted into sufficient chargeable output.

Capacity ratio

This measures the actual professional staff hours spent on client business as a proportion of their total hours worked and is 0.6 percentage points above target this period. This means that a greater proportion of hours than expected were actually spent on clients' business.

Possible causes of variations from target

(i)   **Favourable capacity variance**

- Improved scheduling of clients' business
- Reduced training requirements in the period

(ii)   **Adverse efficiency variance**

- Higher proportion of less experienced staff hours worked
- Efficiency target may have been set too high

(c)   **Factors to consider before investigation of target variations**

(i)   **Materiality**

Small variations in a single period are bound to occur and are unlikely to be significant. If variations are considered to be more significant (ie more material) then investigation is likely to be a worthwhile exercise.

(ii)   **Controllability**

Some variations may be out of the control of the manager responsible for a division or department. For example, worldwide price increases (such as oil) cannot be controlled by an organisation's managers. Therefore, variances which are uncontrollable require standards to be revised rather than investigations to be made.

(iii)   **Variance trend**

Small variations in a single period are unlikely to be significant, whereas small variations that occur consistently may require further investigation. **Variance trend** is important since it provides an indication of whether a variance is becoming out of control.

(iv)   **Other factors**

- Cost versus benefits
- Past experience
- Nature of item of expense

Examiner's marking scheme

			Marks
(a)	Ratios (2 for each)		6
(b)	Report format	1	
	Ratios (1 for each)	3	
	Link between ratios	1	
	Reasons for variation (up to 1½ for each)	3	
			8
(c)	Factors (up to 2 for each)		6
			20

27 QUESTION WITH HELP: PERFORMANCE AND QUALITY

You are a trainee consultant for a consultancy specialising in providing advice for organisations operating within the transport sector. You have been asked to provide some information for a number of clients.

(a) Explain how the control of quality in service industries differs from that in manufacturing industries. (4 marks)

(b) Suggest three appropriate performance measures for quality in a mass transport service. Indicate briefly how the information for the measurements would be obtained.

(4 marks)

(c) A transport company is reviewing the way that it reports vehicle operating costs to the company management. In particular, it is interested in the use of performance ratios which will help to assess the efficiency and effectiveness of the use of its vehicles.

Information on the following items is available for each vehicle for each period.

Costs

Variable costs	*Fixed costs*	*Activity*
Fuel	Road fund licence	Miles driven
Oil	Insurance	Tonnes carried
Hydraulic fluid	Drivers' wages	Journeys made
Tyres	Cleaning	Number of days available for use
Other parts	Depreciation	Number of days vehicle actually
Repairs and maintenance		used

Required

(i) Indicate *six* suitable performance ratios which could be used to monitor the effectiveness and efficiency of the usage of each vehicle.

Three of your ratios should relate to the efficient control of costs and three should relate to the effective usage of vehicles. (6 marks)

(ii) The company directors are concerned by the increase in expenditure on fuel over the last few years. Fuel costs have increased although there were no changes in the number of vehicles and negligible changes in the number of miles driven each year.

The company accountant has gathered information on the fuel costs and has also established a price index for fuel as follows.

Year	*Expenditure on fuel* £	*Fuel price index*
1	18,000	100
2	19,292	106
3	21,468	120
4	23,010	128

Use the index numbers to express all fuel costs in terms of year 4 prices. All figures should be rounded to the nearest £.

Comment on the results you have obtained. (6 marks)

(20 marks)

If you are stuck, look at the next page for detailed help as to how you should tackle this question.

BPP
PROFESSIONAL EDUCATION

APPROACHING THE ANSWER

Step 1.   Base your answer to part (a) on the fact that the problem stems from the simultaneity of production and consumption of the service.

Step 2.   For part (b), begin by thinking about the aspects of the service that affect its quality - such as availability, comfort, friendliness and reliability.

Step 3.   Then consider how the factors can be measured. Comfort might be measured by the crowdedness of an airport whereas friendliness might be measured by staff attitude and helpfulness.

Lastly, give thought as to where the information might come from. Customer surveys and management inspections are possible sources.

Step 4.   Now let's think about part (c). Cost control ratios need to measure a cost (total, variable and/or fixed) per 'something' (mile, day and so on).

Usage ratios need to cover how many days the vehicles were used, how many tonnes were carried, how many miles were driven and so on.

Step 5.   The expenditure can be expressed in year 4 prices by multiplying each year's actual expenditure by (year 4 index/index for year in question). For example, the year 1 calculation would be £18,000 × 128/100 = £.................... .

Step 6.   Your comments need to assess whether the expenditure has increased due to inflation (annual fuel costs in terms of year 4 prices are similar) or due to some other reason.

27   ANSWER TO QUESTION WITH HELP: PERFORMANCE AND QUALITY

(a)   The **problem of quality control** in service industries as opposed to manufacturing industries stems from the **simultaneity of production and consumption**. Quality of service can only be measured *after* the service has been delivered and consumed. A disappointed customer may receive an apology and be assured that control action will be taken to ensure a better quality of service next time, but there is no way that that customer can assess quality without first buying the service.

(b)   Fitzgerald et al, *Performance Measurement in Service Businesses* (CIMA, 1991), identify 12 factors pertaining to service quality and the following tables shows the measures used and the means of obtaining the information by British Airports Authority, a mass transport service.

Service quality factors	Measures	Sources of information
Access	Walking distances	Customer survey and internal operational data
	Ease of finding way around	Customer survey
Aesthetics/appearance	Staff appearance	Customer survey
	Airport's appearance	Customer survey
	Quantity, quality, appearance of food	Management inspection
Availability	Equipment availability	Internal fault monitoring system and customer survey
Cleanliness/tidiness	Cleanliness of environment and equipment	Customer survey and management inspection
Comfort	Crowdedness of airport	Customer survey and management inspection
Communication	Information clarity	Customer survey
	Clarity of labelling and pricing	Management inspection
Competence	Staff efficiency	Management inspection
Courtesy	Courtesy of staff	Customer survey and management inspection
Friendliness	Staff attitude and helpfulness	Customer survey and management inspection
Reliability	Number of equipment faults	Internal fault monitoring systems
Responsiveness	Staff responsiveness	Customer survey
Security	Efficiency of security checks	Customer survey
	Number of urgent safety reports	Internal operational data

(c)   (i)   **Cost control ratios**

Cost per mile
Cost per tonne carried
Cost per tonne/mile
} Each of these ratios could be calculated for fixed and variable costs separately and for each of the fixed and each of the variable costs.

Fixed cost per available day
Fixed cost per working day

Usage ratios

Tonne/miles per period

Days available as a percentage of total working days

Days used as a percentage of available days

Tonne/miles per available day/used day

(ii)   Fuel costs expressed in terms of year 4 prices

Year	Expenditure £	Adjustment for movement in fuel price index £	Expenditure at year 4 prices £
1	18,000	× 128/100	23,040
2	19,292	× 128/106	23,296
3	21,468	× 128/120	22,899
4	23,010	× 128/128	23,010

The increases in expenditure on fuel are mainly the result of increases in fuel prices. When expenditure is adjusted to year 4 prices it is possible to see that **expenditure has not varied significantly in real terms.**

28 **REDIPHONE (6/00)**   *36 mins*

Rediphone provides mobile telephone services to approximately three million people. Growth has been extremely rapid during the four years since the company's formation; there has been little time to set up a comprehensive management accounting system to control the expanding administration function. There are now more than 2,000 people employed over the following three departments: sales administration, handling account queries and credit control.

The need for information is now particularly urgent as the new head office, opened only 12 months ago, is already full. A solution has been proposed, whereby at least half of the staff would be encouraged to work from home, thus reducing the pressure on office accommodation. At the same time, efforts to provide for more attractive and flexible work patterns would be made as staff recruitment is also becoming a serious issue. Most of the tasks in the administration functions are fairly routine by nature and recent advances in information technology will enable workers to do almost all of their normal duties via a computer and modem in their own home.

Rediphone has sought your help in setting up a management accounting system.

Required

(a) Briefly describe THREE qualities of useful management accounting information.

(6 marks)

(b) Briefly explain the term 'cost centre' and describe how Rediphone might set up a system to measure the performance of cost centre managers.   (5 marks)

(c) Suggest TWO financial and TWO non-financial measures by which management might seek to monitor the credit control department.   (4 marks)

(d) Briefly explain how monitoring the output of home workers might be different from office based workers and suggest THREE examples of information that could be produced by a management accounting system to assist in monitoring the EFFICIENCY or EFFECTIVENESS of remote workers.   (5 marks)

(20 marks)

28   ANSWER: REDIPHONE

> **What the examiner said**
>
> Many candidates struggled to identify both a range of suitable performance measures in answer to part (c) and examples of management accounting information in part (d). Candidates are advised that the ability to apply appropriate performance measures will be a key feature of accountancy in the future.

(a)

> **Helping hand**
>
> To help with your revision we have described ten qualities of management accounting information in our answer below. You will **waste valuable examination time** if you do this. Remember to **read the question carefully** and describe only **three** qualities.

Qualities of useful management accounting information

Relevance

Information must be relevant to the purpose for which a manager wishes to use it. For example, **managers at different levels in an organisation require a different degree of detail in their information.** A managing director may need summary information whereas a departmental manager will need more detailed control information. The consequence of irrelevant information is that **managers might be confused by the information and waste time trying to understand it.**

Completeness

A manager must have **all the information necessary to manage effectively.** For example, a customer debt may be reported to a manager as outstanding for four months. The manager might then send a strongly worded letter to the customer, causing problems with customer relations, because the manager had not been informed that a contract had been negotiated with special credit terms of six months.

Accuracy

Management information should be **sufficiently accurate** for its purpose. The appropriate level of accuracy will depend on the purpose for which the information is required. For example, the credit control department will need to ensure that a particular outstanding debt is collected to the exact penny whereas a middle manager who is preparing a sales budget may work with forecasts rounded to the nearest £1,000.

Clarity

A manager cannot use information properly if it is not possible to understand it. For example, accounting jargon may be difficult to understand and any technical terms should always be clearly explained or avoided altogether.

Confidence

Information must be trusted by managers and they should feel confident when using it. Managers should be informed of any assumptions it has been necessary to make when preparing the information.

Communication

Information should be **communicated to the appropriate manager.** For example, a manager cannot act to control expenditure without information about the expenditure to date and how it compares with the budgeted expenditure to date. The information must **be communicated to the person who has the authority to act** on it.

Volume

Reports to managers must be **clear and concise,** otherwise they may be ignored altogether if there is too much information to digest. The **exception principle** may be applied, for example by providing a credit control manager with information about overdue accounts only, and not detailed data concerning every single outstanding account.

Timing

Information which is supplied too late **reduces the value of any management action.** For example, a variance control report which is several weeks late may mean that excessive costs are incurred for longer than necessary. On the other hand, **information which is prepared too frequently wastes resources** and may be ignored.

Channel of communication

Certain types of information may be **communicated more effectively** using different methods of communication. For example, a quick telephone call may be adequate to update an account manager concerning the interim sales figure part way through the month, but routine monthly sales reports would be more appropriately communicated in a written format.

Cost

The benefits obtainable from information must exceed the costs of acquiring it. There will often be **conflict** between the requirements of, for example, cost, accuracy, and timeliness. The most accurate information may be very costly and take an excessive amount of time to produce. **A trade-off is often necessary** to obtain **sufficiently accurate** information, within **a reasonable time period, without incurring excessive costs.**

(b)

What the examiner said

Many candidates managed to write a lot in answer to part (b) without once mentioning the company Rediphone or any other circumstances of the scenario.

Helping hand

Take heed of what the examiner said and **always try to make your answer relevant to the scenario described.** The scenario can sometimes provide useful bits of information to get you started on your answer.

A **cost centre** is **any unit of an organisation to which costs can be separately attributed.** It can be used as a 'collecting place' for costs for control purposes or for further analysis.

The following **steps** might be taken by Rediphone to **set up a system to measure the performance of cost centre managers.**

(i)   **Establish cost centres for which costs can be separately identified**

Examples include the three departments mentioned of sales administration, account query handling and credit control.

(ii) **Establish a coding system so that costs can be charged to the cost centre**

Direct costs can be allocated to each cost centre using the coding system, for example the salaries of sales administration staff and the stationery costs incurred by the credit control department. Indirect costs would need to be apportioned on some equitable basis, for example using the floor space occupied by each cost centre for rent.

(iii) **Provide regular control reports to cost centre managers**

These reports can be used to monitor the performance of cost centre managers.

(1) **Controllable costs,** over which managers can exercise some influence (such as salary costs), should be identified separately.

(2) Information on **non-controllable costs** should also be provided but should not be used as a basis for monitoring management performance.

(3) If possible the costs incurred should be **related to some measure of output,** such as the number of invoices processed or the number of queries handled.

(c)

> **Helping hand**
>
> Many different control measures could be included in your answer to this part. You probably thought of different measures to those we have suggested below. As long as your suggestion can be measured, and it provides a valid basis for monitoring performance by comparison, it should earn full marks.

Two financial performance measures to monitor the credit control department

- Monthly cost centre cost per £ of credit sales
- Salary cost per customer account

Two non-financial performance measures to monitor the credit control department

- Number of customer accounts handled per employee
- Average days of debt outstanding

(d)

> **Helping hand**
>
> You will have to apply a bit of imagination and common sense in this part of the question, as well as your understanding of management accounting systems. You must gain confidence in **applying your knowledge in an unfamiliar situation.** It is highly unlikely that you will have worked in many of the situations described in examination questions!

Monitoring the output of homeworkers

Homeworkers are different from employees who work on an organisation's premises because they cannot be observed and therefore it is impossible to see what they are doing and to note how many hours they are working. The focus must therefore be on **monitoring their output,** rather than their input.

Rediphone will need to devise systems to monitor the output of each individual home worker. Alternatively it may be more appropriate to monitor the output of a team or group of homeworkers. The computer systems used to send work to and collect work from homeworkers should provide the basic information for monitoring their output and efficiency and effectiveness.

Three examples of information to assist in monitoring the efficiency and effectiveness of remote workers

(i) The number of customer complaints related to tasks completed by remote workers

(ii) The number of customer accounts handled by each remote worker

(iii) The average 'turn-around' time between a task being communicated to the remote worker and the job being returned in a satisfactorily completed state

Examiner's marking scheme		**Marks**
(a)	Qualities of useful management information (3 items × 2 marks) (½ mark quality, 1½ marks explanation)	6
(b)	'Cost centre' definition	2
	Use of cost centres to monitor and control	3
		5
(c)	Financial measures	2
	Non-financial measures	2
		4
(d)	Monitoring output of home workers	2
	Performance measures (3 items × 1 mark)	3
		5
		20

29   BARWIN LTD (12/00)   *36 mins*

As a trainee accountant, you have recently been transferred to the marketing department of Barwin Ltd, a company making sports caps which are sold to a wide variety of wholesalers, retailers and sports clubs. Customers are categorised by the size of their account, measured in terms of annual turnover. There are a few large customers, which have a turnover greater than £200,000, mainly high street fashion chains. At the other end of the scale, small customers have an annual turnover of less than £5,000. These mainly comprise of individual sports clubs and societies that tend to place orders for caps with their own club motif sewn on to the cap – the minimum order is £300. Medium-sized customers lie in the range of £5,001 to £200,000. The significance of categorising customers by the size of their account is to allow the application of different gross profit margins for sales quotations – large 10%, medium 20%, small 30%.

The sales manager is presently on holiday. His assistant, Alex Smart, is struggling with a couple of problems that he hopes you can help him with.

Problem 1

Alex has to supply a quotation to a customer. The cost price is £8,000 and Alex has to add on an amount to provide for profit. 'For a medium-sized account the standard margin is 20% of the selling price, but I haven't got the selling price. What am I supposed to do?' he asks you.

Required

Calculate the selling price that is required to provide a margin equal to 20% of the selling price, based on the cost of £8,000.   (2 marks)

Problem 2

Alex has been asked to brief the sales manager on his return on the performance of the sales representatives. The sales manager is particularly keen to see which of Barwin's two regions has the better performance. He wants to give a bonus to the better team according to Alex's recommendation. Alex has compiled the following information from the last period's accounts but is unsure what to do next.

Table 1	*North Region*	*South Region*
Orders taken and delivered	£	£
Large	2,000,000	4,000,000
Medium	1,200,000	2,300,000
Small	1,700,000	1,000,000
Total turnover	4,900,000	7,300,000

Table 2		
Orders as a % of the total company turnover	40.2%	59.8%
New business as a percentage of total orders	32.0%	15.5%
Cancelled orders as a percentage of total orders	9.0%	3.0%
Order value taken per mile travelled	£13.61	£34.76

Table 3		
Sales representatives		
– Number of sales people	12	9
– Total salaries of sales people	£180,000	£171,000
– Fixed expenses – car leasing, telephones, etc	£72,000	£54,000
– Total miles travelled*	360,000	210,000
Sales manager's salary	£32,000	£34,000

* Variable cost per mile = £0.10

Required

(a) Calculate the financial performance of the sales team in both of the two areas based on the gross profit less sales expenses.

Show your results to the nearest £'000. (6 marks)

(b) On the basis of the information supplied and the expenses and profit calculated in part (a), calculate at least FOUR suitable performance ratios that will help Alex to compare the two areas. Show your results in a table. (6 marks)

Note. Such measures should be in addition to the performance measures provided in table 2 of this question.

(c) Write some brief notes to assist Alex in understanding the performance of the two areas. (6 marks)

(20 marks)

29   ANSWER: BARWIN LTD

> **What the examiner said**
>
> Candidates generally achieved their best marks on this question. Common errors included using the turnover figure supplied (rather than calculating gross profit from turnover) and not working to a round £1,000 as requested by the question.

Problem 1

> **Helping hand**
>
> You may find the following useful.
>
> | | % |
> |---|---|
> | Cost | 80 |
> | Plus profit | 20 |
> | Equals sales | 100 |
>
> Profit may be expressed either as a **percentage of cost of sales** (such as **25% (20/80) mark-up**) or as a **percentage of sales** (such as **20% (20/100) margin**).

Margin = 20%

∴ Cost = 80%

∴ Selling price = 100%

∴ £8,000 = 80%

∴ Selling price = (£8,000/80%) × 100% = £10,000

Problem 2

(a)   **Financial performance of sales teams**

	North Region £'000	As % of turnover	South Region £'000	As % of turnover
Gross profit on large orders @ 10%	200		400	
Gross profit on medium orders @ 20%	240		460	
Gross profit on small orders @ 30%	510		300	
Total gross profit	950	19.4%	1,160	15.9%
Sales expenses:				
Salaries	(180)		(171)	
Fixed expenses	(72)		(54)	
Variable mileage costs	(36)		(21)	
Sales manager's salary	(32)		(34)	
Total sales expenses	(320)	6.5%	(280)	3.8%
Gross profit less sales expenses	630	13.0%	880	12.0%

(b)

> **Helping hand**
>
> The question required a minimum of four ratios. Only do more if the calculation is quick, or if you have sufficient time.

Performance ratios

Ratio	North Region	South Region
% of new business (W)	$\dfrac{£1,568,000}{£(1,568,000+1,131,500)} \times 100\%$	$\dfrac{£1,131,500}{£(1,568,000+1,131,500)} \times 100\%$
Gross profit per staff member	£950,000 ÷ 12 = £79,000	£1,160,000 ÷ 9 = £129,000
Orders per staff member	£4,900,000 ÷ 12 = £408,000	£7,300,000 ÷ 9 = £811,000
New business per staff member	£1,568,000 ÷ 12 = £131,000	£1,131,500 ÷ 9 = £126,000
Cancelled orders per staff member	(£4,900,000 × 9%) ÷ 12 = £37,000	(£7,300,000 × 3%) ÷ 9 = £24,000
Average salary per sales person	£180,000 ÷ 12 = £15,000	£171,000 ÷ 9 = £19,000
Miles travelled per sales person	360,000 ÷ 12 = 30,000 miles	210,000 ÷ 9 = 23,000 miles
Sales expenses as % of turnover	$\dfrac{£320,000}{£4,900,000} \times 100\% = 6.5\%$	$\dfrac{£280,000}{£7,300,000} \times 100\% = 3.8\%$
Working New business	£4,900,000 × 32% = £1,568,000	£7,300,000 × 15.5% = £1,131,500

(c)

Helping hand

Try to provide possible reasons for the differences in the performance of the two regions.

The **crude analysis** provided by the figures in part (a) (gross profit as % of turnover, sales expenses as % of turnover and gross profit less sales expenses as % of turnover) provides the following indications.

(i)   The **sales mix achieved by North Region is more profitable.**

(ii)   The **expenses involved in achieving these sales are a higher proportion of revenue in the North Region** and reduce profit considerably.

The **more detailed analysis** in part **(b)** highlights the following.

(i)   **North Region** has a **higher % of new business** and that the **new business generated per staff member** is also **higher**. If this is part of a trend than it would indicate that North Region is achieving **faster growth** in sales.

(ii)   **This growth** may, in time, eliminate the **relative differences in the profitability of sales persons** indicated by the gross profit per staff member and orders per staff member.

(iii)   The **differences in miles travelled per sales person** may be due to **geographical factors** (or to the sales force **working harder**).

(iv)   Differences in **cancelled orders per sales person** may be due, in part, to the relatively **higher percentage of new business** achieved in the **North Region**.

(v)   Looking at the costs, while **salaries per sales person** are significantly **higher in the South Region** (26% greater than the North Region), total fixed costs are considerably **lower** (75% of those in the North Region).

Examiner's marking scheme

		Marks
Problem 1 Method		to 1
Answer		to 1
		2
Problem 2		
(a) Gross profit		to 2
Sales expenses		to 2
Profit		to 1
Format		to 1
		6
(b) Performance measures	(1½ marks × 4 measures)	6
(c) Performance comparison	(1½ marks × 4 points)	6
		20

30   SUPERVANS LTD (6/98)   *36 mins*

Supervans Ltd is a subsidiary of a major international cargo company. The company currently has a total of 230 vans operating from eight depots making urgent deliveries of small parcels to small shops (mainly pharmacies) and businesses across the UK. Parcels to the rest of the world are transferred to the parent company's system. The depot managers are responsible for all the operations within their depot. A typical depot includes the following operations: a depot manager; an administration and accounting department; vehicle maintenance; deliveries; and a sales and marketing team responsible for increasing business.

Required

(a) Explain how the head office of Supervans Ltd might seek to improve control over their depots through the use of accounting responsibility centres and performance measures.

(5 marks)

(b) For each department, and the depot as a whole, identify what type of accounting centre might be appropriate.   (5 marks)

(c) Suggest TWO examples of suitable performance measures for EACH of the five aspects of a depot's operations.   (10 marks)

(20 marks)

Helping hand

The key to providing an excellent answer to this question is to ensure that you make your **points relevant to the scenario presented**. For example, you must describe how Supervans in particular rather than organisations in general can improve control through the use of accounting responsibility centres and performance measures. **Don't identify types of accounting centre or give examples of performance measures in (a),** otherwise you will simply be **duplicating your answers to (b) and (c).**

---

30   ANSWER: SUPERVANS LTD

> **What the examiner said**
>
> The answers of most candidates were disappointing. Marks were awarded in part (c) for answers that demonstrated a practical understanding of both the issues that might be controllable in different responsibility centres and the objectives of those functions.

(a)

> **Helping hand**
>
> Your answer should include **detail of the various types of responsibility centre that exist**. This will focus your mind for part (b), when you need to identify the particular types of centre appropriate for Supervans Ltd.

A responsibility centre is a function or department of an organisation that is headed by a manager who has direct responsibility for its performance. Responsibility centres are usually divided into three types: **cost centres, profit centres and investment centres**. The type adopted will depend on whether it is simply costs which can be attributed to the responsibility centre in question (cost centre), costs and revenues (profit centre) or costs, revenues and a certain level of investment (investment centre). Depending on the type of responsibility centre, the manager's performance will be measured in terms of cost variances and ratios (cost centre), profit (profit centre) or return on capital employed (investment centre), as well as a host of non-financial indicators such as breakdowns per 1,000 miles and so on.

The head office of Supervans Ltd should be able to **improve control** over their depots through the use of responsibility centres and the associated performance measures because **all costs, revenues and activities will be the responsibility of a specific manager**. Each manager will be aware of his area of responsibility and should aim to monitor cost levels, resources used, turnover and return on investment as appropriate. Senior management can then provide an overall control measure, the detail having been carried out by responsibility centre managers.

(b)

> **Helping hand**
>
> As you will see from our answer, in some instances there is **more than one possible suitable type of responsibility centre**. You will be awarded marks if you have justified your suggestion.

Depot manager

Because depot managers are in charge of all operations within their depot, they should be treated as an **investment centre**. This assumes that the manager has **some say over the level of investment** within the depot, however, as well as being responsible for costs and revenues. If the parent company gives depot managers **no control over investment policy**, the manager should be assessed as a **profit centre**.

Administration and accounting department

Depending on the size of the depot, these two functions will be treated as either one or two **cost centres** although it is likely that there will be a manager responsible for each function.

Vehicle maintenance

This function is **most likely** to be operated as a **cost centre**. If the **deliveries** function is **'charged' for the use of the vehicle maintenance service**, however, it could be treated as a **profit centre**. The charge basis might be based on the external cost of the services provided.

Deliveries

This will more than likely be a **profit centre** because, as well as incurring costs and receiving allocations and apportionments of the costs of other responsibility centres, its activities produce the depot's income.

Sales and marketing

This could be treated as a **profit centre**, the **turnover from new business** being matched against the department's costs. Alternatively it could be treated as a **cost centre**.

(c)

Helping hand

Do not simply regurgitate performance measures you have memorised. Make sure that they are relevant to the scenario in question.

Here are some examples of performance measures for each of the five areas of a depot's operations.

Depot manager

- Depot net profit compared with budget
- Return on capital employed (ROCE) (if investment centre)
- Turnover (local and transferred to parent company)

Administration and accounting department

- Cost per 1,000 deliveries
- Departmental cost compared with budget
- Time to prepare accounts at period end
- Level of bad debts

Vehicle maintenance

- Breakdowns per 10,000 miles
- Maintenance cost per 1,000 miles
- Vehicle days lost per period (due to breakdowns, repairs etc)

Deliveries

- Cost per parcel mile
- Number of lost parcels/claims per period
- Departmental profit compared with budget

Sales and marketing team

- Total new business generated in total and per salesperson
- Proportion of new customers retained after 12 months
- Cost (against budget) for the department, per salesperson, per new customer, per £1,500 of new sales

Examiner's marking scheme

			Marks
(a)	Definition	- responsibility centres	to 3
		- performance measures	to 2
			5
(b)	Each department - identification of appropriate accounting treatment		to 5 5
(c)	Each department - suggestion of appropriate performance measures - 1 mark per measure		to 10
			<u>10</u>
			<u>20</u>

31   HIGHLAND AND LOWLAND (6/99)   *36 mins*

Highland and Lowland make a similar product, but each firm sells its product to customers in different parts of the country. Both organisations have been experiencing pressure in their individual markets from cheaper goods, imported from overseas. Recently, the two senior managers have agreed to co-operate by sharing management accounting information, on the basis that each firm might be able to improve its own operating performance.

As the assistant accountant in Highland, you have been asked to produce a report for management on the potential for reducing costs. The following information is available.

MANAGEMENT ACCOUNTS FOR YEAR ENDED 31 MARCH 20X9

	Highland		Lowland		*
Production	200,000 units		200,000 units		
	£'000	£'000	£'000	£'000	%
Materials		53,000		48,545	–8.4
Labour		13,700		15,029	+9.7
Prime costs		66,700		63,574	–4.7
Add: overheads					
Production: fixed (depreciation)	3,500		4,000		+14.3
variable	2,600		3,123		+20.1
		6,100		7,123	
Production cost		72,800		70,697	
Add: selling and distribution expenses					
Marketing	1,500		2,000		+33.3
Distribution	1,750		1,300		–25.7
Total		3,250		3,300	
Total costs		76,050		73,997	–2.7

* Difference in cost expressed as a percentage of Highland's cost.

EXTRACT FROM BALANCE SHEETS AS AT 31 MARCH 20X9

	Highland £'000	Lowland £'000
Fixed assets		
Production equipment at cost	35,000	40,000
Cumulative depreciation	31,500	20,000
Written down value at 31.3.X9	3,500	20,000

Required

Write a report to the management of Highland comparing the performance between the two companies with a view to cost reduction. In your report you should do the following.

(a) Distinguish between the terms 'cost reduction' and 'cost control'.   (6 marks)

(b) Comment on the table of costs, suggesting likely reasons for the significant differences (positive or negative) between the two firms.   (10 marks)

(c) Briefly describe two problems commonly associated with cost reduction campaigns.   (4 marks)

(20 marks)

Helping hand

Don't forget to use a report format for your answer. Marks are always awarded for appropriate presentation.

---

31   ANSWER: HIGHLAND AND LOWLAND

What the examiner said

Many candidates struggled to distinguish adequately between the terms 'cost reduction' and 'cost control'.

REPORT

To: Management of Highland
From: Assistant accountant
Date: XX.X.XX
Subject: The potential for reducing costs

This report compares the performances of Highland and Lowland with a view to identifying potential areas for cost reduction.

(a)

Helping hand

It is common to confuse 'cost control' with 'cost reduction', which is probably why the examiner has asked you to distinguish between the two!

Cost reduction and cost control

Cost control is concerned with **regulating costs** and **keeping them within acceptable limits.** If costs exceed these limits then cost **control action** may be necessary. The limits will usually be the standard cost limits set out in the formal budget, but the focus is on **monitoring costs** and there is not necessarily any attempt to reduce costs below their current levels.

Cost reduction is a **planned and positive approach to reducing the costs** of goods and services without impairing their suitability for the use intended. Whereas cost control aims to control costs at the budgeted or standard level, cost reduction aims to **reduce costs to below budget or standard level,** as standards do not necessarily reflect the conditions which minimise costs.

(b)

Helping hand

It is a good idea to try to **demonstrate any interrelationships** which exist between the costs. For example, lower materials costs may indicate poor quality material which is more difficult to process, thus leading to higher labour and variable overhead costs. You may be able to identify other examples of possible interrelationships. In this question the comparison of costs is relatively straightforward because both companies produced the same volume of units. **If the volumes had been different it would not be possible to compare the absolute cost figures directly**. You would have needed to allow for the different volumes before making any comparisons of variable costs.

Comparison of costs in Highland and Lowland

Material costs

The **difference** in materials cost is **significant in absolute terms** (Lowland costs are £4,455,000 lower) **and in percentage terms** (Lowland costs are 8.4% lower than those of Highland). Possible **reasons for the difference** are as follows.

(i)   Lowland used lower quality, cheaper material.

(ii)   Lowland labour was more efficient at processing the material and so wastage was lower.

(iii)   Lowland's production equipment is newer than Highland's (see below*) and may therefore have processed the material more efficiently or economically. There may have been less wastage or a lower reject rate, thus leading to a lower usage of materials.

* The annual depreciation charges of £3,500,000 for Highland and £4,000,000 for Lowland indicate that both companies are depreciating the original cost of their production equipment using a straight line basis over ten years. Their fixed asset data are therefore directly comparable. Highland's fixed assets have only one year of life remaining, whereas Lowland's production equipment is only halfway through its useful life.

Labour costs

The difference in labour cost is **significant in absolute terms** (Lowland costs are £1,329,000 higher) **and in percentage terms** (Lowland costs are 9.7% higher than those of Highland). Possible **reasons for the difference** are as follows.

(i)   It has already been noted that Lowland may have been using lower quality material. This may have been more difficult to process, resulting in higher labour costs.

(ii)   Lowland may have been using more highly skilled and therefore more costly labour. Material cost savings may have resulted, however, as mentioned earlier in the report.

Fixed production overhead: depreciation

Lowland's depreciation charge is £500,000 higher than the annual depreciation charge of Highland. This is **not a particularly significant difference,** but it may be due to the purchase of more expensive sophisticated equipment, or prices for plant and equipment may have increased so that Lowland's more recent purchase of equivalent equipment was more expensive.

Variable production overhead

Lowland's variable production overhead is £523,000 (20.1%) higher than that of Highland. The difference is **not significant in absolute terms** and the possible reasons are similar to those for the difference in labour costs.

Marketing expenses

Lowland's marketing expenses are £500,000 (33.3%) higher than those of Highland. This is **not significant in absolute terms,** but possible reasons could be higher advertising costs or more highly-paid sales staff.

Distribution expenses

Lowland's distribution expenses are £450,000 (25.7%) lower than those of Highland. This is **not significant in absolute terms,** but possible reasons could include the use of cheaper premises for storage or an older distribution fleet with lower depreciation costs.

(c)

Helping hand

You are asked to describe two problems, so do not waste valuable examination time by providing more than two. We have included more for revision purposes.

Problems commonly associated with cost reduction campaigns

(i)   There may be **resistance from employees** to the pressure to reduce costs, usually because the nature and purpose of the campaign has not been properly explained to them, and because they feel threatened by the change.

(ii)   The programme may be limited to a small area of the business with the result that **costs are reduced in one cost centre, but this reduction causes extra costs to be incurred in another cost centre.** For example, savings from the purchase of lower quality material may lead to increased processing costs.

(iii)   Cost reduction campaigns are often **introduced as a rushed measure** instead of as a carefully thought out, well-planned exercise.

(iv)   **Cost reduction in the short term may lead to higher costs in the longer term.** For example a decision to reduce the size of a company's quality control department or its internal audit section might reduce staff costs in the short term but increase costs in the longer term.

(v)   The **costs** incurred in carrying out the cost reduction campaign may **outweigh any cost savings achieved.**

Examiner's marking scheme

		Marks	
(a)	Use of report format	to 2	
	Definition of terms (× 2 marks each)	to 4	
			6
(b)	Comment on materials and labour	to 4	
	Identification of issues re age of production equipment	to 3	
	Comment on other costs	to 3	
			10
(c)	Identification of 2 problems (× 2 marks each)	4	
			20

32   FRESH SLICE LTD (12/99)   *72 mins*

Fresh Slice Ltd (FS) prepares sandwiches with a variety of fillings for sale to shops, garages and other retail outlets. The firm has experienced rapid growth over the past four years and now employs over 40 staff. The business is split into two separate divisions, food preparation and sandwich distribution - employing 30 and 10 members of staff respectively.

So far, it has been relatively straightforward for management to organise and control the business. Each day, bread and fillings are purchased, which are then made up into sandwiches for delivery to shops, for sale on the same or following day. Thus there are no significant stocks of ingredients. Overheads have been kept to a minimum, as the sandwich preparation process has been essentially a manual operation, with piece-rates being the main basis of labour remuneration.

Recently, the market has become more sophisticated as customer tastes and expectations have risen. There has also been a consolidation in terms of the number of companies involved in the industry. As a result of both pressures, there is an urgent need to introduce automated production processes and to introduce additional functions such as refrigeration facilities (to store bulk deliveries of ingredients on-site) and a bakery to provide speciality breads freshly baked on the premises.

The directors, who are also shareholders of FS, are fairly traditional in their outlook and so far have only seen the necessity to produce accounts on an annual basis, principally to meet the statutory obligations of being a 'limited' company. These financial accounts have been produced by Jones and Bell, a local firm of accountants. The senior partner, Mr Jones, has suggested that, as the complexity of the business increases, FS should consider appointing its own accountant to prepare monthly management accounts and to support all levels of management in decision making.

Required

As the assistant to Mr Jones, prepare a report for the directors of Fresh Slice Ltd. Your report should include reference to the following.

(a) A table summarising the principal differences between management accounting and financial accounting.   (6 marks)

(b) An explanation of how a management accountant might contribute to the running of the business by providing information for the following.

    (i)   Analysis   (3 marks)
    (ii)   Planning   (3 marks)
    (iii)   Control   (3 marks)

(c) A brief outline of the steps involved in the decision-making process   (4 marks)

(d) FOUR examples of suitable performance measures to enable management to monitor the performance of the sandwich delivery division. *Note.* Two of the measures should be non-financial performance measures.   (4 marks)

For report format   (2 marks)

END OF REPORT STAGE

Two basic types of sandwich are prepared, luxury and standard, both with a variety of fillings. Luxury sandwiches are more popular in the summer when people have outdoor picnics.

Annual production	- luxury sandwiches	600,000 units
	- standard sandwiches	900,000 units
Weekly production during 16-week summer period	- luxury sandwiches	20,000 units
	- standard sandwiches	24,000 units
Estimated labour time per sandwich	- luxury	- 3.00 minutes
	- standard	- 2.00 minutes
Present piece-work rate per sandwich	- luxury	- £0.24
	- standard	- £0.16

Present payment system

The normal working week is 40 hours but for 16 weeks in the summer, when demand rises, an overtime premium of £2.40 per hour is paid in addition to normal piece-rate earnings. The factory operates for 50 weeks in each year.

Proposed payment system

One of the key decisions presently facing the directors of FS is whether or not to place all the 30 production staff in the food preparation division on an annual-hours contract. This would involve a guaranteed annual salary of £10,000, payable as a fixed monthly wage. The contract would be based on 2,000 hours per year (50 weeks of 40 hours per week) at £5.00 per hour, rather than the present piece-work rates. Under an annual-hours contract, time is worked as directed by management. Hours are increased or reduced at management's discretion at different times of the year. Thus, hours will stay within a previously agreed total number of hours per worker per year - in this case 2,000. Under the new scheme 30 production staff are sufficient to achieve the budgeted annual production.

Required

(e) Calculate the following.

    (i) The total annual wages paid under the present system   (6 marks)

    (ii) The annual wages under the proposed system   (3 marks)

(f) On the basis of your answers to part (e), briefly outline the advantages and disadvantages of moving from the present piece-work system to the proposed annual-hours contract for the following.

    (i) The company   (3 marks)

    (ii) The employees of the food preparation division   (3 marks)

(40 marks)

Helping hand

Notice the **presentation methods** required: a report for parts (a) to (d) and a table in (a).

Do not provide a general discussion on the role of the management accountant in (b). You must explain how he/she might contribute to the running of the business by providing information for three particular activities.

Part (c) is only worth four marks. Check your **time allocation** carefully.

Provide measures **appropriate** to the scenario in (d). General measures such as earnings per share will not earn you full marks.

You need to rely on **knowledge from Paper B2** in the second part of the question. The calculations in (e) are very straightforward so don't think you've not understood the question if you find them easy to do.

---

32   ANSWER: FRESH SLICE LTD

> **Helping hand**
>
> Notice that the use of a **report** format is worth **2 marks**. Don't waste those marks, they might represent the difference between a pass and a fail.
>
> **What the examiner said**
>
> Part (a) was handled well by the majority of candidates, although some were tempted to explain the general role of management accounting and financial accounting without drawing out the distinction between the two.
>
> The examiner was disappointed that, despite previous questions on performance measures and an article in *Technician Bulletin*, candidates were, on the whole, unable to suggest appropriate performance measures in part (d).
>
> There were few fully correct answers to part (e). Markers did give credit where candidates' workings showed evidence of understanding the principles. But in cases where insufficient detail was provided or detail was not clear, marks could not be given.

REPORT

To: Directors of Fresh Slice Ltd
From: A N Assistant, Jones and Bell
Date: 13 November 20X0
Subject: Management accounting at Fresh Slice Ltd

This report is intended to **provide additional information** to support our senior partner's suggestion regarding the appointment of a management accountant at Fresh Slice (FS) Ltd to prepare monthly management accounts and to support all levels of management in decision making.

(a)

> **Helping hand**
>
> Instead of diving straight into a table summarising the differences between financial and management accounting, try to include a very **short introduction** as to why the table is included. It will make your report easier to read and follow.

Management accounting compared with financial accounting

Our firm currently prepares financial accounts for your organisation on an annual basis in order to comply with the statutory obligations of being a limited company. These **financial accounts** are **unlikely to provide you with the level of management information that you will require as the complexity of your business increases**, however. Such management information, which will allow you to plan, control and make decisions in a more complex business environment, can be provided by a management accounting system.

In order to **appreciate the value and benefits provided by a management accounting system,** you may find it useful to consider the **differences between management accounting and financial accounting.**

Management accounting	**Financial accounting**
A management accounting system produces information that **is used within an organisation,** by managers and employees.	A financial accounting system produces information that is **used by parties external to the organisation**, such as shareholders, banks and creditors.
Management accounting **helps management to record, plan and control activities and aids the decision-making process** (see (b) below).	Financial accounting provides a **record of the performance** of an organisation over a defined period and the **state of affairs** at the end of that period.

189

Management accounting	Financial accounting
There is **no legal requirement** for an organisation to use management accounting.	Limited companies must, **by law**, prepare financial accounts.
Management accounting can **focus on specific areas of an organisation's activities** (such as the sandwich delivery division). Information may aid a decision rather than be an end product of a decision.	Financial accounting **concentrates on the organisation as a whole**, aggregating revenues and costs from different operations. Financial accounts are an end in themselves.
Management accounting information may be **monetary or** alternatively **non-monetary** (such as number of orders delivered late).	Most financial accounting information is of a **monetary** nature (such as the cost of ingredients used during the year).
Management accounting provides both an **historical record** (number of sandwiches produced on a particular day) and a **future planning tool** (the cost of baking bread on the premises compared with that associated with buying it in).	Financial accounting presents an essentially **historic picture** of past operations.
No strict rules govern the way in which management accounting operates. Your management accounts and information would be in a **format that was of use to you and the organisation**.	Financial accounting must operate within a **framework determined by law, by SSAPs and by FRSs**. In principle the financial accounts of different organisations can be easily compared.

It should therefore now be evident that there are huge differences between financial accounting and management accounting and hence between the information each provides and the value of that information for particular purposes.

(b)

> **Helping hand**
>
> 'Analysis' is quite a **vague** term and so you may find that you have not interpreted its meaning as we have done. Don't forget to **relate** your answer to FS Ltd.

The contribution of a management accountant to the running of your business

(i)   **By providing information for analysis**

The provision of information for analysis could be given as the **general, overriding role** of the management accountant. The majority of the information that he or she provides would be analysed in some way by the management team to **assist with planning, control and decision making**.

(1)   The management accountant may provide past data on sales revenue for the purposes of **time series analysis** so that accurate forecasts are incorporated into the budget (indeed, he or she may well carry out the analysis him/herself).

(2)   The management accountant would also provide information for, and also carry out, **variance analysis**, to determine the component differences between planned and actual costs and revenues.

(3)   He/she may use, or provide the information for, a decision-making technique known as **limiting factor analysis** (which would determine the most profitable mix of sandwiches to prepare if one of the resources you use (say cheese) was in short supply).

(ii)   **By providing information for planning**

The planning information provided by a management accountant may be focused on a number of different areas, such as the following.

(1)   **Pricing** (suggested price for sandwiches developed for more sophisticated customer tastes).

(2)   **Product costs** (the cost of sandwiches prepared without on-site refrigeration facilities compared with the expected cost of those prepared after the installation of the facilities).

(3)   **Competition** (prices and range of sandwiches offered by competitors).

In the short-term planning process of **budgeting**, a management accountant would provide invaluable information on past costs and revenues (which can be used for forecasting purposes) and he or she would also be deeply involved in the budgeting process itself.

(iii)   **By providing information for control**

A management accountant would provide **performance reports** that would **compare actual performance** (number of each type of sandwich sold, revenues, costs, sales to particular customers and so on) **with planned performance**.

Those activities that were not conforming to plan (possibly the sale of sandwiches with particular fillings, or sales to particular outlets) would therefore be highlighted as potential problem areas so that the **management team could take control action**. Such action would result in activities conforming to plan in future or to the plan being amended to take account of information not known when it was set.

(c)

Helping hand

This is **standard text book material** but to obtain marks you must **refer** in your answer to **FS Ltd**.

The decision-making process

The management accountant would be a vital cog in your organisation's decision-making process (which, despite its name, also incorporates planning and control). A brief outline of the process is set out below.

Step 1.   **Identify objectives**

The organisation's goals or objectives must be defined to ensure that managers are able to assess which of the courses of action available is the most appropriate for the organisation. Your overriding objective may be the maximisation of profit and/or to become the sandwich company most in tune with customer tastes and expectations and so the decision option chosen should reflect this.

Step 2.   **Search for alternative courses of action**

The next step is to find a number of possible courses of action that would enable the company's objectives to be achieved. For FS Ltd these might include the following.

(i)   Develop new styles of sandwiches to sell in existing markets
(ii)   Develop new styles of sandwiches to sell in new markets
(iii)   Develop new markets in which to sell existing styles of sandwiches

Step 3.   **Collect data about alternative courses of action**

The type of data that needs collecting will depend on the type of decision. If the decision is about the long-term future of the organisation, the management accountant will need to collect data about the environment within which FS Ltd operates (competitors, consumer tastes and so on) and about the organisation's capabilities (such as distribution network and capacity to expand).

Step 4.   **Select the appropriate course of action**

The course of action that best satisfies the organisation's objectives should be selected.

Step 5.   **Implement the decision**

Suppose you decided to repackage and then raise the price of your vegetarian range of sandwiches by 15% from £1 per packet for sale in a new market. The actual price charged in the market would need to be increased to £1.15 per packet and the sales budget prepared on the basis of a selling price of £1.15.

Step 6.   **Compare actual and planned outcomes and take any necessary corrective action if the planned results have not been achieved**

The price charged in the new market for vegetarian sandwiches might reduce demand to such an extent that sales revenue on that line was significantly below budget. The price may need to be lowered or a promotional campaign launched.

(d)

Helping hand

You were only expected to provide **four measures** (although did you note that **two** had to be **non-financial**?). Remember this is a sandwich delivery service so a 'cost per tonne delivered' measure is unlikely to be useful!

Performance measures

Performance measurement would also be enhanced by the appointment of a management accountant, who could prepare for the organisation's divisions or activities suitable measures to **enable management to monitor performance**. Examples of those that could be used for the sandwich delivery division include the following.

Financial

(i)   Average total cost per delivery
(ii)   Average labour cost per delivery
(iii)   Average transport cost per delivery
(iv)   Average variable cost per delivery
(v)   Cost of late deliveries

Non-financial

(i)   Proportion of orders delivered late
(ii)   Number of orders not delivered
(iii)   Number of complaints about service provided by delivery staff
(iv)   Number of orders which include incorrect items

I hope this information has proved useful and has served to highlight the benefit of introducing a management accounting function to FS Ltd. If you have any questions or I can provide any further assistance, please do not hesitate to contact me.

(e)

> **Helping hand**
>
> In part (i) you need to calculate the annual piece-rate payments *and* the additional payments during the summer.

(i) **Total wages paid under the present system**

	£'000	£
Annual piece-rate payments		
Luxury sandwiches (600,000 × £0.24)	144	
Standard sandwiches (900,000 × £0.16)	144	
		288,000
Additional payments during summer		
Hrs required per week – luxury sandwiches		
20,000 × 0.05 hr =	1,000	
Hrs required per week – standard sandwiches		
24,000 × 2/60 hr =	800	
Total hrs required per week	1,800	
Normal hrs worked per week (30 × 40 hrs)	1,200	
Overtime hours per week	600	
∴ Additional payment = 600 × 16 wks × £2.40		23,040
Total wages paid		311,040

(ii) **Annual wages under the proposed system**

	£
30 staff × annual salary of £10,000	300,000

(f)

> **Helping hand**
>
> You should have tried to think of **three points for the company** and **three for the employees**, given that each of the parts is worth three marks.

Impact on moving from the present piece-work system to the proposed annual-hours contract

(i) **On the company**

Advantages

(1) The **wages paid will decrease** by £11,040.

(2) Time is worked as directed by management and so additional payments need not be made if workers have to work longer than 40 hours per week (provided the annual total number of hours is 2,000 or less). This gives management the **flexibility** to respond to changes in demand at short notice, without increasing costs for the company.

(3) **Quality may improve.** Workers are not under time pressure to prepare sandwiches within a particular time.

Disadvantages

(1) If demand increases rapidly during the year, the total number of hours required may be in excess of the 2,000 agreed, with the result that **additional payments need to be made** if demand is to be met.

(2) Workers may **not work as quickly,** and hence may not prepare as many sandwiches as anticipated, if not paid on a piece-work basis. Demand may not be met and/or more workers may need to be taken on, increasing the wages cost.

(3) The **cost** of paying staff who are **absent through illness** must be met.

(ii) **On the employees**

Advantages

(1) They will receive a **guaranteed income** of £10,000 even if they work less than the standard hours offered under the piece-work scheme.

(2) They will have a **more even payment pattern** and the protection of **salaried status.**

(3) They are under **less time pressure** and can therefore ensure that they are producing a **quality** product.

Disadvantages

(1) **Hours can be increased or decreased at management's discretion** at different times of the year. Employees could find themselves working 20 hours one week and 60 hours the next.

(2) Their **total pay will fall** by £11,040/30 = £368 each (on average).

(3) The new system will **favour inexperienced/slower workers.**

Examiner's marking scheme

			Marks
(a)	Differences between management and financial accounting Four differences both sides (1½ marks × 4)		to 6
(b)	Management accountant's role in providing information 3 marks for each subheading		to 9
(c)	Steps in decision-making process – six steps and description		to 4
(d)	Four performance measures × 1 mark per measure		to 4
For report format			to 2
			25
(e)	(i)	Annual wage calculation – present system	
		- cost of piece-rate earnings	to 2
		- cost of summer overtime	to 3
		- total annual wages	to 1
	(ii)	Annual wage calculation – proposed system	to 3
			9
(f)	Two advantages and two disadvantages of changing systems	
	(i)	- for management – three factors × 1 mark	to 3
	(ii)	- for employees – three factors × 1 mark	to 3
			$\frac{6}{40}$

DO YOU KNOW? – DECISION MAKING

- *Check that you can fill in the blanks in the statements below before you attempt any questions. If in doubt, you should go back to your BPP Interactive Text and revise first.*

- The high-low method can be used to determine the .... and .... elements of semi-variable costs.

- Over a long period of time, virtually all costs are .... Within short time periods, costs will be fixed or variable in relation to .... In the very, very short term, costs which are normally considered to be .... may be ....

- .... costing provides more useful decision-making information than .... costing.

- A .... cost is a future cash flow arising as a direct result of a decision.

- .... cost is the benefit which could have been earned, but has been given up, by choosing one option instead of another.

- The total relevant cost of a scarce resource consists of the following.
  - . . . .
  . . . .
  - . . . .

- In a make or buy situation with no scarce resources, the relevant costs are .... plus ....

- In a situation where a company must subcontract work to make up a shortfall in its own in-house capabilities, its total costs will be minimised if those units bought have the lowest extra .... cost of buying per unit of .... saved by buying the products in question.

- The .... is the activity level at which there is neither profit nor loss. It is calculated as .... ÷ ....

- A .... chart is a chart which shows approximate levels of profit or loss at different sales volume levels within a limited range. A .... chart provides a simple illustration of the relationship of costs and profit to sales.

- There are many influences on an organisation's pricing policy.
  - ....
  - ....
  - ....
  - ....
  - ....
  - ....

  - ....
  - ....
  - ....
  - ....
  - ....
  - ....

- The price elasticity of demand measures ....

- The .... approach to pricing involves determining a profit-maximising price.

- Using .... pricing, the sales price is determined by calculating the full cost of the product and adding a percentage mark-up for profit. The approach is unlikely to arrive at a profit-maximising price.

- .... pricing involves adding a profit margin to the marginal cost of production (or sales).

- The opportunity cost approach to pricing involves including .... and then adding a profit margin.

- Fixed price tenders involve an analysis of .... costs. A margin is often added to the ....

TRY QUESTIONS 33-40

- *Possible pitfalls*

  Write down the mistakes you know you should avoid.

195

DID YOU KNOW? – DECISION MAKING

- *Could you fill in the blanks? The answers are in bold. Use this page for revision purposes as you approach the exam.*

- The high-low method can be used to determine the **fixed** and **variable** elements of semi-variable costs.

- Over a long period of time, virtually all costs are **variable**. Within short time periods, costs will be fixed or variable in relation to **changes in activity level**. In the very, very short term, costs which are normally considered to be **variable** may be **fixed**.

- **Marginal** costing provides more useful decision-making information than **absorption** costing.

- A **relevant** cost is a future cash flow arising as a direct result of a decision.

- **Opportunity** cost is the benefit which could have been earned, but has been given up, by choosing one option instead of another.

- The total relevant cost of a scarce resource consists of the following.

   ◦ **The contribution foregone from the next-best opportunity for using the scarce resource (its opportunity cost)**

   ◦ **The variable cost of the scarce resource**

- In a make or buy situation with no scarce resources, the relevant costs are **the differences in unit variable costs** plus **differences in directly attributable fixed costs.**

- In a situation where a company must subcontract work to make up a shortfall in its own in-house capabilities, its total costs will be minimised if those units bought have the lowest extra **variable** cost of buying per unit of **scarce resource** saved by buying the products in question.

- The **breakeven point** is the activity level at which there is neither profit nor loss. It is calculated as **total fixed costs ÷ contribution per unit**.

- A **breakeven** chart is a chart which shows approximate levels of profit or loss at different sales volume levels within a limited range. A **profit/volume (P/V)** chart provides a simple illustration of the relationship of costs and profit to sales.

- There are many influences on an organisation's pricing policy.
   ◦ **Price sensitivity**   ◦ **Competitors**
   ◦ **Income**   ◦ **Price perception**
   ◦ **Suppliers**   ◦ **Product range**
   ◦ **Quality**   ◦ **Inflation**
   ◦ **Ethics**   ◦ **Intermediaries**
   ◦ **Newness**   ◦ **Substitute products**

- The price elasticity of demand measures **the extent of change in demand for a good following a change in its price.**

- The **demand-based** approach to pricing involves determining a profit-maximising price.

- Using **full cost plus** pricing, the sales price is determined by calculating the full cost of the product and adding a percentage mark-up for profit. The approach is unlikely to arrive at a profit-maximising price.

- **Marginal cost plus (mark-up)** pricing involves adding a profit margin to the marginal cost of production (or sales).

- The opportunity cost approach to pricing involves including **the opportunity costs of the resources consumed in making and selling the item in the cost of the product** and then adding a profit margin.

- Fixed price tenders involve an analysis of **relevant** costs. A margin is often added to the **minimum price**.

   TRY QUESTIONS 33-40

- *Possible pitfalls*
   ◦ **Using absorption costing information for decision-making purposes**
   ◦ **Classifying sunk costs, committed costs and notional costs (eg depreciation) as relevant costs**
   ◦ **Failing to consider the non-financial aspects of decision options**

33   QUESTION WITH HELP: DECISION MAKING

A cinema chain, based in Oxford, owns three cinemas in the towns of Newbury, Reading and Basingstoke. As the chain's finance assistant, you have prepared budgets for the coming year based upon a ticket price of £4.

	Reading £	Newbury £	Basingstoke £	Total £
Budgeted ticket receipts	1,600,000	1,200,000	800,000	3,600,000
Costs				
Film hire	500,000	400,000	390,000	1,290,000
Wages and salaries	300,000	250,000	160,000	710,000
Overheads	500,000	400,000	350,000	1,250,000
	1,300,000	1,050,000	900,000	3,250,000

Included in the overhead figures are the Oxford head office fixed costs that amount to £720,000. These have been allocated to each cinema on the basis of budgeted ticket receipts. All other costs are variable.

The management are concerned about the Basingstoke cinema and the fact that it is showing a budgeted loss and is considering closing the cinema and selling the site to a property developer. You have been asked to look into the proposal.

Required

(a) Prepare marginal costing statements to show contributions for each cinema and contribution and profit for the overall chain on the following bases.

  (i)   The original budget
  (ii) If the Basingstoke cinema is closed   (8 marks)

(b) State whether, on the grounds of profitability, you think that the Basingstoke cinema should be closed. Give a reasoned explanation of your decision.   (3 marks)

(c) Calculate the contribution per ticket sale at each cinema.   (3 marks)

(d) Calculate the margin of safety in revenue for the chain at the budgeted level of activity in the following circumstances.

  (i)   If the Basingstoke cinema is kept open
  (ii) If the Basingstoke cinema is closed   (3 marks)

(e) If the Basingstoke cinema is kept open management want an increase in profitability. One suggestion is that receipts at the cinema can be increased by 50% by an advertising campaign directed at Basingstoke that will add £40,000 to the chain's fixed costs.

  Explain whether the advertising campaign should be undertaken to improve the cinema's profitability. Give reasons for your decision.   (3 marks)

(20 marks)

If you are stuck, look at the next page for detailed help as to how you should tackle this question.

APPROACHING THE ANSWER

Step 1. Begin part (a) by preparing a working to determine variable overheads (overheads minus apportioned head office costs) for each cinema and in total. The apportioned head office costs for Reading are calculated as:

(budgeted ticket receipts/total receipts) × £720,000

= 1,600,000/3,600,000 × £720,000

Step 2. Draw up the (original budget) marginal costing statement to show, for each cinema and in total, ticket receipts, variable costs and contribution. From the contribution in the 'Total' column deduct head office fixed costs to arrive at the budgeted profit.

Step 3. Draw up a revised marginal costing statement which, because it does not include Basingstoke, will have a number of different values in the 'Total' column. (Not all of them will be different, however!).

Step 4. For part (b) you need to compare the statements in (a)(i) and (ii). Basingstoke should remain open if profit decreases if it is closed.

Step 5. Contribution per ticket sale for part (c) is calculated as total contribution ÷ number of tickets, so you need to work out, for each cinema, the number of tickets sold. You do this by dividing budgeted ticket receipts by the ticket price. You can get total contribution for each cinema from your statements prepared in part (a)(i).

Step 6. Margin of safety required for part (d) is the difference between breakeven point in revenue and budgeted revenue. You can obtain budgeted total revenue for the two scenarios from your statements in (a).

Step 7. Calculate the breakeven point in revenue by dividing total fixed costs by the total C/S ratio. You can get contribution and sales for both scenarios from your statements in (a). Fixed costs are the same under both scenarios.

Step 8. Work out the margin of safety for each scenario by deducting breakeven revenue from budgeted revenue.

Step 9. To ascertain whether the campaign should be undertaken (part (e)), compare the possible increase in contribution (50% of present *contribution*, not turnover, because if turnover increases, variable costs increase) with the cost of the campaign. If the increase in contribution is greater than the cost, the campaign should go ahead.

33   ANSWER TO QUESTION WITH HELP: DECISION MAKING

(a)   *Working*

	Reading	Newbury	Basingstoke	Total
	£'000	£'000	£'000	£'000
Overheads	500	400	350	1,250
Apportioned head office costs	320	240	160	720
Variable overheads	180	160	190	530

(i)   **Marginal costing statement based on original budget**

	Reading		Newbury		Basingstoke		Total
	£'000	£'000	£'000	£'000	£'000	£'000	£'000
Ticket receipts		1,600		1,200		800	3,600
Variable costs							
Film hire	500		400		390		1,290
Wages and salaries	300		250		160		710
Variable overhead	180		160		190		530
		980		810		740	2,530
Contribution		620		390		60	1,070
Head office fixed costs							720
Profit							350

(ii)   **Marginal costing statement if the Basingstoke cinema is closed**

	Reading	Newbury	Total
	£'000	£'000	£'000
Ticket receipts	1,600	1,200	2,800
Variable costs	980	810	1,790
Contribution	620	390	1,010
Head office fixed costs			720
Profit			290

(b)   On the grounds of profitability, the **Basingstoke cinema should not be closed,** because **it earns a contribution of £60,000.** The overall profit for the cinema chain would fall by £60,000 because ticket revenue of £800,000 would be lost and variable costs of only £740,000 would be saved. The £160,000 of **head office fixed costs apportioned to the Basingstoke cinema would still be incurred** if it was closed down.

(c)

	Reading	Newbury	Basingstoke
Budgeted ticket receipts (£'000)	1,600	1,200	800
Number of tickets ('000) (÷ £4)	400	300	200
Contribution (£'000)	620	390	60
Contribution per ticket	£1.55	£1.30	£0.30

(d)   **Breakeven point in revenue** $= \dfrac{\text{fixed costs}}{\text{C/S ratio}}$

	Basingstoke open	Basingstoke closed
Contribution/sales ratio	1,070/3,600	1,010/2,800
	= 29.72%	= 36.07%
Breakeven point in revenue	720/0.2972	720/0.3607
	= £2,422,611	£1,996,119
Budgeted revenue	£3,600,000	£2,800,000
Margin of safety in revenue	£1,177,389	£803,881

(e) **Increase in contribution as a result of campaign** = **50% × present contribution**

	=	50% × £60,000
	=	£30,000
Cost of advertising campaign		£40,000
Reduction in profit		£(10,000)

The **advertising campaign should not be undertaken** because the **extra contribution is less than the cost of the campaign**. In addition the extra fixed cost will increase the breakeven point and will reduce the margin of safety.

34   BURGERTOWN (12/98)   *72 mins*

Burgertown is a fast-food restaurant (take-away and eat-in quick-food) established 12 months ago by Bill Webster in the town of Woodhampton. As a result of the success of the first restaurant, he is currently looking to open a further restaurant, of a similar size, in Parkwich, a nearby town. The planning process for the first restaurant relied on Bill's own intuition; no detailed forecasts of income and expenditure were prepared. The start up cost of £250,000 for shop fitting and equipment was provided from the sale of Bill's former business. This time, however, he will require a bank loan. The manager of the bank has asked for detailed estimates of the costs and expected returns. Bill has sought your help in preparing a report for the bank manager. Bill has provided the following information as a result of his first 12 months of trading at the Woodhampton restaurant.

1   Total number of meals sold during the year was 260,000, at an average value of £2.70. The total cost of the meals served (food, drink, cooking oil, packaging etc) was £312,000.

2   A combination of full-time and part-time staff are employed. In busy periods more staff are called in to work. Bill feels that the first six months of operation were not typical months, due to the need for staff training. He has therefore provided the following summary of the cost of staff wages in the last six months.

Month	Cost	Meals sold
	£	
7	15,867	21,605
8	13,343	15,025
9	14,027	16,123
10	17,519	26,002
11	18,657	28,310
12	15,539	20,599

Note. Assume that all months are of equal duration.

3   Other cash expenses for the year, all assumed to be fixed, were as follows.

	£
Rent of premises	40,000
Business rates	16,000
Electricity for cooking, heat and light	7,000
Maintenance and cleaning materials	4,000
Miscellaneous	16,000
Total	83,000

4   The cost of shop fitting and equipment for the new Parkwich restaurant is estimated at £250,000. Bill expects that a total refit will be required at the end of 10 years - you have already suggested to Bill that straight-line depreciation would be most appropriate.

5   The interest charge on the proposed bank loan of £250,000 is 12%. Assume there are no requirements for working capital.

Required

(a)   Using the high-low method, calculate the variable labour cost per meal and (to the nearest £'000) the annual fixed labour cost in the Woodhampton restaurant.

(5 marks)

(b)   On the basis that Bill expects the Parkwich restaurant to have the same annual sales and a similar cost behaviour pattern to his first site, and taking into account notes 4 and 5, produce a detailed statement of the estimated annual income and expenditure of the proposed Parkwich restaurant, in a marginal costing format (showing figures to nearest £'000). (8 marks)

(c) Calculate the breakeven point in meals for the proposed Parkwich restaurant. Show all your workings. (4 marks)

(d) Calculate the margin of safety ratio for the proposed Parkwich restaurant. (3 marks)

(e) Draw a breakeven chart to show Bill and the bank manager the effect of sales volume on the profitability of the Parkwich restaurant. (7 marks)

(f) Bill feels that the Parkwich restaurant will generate significantly higher sales than the original one in Woodhampton if a site close to the main shopping and entertainment district of Parkwich is chosen. This will result in a higher rent, however, £130,000 in total, but Bill would expect the average selling price of a meal to rise to £2.90. To compensate for the additional risk involved, Bill expects that the annual profit on the Parkwich restaurant should be £50,000 higher than on the Woodhampton site.

Calculate, in percentage terms, how many extra meals would need to be sold to achieve this higher level of profit. Show all your workings. (5 marks)

(g) Before Bill presents his plan to the bank, explain to him some of the limitations of the breakeven analysis you have prepared. (8 marks)

(40 marks)

Helping hand

You will earn high marks in this question if you read the **requirements** carefully and **follow them exactly.**

- In part (a), calculate the annual fixed labour cost **to the nearest £'000.**

- In part (b), show figures to the nearest £'000. Take into consideration both the fact that the Parkwich restaurant will have the **same annual sales** and a **similar cost behaviour pattern** to the first site and the detail in **notes 4 and 5.**

- In part (c), calculate the breakeven point in terms of **meals** (not revenue).

- Calculate the margin of safety as a **ratio** in part (d) (not in terms of meals).

- The graph in (e) should be a **breakeven chart** and not a P/V chart.

- Calculate the extra meals needed in **percentage terms** for part (f).

- Provide only **limitations** (not advantages) of breakeven analysis in (g).

34   ANSWER: BURGERTOWN

> **Helping hand**
>
> Key to this question is an appreciation of the principles of cost behaviour and, specifically, how the financial implications of various scenarios might be evaluated through an understanding of the relationships between revenue, fixed costs, contribution per unit and profit.
>
> **What the examiner said**
>
> Part (g), although providing an opportunity to gain 20% of the total marks available for the question, was not answered well.

(a)

> **Helping hand**
>
> Remember that you use the costs associated with the **highest and lowest activity levels**, not the highest and lowest costs, for the high-low method.

Using the high-low method:

	Meals sold	Labour cost £
High activity level	28,310	18,657
Low activity level	15,025	13,343
Difference	13,285	5,314

Variable labour cost of 13,285 meals = £5,314

$\therefore$ **Variable labour cost per meal** $= \dfrac{£5,314}{13,285} = £0.40$ per meal

To find the fixed cost:

	£
Total cost of 28,310 meals	18,657
Variable cost of 28,310 meals ($\times$ £0.40)	11,324
Fixed cost per month	7,333

$\therefore$ **Annual fixed labour cost**, to the nearest £'000 $= £7,333 \times 12$
$= £88,000$

(b)

> **Helping hand**
>
> 'In a **marginal costing format**' means that you must **highlight separately variable costs, contribution** and **fixed costs.**

PARKWICH RESTAURANT
STATEMENT OF ESTIMATED ANNUAL INCOME AND EXPENDITURE

	£ per meal	£'000	£'000
Sales revenue	2.70		702
less variable costs:			
cost of meals served	1.20	312	
staff	0.40	104	
			416
Contribution	1.10		286
less fixed costs:			
full-time staff (from (a))		88	
rent of premises		40	
business rates		16	
electricity		7	
maintenance and cleaning materials		4	
miscellaneous		16	
depreciation of shop fittings and equipment ($\frac{£250,000}{10}$)		25	
loan interest (£250,000 × 12%)		30	
			226
Profit			60

(c)

> **Helping hand**
>
> If you had trouble with this calculation you **must** go back to your Interactive Text and revise.

$$\textbf{Breakeven point} = \frac{\textbf{total fixed costs (from (b))}}{\textbf{contribution per meal (from (b))}} = \frac{£226,000}{£1.10} = 205,455 \text{ meals}$$

(d)

> **Helping hand**
>
> You may not have known how to calculate the margin of safety ratio but you would have **earned some marks from calculating the margin of safety in terms of meals**.

	Meals
Forecast number of meals	260,000
Breakeven point (from (c))	205,455
Margin of safety	54,545

$$\textbf{Margin of safety ratio} = \frac{\textbf{margin of safety meals}}{\textbf{forecast number of meals}} = \frac{54,545}{260,000} = 21\%$$

(e)

> **Helping hand**
>
> Notice how marks are earned for the chart. You could earn one mark for a sensible scale, one mark for identifying the breakeven point and so on. It is **easy to pick up marks for simple things**. Don't throw away mark-earning opportunities.

Basic data for breakeven chart (from (b))

Fixed costs = £226,000

Total cost for 260,000 meals:

	£
variable cost	416,000
fixed cost	226,000
	642,000

Sales revenue for 260,000 meals = £702,000

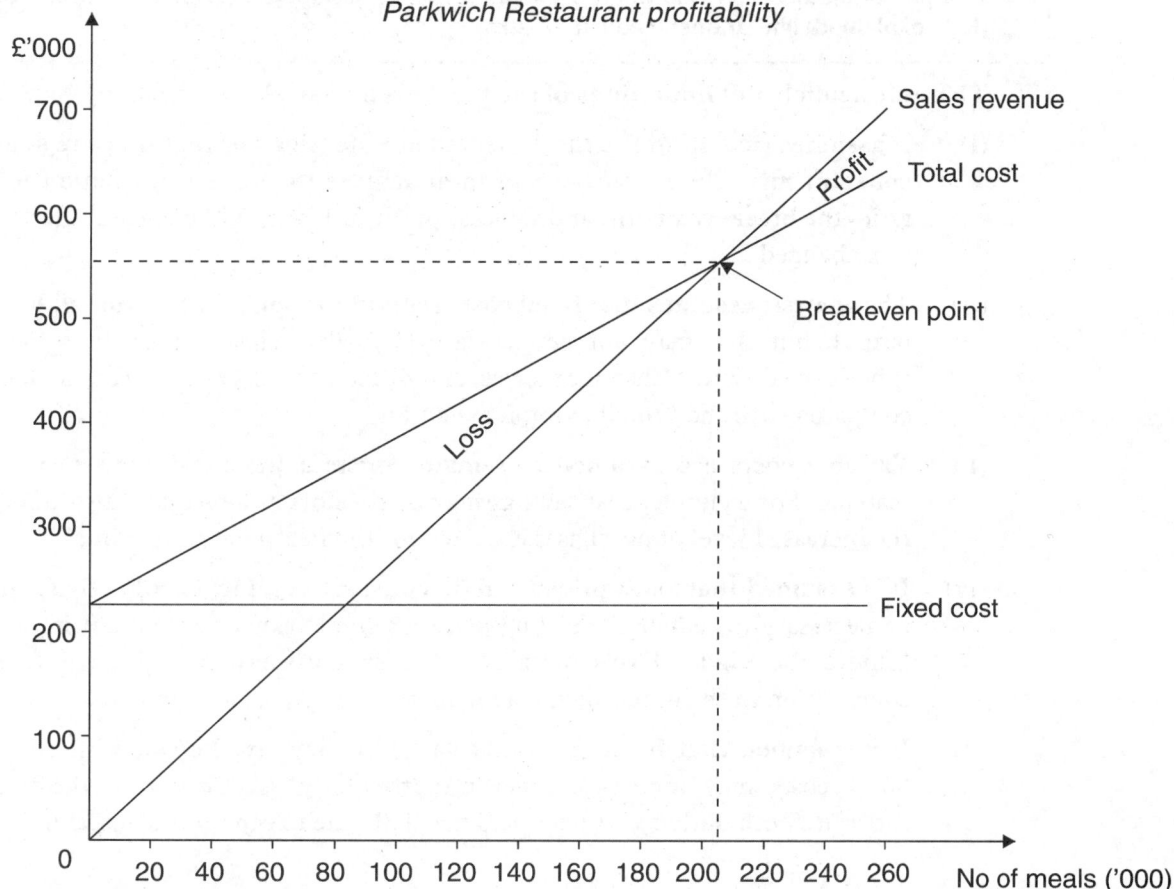

Breakeven chart to show the effect of sales volume on Parkwich Restaurant profitability

(f)

Helping hand

A **percentage increase** is calculated as **(difference between the two figures ÷ original figure) × 100%**.

Contribution required to cover fixed costs and required level of profit:

	£'000	£'000
Original fixed costs (from (b))	226	
Increase in rent (£130,000 – £40,000)	90	
Revised fixed costs		316
Original profit requirement (from (b))	60	
Increase to compensate for risk	50	
		110
Total contribution required		426

Contribution per meal = £2.90 – £1.60 = £1.30

	Meals
∴ Number of meals required (£426,000/£1.30)	327,692
Original number of meals	260,000
Increase required	67,692

Percentage increase $= \dfrac{67,692}{260,000} \times 100\% = 26\%$

(g)

> **Helping hand**
>
> This part of the question was worth eight marks so realistically you needed to provide **four (fully explained) limitations** to earn full marks.

There are a number of **limitations of the breakeven analysis** prepared.

(i) It **assumes that all of the meals served are identical, or that they are sold in a constant mix.** Unless all types of meal achieve the same contribution to sales ratio, the breakeven point and forecast profit or loss would change if the product mix changed.

(ii) The analysis **assumes that fixed costs remain the same in total for all levels of output,** but this may not be the case. The Parkwich restaurant is likely to experience different customer levels, and different peaks and troughs in demand, compared with the Woodhampton restaurant.

(iii) **Variable costs are assumed to remain constant per meal.** This may not be realistic. For example, cost savings may be possible as a result of discounts from the increased level of purchases expected for the Parkwich restaurant.

(iv) It is **assumed that sales prices will be constant at all levels of activity.** It may be necessary to reduce the selling prices in the Parkwich restaurant in order to achieve the higher levels of sales, however. Furthermore, different levels of competition in the other town may require different pricing policies.

(v) It is **assumed that fixed costs and variable costs are known with certainty.** Some costs may increase, however (particularly as a result of the need to supervise both outlets), while others may fall (due to economies of scale).

Examiner's marking scheme

			Marks
(a)	High-low method		
	- correct method and application	to 3	
	- monthly variable cost	to 1	
	- annual fixed cost	to 1	
			5
(b)	Income and expenditure statement		
	- variable costs	to 1	
	- cost per unit shown	to 1	
	- contribution	to 1	
	- depreciation	to 1	
	- interest payments	to 1	
	- other costs	to 1	
	- total cost	to 1	
	- profit	to 1	
			8
(c)	Breakeven point		
	- formula/method	to 2	
	- correct figures	to 1	
	- breakeven point calculation	to 1	
			4
(d)	Margin of safety		
	- formula/method	to 1	
	- correct figures	to 1	
	- margin 21.0%	to 1	
			3
(e)	Breakeven chart		
	- presentation for management	to 2	
	- sensible scale	to 1	
	- two cost lines	to 1	
	- sales line	to 1	
	- breakeven point correctly identified	to 1	
	- relevant range covered	to 1	
			7
(f)	Additional meals		
	- new costs, rent and profit	to 2	
	- new contribution figure	to 1	
	- method	to 1	
	- answer in meals and percentage terms	to 1	
			5
(g)	Limitations of breakeven analysis		
	- four limitations with reference to case (2 marks each)		8
			40

BPP
PROFESSIONAL EDUCATION

35   CES (12/98)   *36 mins*

CES specialises in providing contract services to the electricity supply industry. Powerco plc has asked CES to submit a tender to overhaul one of the four steam turbines in its Derwent power station. The work is scheduled to take place in three months' time, when demand for electricity will be low. The CES contracts manager has supplied the following estimates.

1   *Labour*

	Task	Skill level required	Number of workers	Number of days
(i)	Strip down and rebuild	fitter	6	8
(ii)	Overhaul turbine	fitter	4	19
		engineer	5	19
(iii)	Test and commission	engineer	2	4

Each fitter costs £100 per day and the engineers £210 per day.

Each of the three tasks has to be completed before the next task can commence.

2   *Materials*

Total material requirement has been estimated at a stores issue price of £57,800. In pricing for tenders, CES apply a mark-up to the stores issue price of plus 20%.

3   *Travel and hotel accommodation*

Expenses of £30 per day per worker will be paid to all workers.

4   *Overheads and profit*

It is the company's policy to include an amount of £120 per worker per day, to cover the company's overheads. Profit is provided by adding a margin of plus 30% to total cost.

5   *Additional information*

At the time of the contract, CES will only have three fitters available. The remaining fitters will have to be hired from an employment agency at a rate of £150 per day, plus travelling expenses at the rate of £30 per day.

Two of the engineers required for the overhaul stage are on secondment to another contractor at a rate of £400 per day. They can be recalled from this contract, subject to written notice.

Included in the cost of materials is £19,000 which relates to bearing sets bought three years ago for a similar job which was cancelled. It is the contract manager's view that these components are unlikely to be used elsewhere, as almost all other power stations now use an upgraded bearing specification. All other materials are in constant usage and no price changes are envisaged in the near future.

Required

(a)   Prepare a tender for submission to Powerco plc on EACH of the following assumptions.

   (i)   That there are no constraints on worker availability and the contract can therefore be based on CES's normal pricing policy (referring to notes 1 to 4 only).   (8 marks)

   (ii)   That CES is keen to start dealing with Powerco plc and the managing director is prepared to submit a tender based on the lowest relevant cost to CES, after the circumstances mentioned in note 5 above have been taken into consideration.
                                                                                                  (7 marks)

(b) State what your advice to CES might be regarding the lowest relevant cost tender. Include any points of caution that CES should be made aware of.   (5 marks)

(20 marks)

Helping hand

Part (a)(ii) is probably the trickiest part of this question, especially the calculation of the relevant labour cost. You will need to **calculate the costs of CES fitters and agency fitters separately**. Note that each of the three tasks has to be completed before the next task can commence.

---

35   **ANSWER: CES**

> **What the examiner said**
>
> Only a minority of candidates were able to demonstrate in part (b) that they appreciated the commercial implications of preparing tenders on the basis of relevant cost.

(a)   (i)

> **Helping hand**
>
> Ignore completely the information in **note 5** when you do this part of the question.

Referring to notes 1 to 4 only

	No of workers	No of days	Worker days	Rate per day £	£	£
Labour						
Strip down and rebuild	6	8	48	100		4,800
Overhaul turbine: fitters	4	19	76	100		7,600
engineers	5	19	95	210		19,950
Test and commission	2	4	8	210		1,680
			227			34,030
Materials						
Stores issue price					57,800	
Mark up of 20%					11,560	
						69,360
Travel and hotel accommodation						
Expenses - 227 worker days (as above) × £30						6,810
Overheads						
227 worker days × £120						27,240
Total cost						137,440
Profit mark up of 30%						41,232
Tender price						178,672

(ii)

> **Helping hand**
>
> In relevant cost questions it is important to state any assumptions that you need to make.
>
> You should note that **each of the three tasks have to be completed before the next task can commence**. This means that only one fitter has to be hired from an agency to overhaul the turbine.

Tender based on lowest relevant cost

	No of workers	No of days	Worker days	Rate per day £	Note	£
Labour						
Strip down and rebuild:						
CES fitters	3	8	24	100		2,400
Agency fitters	3	8	24	150		3,600
Overhaul turbine:						
CES fitters	3	19	57	100		5,700
Agency fitters	1	19	19	150		2,850
Engineers	3	19	57	210		11,970
Recalled engineers	2	19	38	400	(1)	15,200
Test and commission	2	4	8	210		1,680
			227			43,400
Materials						
Stores issue price (£57,800 less £19,000)					(2)	38,800
Travel and hotel accommodation (as before)					(3)	6,810
Overheads					(4)	-
Total relevant cost - lowest tender cost						89,010

Notes

1. This is the **opportunity cost** of the income foregone from the secondment.

2. **Assumption**. The company does not intend to apply any mark-up: the relevant cost will be used as the lowest tender price.

3. All workers, including agency fitters, receive £30 per day for expenses.

4. **Assumption**. Company overheads are all fixed and will not be affected by this contract. Their relevant cost is therefore nil.

(b)

Helping hand

Lowest relevant cost tenders provide no profit and so should **only be considered if it is vital that the organisation is awarded the contract**, perhaps to secure future business.

The **lowest relevant cost tender** should be used **if it is important for CES to be awarded the contract**. At this price they will recover their future costs but will not earn a profit mark-up on these costs. In particular, the usual **mark-up on materials cost has not been included**. This may be intended to recover the cost of small items of material, consumables and so on. If this is the case, then this part of the mark-up should be added to the lowest cost tender.

The company should attempt to ascertain whether or not any other companies are bidding for the work and their estimated tender price, however. If there is no competition, a lowest relevant cost tender may not be necessary.

A few **further points of caution** should also be noted.

(i) This low price is a one-off which **could not be repeated** for future tenders. This is because the bearing sets would not be available as obsolete stock, and CES would need to recover overheads if this customer placed orders on a regular basis. There is a danger that the customer will expect all tenders to be at this low level.

(ii) **Other customers may hear about this low price** and begin to demand similar prices for their contracts.

(iii) **Have all other opportunities for work been identified?** If other work is foregone as a result of this contract then the opportunity cost of this work should also be considered.

(iv) The relevant cost price **assumes that overheads are all fixed** and are not affected by the contract. This is unlikely to be the case in reality.

(v) The **relevant cost of the bearings may not be nil**. They may have a scrap value.

(vi) CES should **ensure that all relevant expenses have been correctly identified and analysed.** Variable costs may have been incorrectly coded to overheads, for example.

Examiner's marking scheme

			Marks
(a)	Tender preparation		
	(i) Normal policy		
	- labour cost	- fitters	to 2
		- engineers	to 2
	- materials		to 1
	- travelling costs		to 1
	- overheads and profit		to 1
	- final price		to 1
			8
	(ii) Relevant costing		
	- extra fitting cost		to 2
	- opportunity cost of engineers		to 1
	- total relevant labour cost		to 1
	- materials cost		to 1
	- travelling cost		to 1
	- relevant tender costs		to 1
			7
(b)	Advice to management		
	- correct cost classification		to 2
	- implications for future Powerco tenders		to 2
	- materials mark-up		to 1
			5
			20

---

36   DILEMMA LTD (6/99)   *36 mins*

Dilemma Ltd makes a product that is aimed at the teenage leisure market in the UK. After a number of successful years they are considering whether to expand their production capability by a factor of 50% to take advantage of rising demand. The accountant has produced the following information.

- Current sales per year are 500,000 units at £1.70 per unit.

- Variable costs are £1.40 per unit.

- Fixed costs are £96,000 per year.

- If production is increased it is anticipated that:

    ° fixed costs will increase by £34,000;

    ° variable costs are expected to fall by £0.05 per unit due to bulk purchasing of raw material;

    ° the selling price is expected to fall by £0.10 per unit for all units.

At a recent management meeting the following comments were noted.

- The production director expressed concern at the revenue projections. In his opinion there are a number of risks inherent in the new strategy. His main concern is that the total number of teenagers is falling, although he conceded that perhaps future teenagers may have more money to spend per head. He also asked if future changes in raw material prices and wage rates had been fully taken into account.

- The sales director stated that she felt much more confident about the plan and said that sales had been rising for some time and, in her opinion, the number of teenagers is increasing. She also thought that inflation should not be too much of a problem.

Required

(a) For both the present and proposed situations calculate the following.

(i)	The breakeven point in units and sales revenue	(3 marks)
(ii)	The annual profit	(2 marks)
(iii)	The margin of safety ratio	(1 mark)

Note. Show all your workings.

(b) Summarise your results from part (a) in a table.   (2 marks)

(c) On the basis of your answers to part (a), state, with reasons, what your advice would be to Dilemma Ltd.   (4 marks)

(d) In view of the differences of opinion expressed by the directors regarding future population and economic trends, suggest four external sources of information, in total, that might be useful in assessing projections for sales and costs. For each source, give an example explaining the type of information available and its relevance to Dilemma Ltd.   (8 marks)

(20 marks)

Helping hand

Read part (a) carefully. You need to do calculations for both the **present and proposed** situations.

Don't forget to explain the **relevance** of the information to **Dilemma Ltd** in part (d).

---

36 ANSWER: DILEMMA LTD

(a)

Helping hand

The margin of safety is the **difference (in units) between the budgeted sales volume and the breakeven sales volume. If it is expressed as a percentage of the budgeted sales volume** it is known as the **margin of safety ratio**. It is an indication of the percentage by which sales can fall before losses are made.

		Present situation	*Proposed situation*
(i)	Breakeven point = $\dfrac{\text{fixed costs}}{\text{contribution per unit}}$	$=\dfrac{£96,000}{£(1.70-1.40)}$	$\dfrac{£130,000}{£(1.60-1.35)}$
		$=\dfrac{£96,000}{£0.30}$	$=\dfrac{£130,000}{£0.25}$
	∴ **Breakeven point in units**	= 320,000 units	= 520,000 units
	× selling price per unit	× £1.70	× £1.60
	Breakeven point in sales revenue	= £544,000	= £832,000
(ii)	**Annual sales units**	500,000	(+ 50%) 750,000
	× contribution per unit (from (i))	× £0.30	× £0.25
	Total contribution	£150,000	£187,500
	Less fixed costs	£96,000	£130,000
	Annual profit	£54,000	£57,500
(iii)	**Annual sales units**	500,000	750,000
	Breakeven sales units (from (i))	320,000	520,000
	Margin of safety in units	180,000	230,000
	Margin of safety ratio = $\dfrac{\text{margin of safety}}{\text{budgeted annual sales}}$	$\dfrac{180,000}{500,000}\times100\%$	$\dfrac{230,000}{750,000}\times100\%$
		= 36.0%	= 30.7%

(b)

Helping hand

You should **earn marks for the presentation** of your table, even if your data from part (a) is incorrect.

Dilemma Ltd
Proposal for expansion of production capability

	Present situation	*Proposed situation*
Breakeven point in units	320,000	520,000
Breakeven point in sales revenue	£544,000	£832,000
Annual profit	£54,000	£57,500
Margin of safety ratio	36.0%	30.7%

(c)   In view of the projected **increase in profit**, the **proposals** are **worthwhile** and should be adopted. The profit increase is only small, however, and the proposed changes would result in a much **more risky situation** for Dilemma Ltd. The breakeven point would increase by more than 60 per cent to 520,000 units and the margin of safety ratio would reduce to 30.7%.

Sales have been **rising** for some time and this would tend to **indicate that expansion is worthwhile**. In view of the **doubts expressed about the future potential market and changes in raw material prices and wage rates,** however, Dilemma Ltd would need to be **more confident about its forecasts** before exposing the organisation to this increased level of risk.

(d)

Helping hand

We have suggested more than four sources of information so that you can use the solution for revision purposes. **Don't forget to explain why you have suggested each information source.**

Possible **external sources of information** include the following.

(i)   **Government statistics** supplied by the **Office for National Statistics**

(1)   **The Annual Abstract of Statistics.** This includes data on population trends for each age group. Dilemma Ltd should examine the trends for teenagers and younger children, in view of the conflicting views about whether the number of teenagers is rising or falling.

(2)   **The United Kingdom National Accounts (The Blue Book).** This publication gives a clear indication of how the nation makes and spends its money. The trends indicated may help to substantiate or disprove the production director's comment that future teenagers may have more money to spend per head.

(3)   **Social Trends.** This publication will also provide information about trends in income, to help with assessing teenagers' future spending power.

(ii)   Other statistics supplied by **government departments**, for example **British Business.** This is published by the Department of Trade and Industry, and includes data on production, prices and trade. The directors' concerns about raw material prices, wage rates and inflation may be alleviated or confirmed by an analysis of this data.

(iii) **Trade journals** will provide information about industry costs and prices, new developments in the industry, articles on competitors' products and so on. This will help Dilemma Ltd to assess the future conditions in its market in terms of demand, prices, costs, intensity of competition and so on.

(iv)   Information from **consultancies,** including **general market research organisations** such as MORI and Gallup. There are also **specialist market research companies** which will provide specific data on Dilemma Ltd's industry, in terms of prices, demand and so on.

(v)   **Specific reference works.** Different businesses have different reference works or so called 'bibles' which Dilemma Ltd may find useful as a point of reference for trends in demand, prices, costs and so on.

(vi)   **Electronic sources** such as **teletext** and the **internet** can provide information about a wide variety of matters. For example, key suppliers may have a website which may provide information on past and future trends in prices.

Examiner's marking scheme

			Marks	
(a)	Breakeven analysis			
	(i)	Calculation of contribution per unit	to 1	
		Calculation of breakeven point	to 1	
		Calculation of sales amount	to 1	
	(ii)	Calculation of annual profit	to 2	
	(iii)	Calculation of margin of safety ratio	to 1	
				6
(b)	Table of results from (a)			2
(c)	Advice to proceed with proposal		to 1	
	Reasons		to 3	
				4
(d)	Sources of information with examples (4 sources × 2 marks each)			8
				20

37   INTERTOWN (12/99)   *36 mins*

Intertown operate a number of railway routes under a franchise agreement with the government. The company is considering whether to place an order to lease 20 new trains at a cost of £300,000 per train per annum. Fixed annual running costs are estimated at £150,000 per train.

The trains would be used to provide new services within the franchise area. All seats would be standard class. The following information is available.

Maximum capacity of each train	120 people seated (standing not allowed)
Average return journey per train	50 miles
Operating cost per mile	£10.00
Operating days per unit	300 days
Return journeys per train per day	3

A firm of transport consultants has been engaged to undertake a study of passenger demand on other public transport routes. Their findings have indicated that demand will vary in accordance with fare levels as follows.

Fare (return)*	Capacity
£	%
11	90
12	80
13	70
14	60
15	50
16	40

* Represents the fare for the average return journey per passenger

Notes

1   At the 80% capacity level and above, fixed costs would rise by £60,000 per annum in total, due to the need to introduce a seat reservation system to manage peak demand without losing passengers when peak-time trains are full. The reservation system involves the rental of operating hardware and software for a minimum five-year period.

2   At the 50% capacity level and below, there will be a saving of 20% in variable costs, due to the lower passenger weight and some economies in cleaning etc.

Required

(a)   For each of the six potential capacity levels, calculate the profit that would arise per train per annum and show your results in a table.

   Remember to show all your workings.   (8 marks)

(b)   State, with reasons, the fare level you would recommend management adopt to maximise profit.   (3 marks)

(c)   Outline any reservations that you may have in terms of your recommendation in part (b) above.   (3 marks)

(d)   Suggest, with a brief explanation, THREE examples of further information that would be useful in evaluating the leasing proposal.   (6 marks)

(20 marks)

Helping hand

Don't be confused by the **relative simplicity** of the calculations needed in (a), and don't forget to show your results in a **table** otherwise you'll lose 1 mark (the difference between a pass and a fail!). You are asked for **information** in (d), not problems or solutions.

---

37   ANSWER: INTERTOWN

(a)

> **Helping hand**
>
> The wording in the question relating to the **fixed costs of £60,000** is **extremely ambiguous**. The ACCA Official solution indicates that the fixed costs **per train** rise by £60,000 but in our opinion you would have been perfectly justified in assuming that the increase is a general fixed overhead.

At each capacity level

Revenue per train per annum

= fare × capacity level × maximum capacity (120) × number of return journeys (3) × number of operating days (300)

= fare × capacity level × 108,000

Operating costs per train per annum = (operating cost per mile (£10) × average return journey per train (50 miles) × number of return journeys (3) × number of operating days (300)) × 80% if capacity 50% or less

= £450,000 if capacity 60% or above *or* £360,000 if capacity 50% or less

Fixed costs

= lease cost of train (£300,000) + fixed annual running costs (£150,000) + additional costs (£60,000) if capacity 80% or above

= £450,000 if capacity 70% or less *or* £510,000 if capacity 80% or above

90% capacity

	£	£
Revenue (£11 × 90% × 108,000)		1,069,200
Costs: operating	450,000	
fixed	510,000	
		(960,000)
Profit		109,200

80% capacity

	£	£
Revenue (£12 × 80% × 108,000)		1,036,800
Costs: operating	450,000	
fixed	510,000	
		(960,000)
Profit		76,800

70% capacity

	£	£
Revenue (£13 × 70% × 108,000)		982,800
Costs: operating	450,000	
fixed	450,000	
		(900,000)
Profit		82,800

60% capacity		£	£
Revenue (£14 × 60% × 108,000)			907,200
Costs: operating		450,000	
fixed		450,000	
			(900,000)
Profit			7,200

50% capacity		£	£
Revenue (£15 × 50% × 108,000)			810,000
Costs: operating		360,000	
fixed		450,000	
			(810,000)
Profit			-

40% capacity		£	£
Revenue (£16 × 40% × 108,000)			691,200
Costs: operating		360,000	
fixed		450,000	
			(810,000)
Loss			(118,800)

Potential annual profitability per train	
Capacity level	**Profit/(loss)**
%	£
90	109,200
80	76,800
70	82,800
60	7,200
50	-
40	(118,800)

(b)

> **Helping hand**
>
> You are asked for the **profit-maximising fare**, not capacity level.

Profits are maximised at a **capacity level of 90%**. Management should therefore charge a **fare of £11 per return journey** to maximise profits at £109,200.

(c)

> **Helping hand**
>
> In (c) and (d) your answers may be completely different to ours. Don't worry. As long as your **suggestions are grounded in common sense** you will **earn marks**.

There are a number of **reservations** associated with recommending a **fare of £11 per return journey**.

(i) The recommendation has been based to a large extent on the results of a study of passenger demand on other public transport routes. Demand for services on **Intertown's routes may not necessarily follow the pattern determined by this study.**

(ii) If trains were to break down/require maintenance, or if weather conditions were adverse, the trains may **not be able to make three return journeys per day and**

not run on 300 days per year. Cost and revenue predictions determined in (a) above could therefore be inaccurate.

(iii)   The **estimate of fixed annual running costs** may be **inaccurate** and/or may be a **step cost** and vary with capacity level.

(iv)   If demand against price estimates turn out to be particularly optimistic such that even the 80% capacity level is not reached, the **cost of the investment in the reservation system will not be justified.** It might therefore be preferable to **set a price based on the 70% capacity level,** thereby giving a reasonable return without having to commit to the cost of the reservation system.

(v)   If **competition** from another form of public transport were to occur within Intertown's franchise area (such as a new coach service), the findings of the consultants may no longer hold.

(vi)   Despite the implementation of a seat reservation system, **passengers may still be lost** when peak time trains are full, impacting on revenue predictions at the higher capacity levels.

(vii)   Intertown would be **committed to renting** the seat reservation system hardware and software for a minimum of **five years**. They may decide to discontinue the new services within this time period, however, or their franchise may be terminated.

(viii)   **Demand may vary** across Intertown's routes and hence some trains may not be as profitable as others. The recommendation makes no suggestion as to **whether all 20 trains should be leased.**

(d)   **Additional information** that would be useful in evaluating the leasing proposal includes the following.

(i)   An assessment of the **reliability of the consultants.**

(ii)   An analysis of potential **competition** from other forms of public transport within Intertown's franchise area in order to determine the extent to which demand levels will remain as predicted.

(iii)   An appraisal of whether it may be more profitable to **buy the trains** rather than lease them. Factors to take into account would include the expected life of a train, the length of the franchise agreement, possible competition, maintenance costs as trains get older and so on.

(iv)   An assessment of whether the **additional fares generated by the seat reservation system** are likely to be **greater than its cost.** If, over five years, £300,000 of fares cannot be generated, the system should not be implemented.

(v)   An **analysis of demand on individual routes** to determine whether or not all 20 trains are required.

(vi)   An analysis of the way in which **future demand** is likely to move (up or down).

(vii)   An assessment of the likely impact of inflation and interest rates on **future costs.**

(viii)   Information on the **reliability of the trains** (to assess whether three return journeys per day, 300 days per year per train, is feasible).

(ix)   An appraisal of the **impact on existing services.**

Examiner's marking scheme

			Marks
(a)	*Profitability calculations*		
	Number of passengers and annual journeys (½ mark each)	to 1	
	Revenue per annum	to 1	
	Adjustments	to 1	
	Annual overheads	to 2	
	Profit/loss per annum	to 1	
	Tabular presentation	to 2	
			8
(b)	Advice to management (identification of most profitable option)		3
(c)	Reservations		3
(d)	Suggestions for further information (three items × 2 marks each)		6
			20

38   BAKO (6/00)   *72 mins*

Bako is a small bakery supplying local shops with bread and pastries. The company is in the process of producing its management accounts for the year ended 30 June 20X0 and making decisions about possible prices and sales quantities for the following year ending 30 June 20X1. Unfortunately, the accountant left the company just before the year end, leaving both the accounts and the sales forecasts unfinished. You work for a firm of certified accountants and have been asked to produce a profit and loss statement for the year just ended and also to help the management of Bako with its planning for the year just starting. The following information is available.

1   Bako has two divisions, one producing loaves of bread, the other producing a variety of sweet and savoury pastries. Both divisions occupy separate parts of the factory but share a fleet of delivery vehicles, plus central administration and marketing functions.

2   An extract from the trial balance shows the following entries as at 30 June 20X0. Note that there were no stocks of raw materials, work in progress or finished goods at either the start or the end of the year.

		Bread	*Pastries*	*Total*
		£'000	£'000	£'000
	Notes			
Sales	(a)	480	220	700
Ingredients		200	80	280
Labour		60	40	100
Variable overheads		20	7	27
Administration	(b)			78
Marketing expenses	(b)			36
Delivery transport	(c)			84
Fixed assets:				
Production equipment at cost		85	75	160
Cumulative depreciation 1.7.W9	(d)	34	30	64
Factory rent	(e)			50

Notes

(a)   Average selling prices per unit are £0.40 per loaf and £1.00 per pastry.

(b)   Administration and marketing costs are to be shared equally between the two divisions.

(c)   There is a fleet of 8 delivery vans. The cost shown includes all vehicle leasing and running costs plus the wages of the drivers. It has been estimated that 50% of the delivery costs are variable and should be apportioned in relation to the number of units delivered per division. The remaining delivery costs are fixed, and in the past these have been apportioned equally between the two divisions.

(d)   Depreciation is calculated on a straight-line basis over five years. (No individual asset was fully depreciated at 1.7.W9)

(e)   Factory rent is to be split in the ratio 3:2 between bread and pastries respectively.

3   On the basis of research undertaken by a firm of marketing consultants, the following projections of unit sales at differing selling prices have been prepared for the year ending 30 June 20X1. The previous accountant had estimated the total cost per division based upon the projected unit sales for each of the two options, after allowing for forecast price increases, but the working papers showing the build up of cost are not available. The only information that is available is shown below.

	Bread	*Pastries*
Option 1 – increase prices		
Selling price per unit	£0.43	£1.20
Estimated sales units	1,100,000	210,000
Total cost	£438,000	£262,800
Option 2 – reduce prices		
Selling price per unit	£0.39	£0.90
Estimated sales units	1,500,000	240,000
Total cost	£550,000	£283,200

Required

(a) For each division, and in total, produce a profit and loss statement for the year ended 30 June 20X0, in a marginal costing format. Show your results to the nearest £'000.

(10 marks)

(b) On the basis of the financial results calculated in part (a) above, state what your advice would be to management, together with any reservations that you may have. (5 marks)

(c) For each of the two proposed pricing options, produce a profit and loss statement showing the projected results for each division for the year ended 30 June 20X1, in a marginal costing format. Show your results to the nearest £'000.   (8 marks)

Note. You should use the high/low method in arriving at the split between variable and fixed costs.

(d) Using your results from part (c), calculate for each option in the BREAD DIVISION ONLY, the following information and show your results in a table.

  (i)   The contribution per unit   (2 marks)
  (ii)   The breakeven point in units   (2 marks)
  (iii) The margin of safety ratio   (2 marks)

(e) Calculate the contribution to sales ratio for BOTH the bread and the pastries divisions under Option 1 – increase prices.   (3 marks)

(f) On the basis of your answers to parts (a) to (e) above, advise management about the best course of action, together with any reservations you might have, for the following.

  (i)   The bread division   (4 marks)
  (ii)   The pastry division   (4 marks)

(40 marks)

38   ANSWER: BAKO

> **What the examiner said**
>
> Many candidates appeared to be confused by the need to apportion fixed overheads between the two divisions when undertaking a marginal costing approach.

(a)

> **Helping hand**
>
> A marginal costing format should highlight the **contribution from each division** and so you will need to **separate the fixed and variable costs.** Follow the detailed instructions concerning the **apportionment of fixed costs.** Remember to **show all your workings,** since credit can sometimes be given for the **logic of your approach** even if you make errors in your calculations.

Profit and loss statement for the year ended 30 June 20X0

	Working	Bread		Pastries		Total	
Sales units	1	1,200,000		220,000		1,420,000	
		£'000	£'000	£'000	£'000	£'000	£'000
Sales revenue			480		220		700
Less variable costs							
Ingredients		200		80		280	
Labour		60		40		100	
Variable overheads		20		7		27	
Delivery transport	2	35		7		42	
			315		134		449
Contribution			165		86		251
Less fixed costs							
Administration		39		39		78	
Marketing expenses		18		18		36	
Delivery transport	2	21		21		42	
Depreciation	3	17		15		32	
Factory rent	4	30		20		50	
			125		113		238
Net profit/(loss)			40		(27)		13

Workings

1   Bread sales units = 480,000/0.40 = 1,200,000

Pastries sales units = 220,000/1.00 = 220,000

2

	£'000
Total delivery transport costs	84
Variable element of cost (50%)	42
Apportioned:	
bread (1,200/1,420)	35
pastries (220/1,420)	7

3   *Assumption.* The production equipment will have no residual value at the end of its useful life.

	£'000
Production equipment depreciation:	
Bread division (£85,000/5)	17
Pastries division (£75,000/5)	15

4   Factory rent apportionment:

	£'000
Bread division (3/5 × £50,000)	30
Pastries division (2/5 × £50,000)	20
	50

(b)

> **Helping hand**
>
> The important issues are that the pastries division makes a **contribution towards fixed costs,** and that consideration must be given as to **whether any of the fixed costs would be saved** if the manufacture of pastries was discontinued.

Advice to management

It appears that the pastries division is incurring a loss and that its activities should be discontinued. **The division is making a contribution** of £86,000 towards fixed costs, however, and **the loss result depends on the validity of the apportionment of fixed costs.**

If none of the fixed costs are **specific to the division** (they would not be saved if the division was discontinued), Bako's profits would reduce by £86,000 if the division was closed. Furthermore, **the sales of pastries and bread may be interdependent,** with the result that sales of bread would reduce if pastries were not also available to customers.

Management are therefore advised to **continue with the sale of pastries** and to look for opportunities to increase the sale of pastries (as the contribution to sales ratio of pastries (39%) is higher than that of bread (34%)).

Management should also **review the validity of the fixed cost apportionment,** and should see whether any specific fixed costs can be identified. These costs should be highlighted separately so that management are better informed as to the relative profitability of each division.

(c)

> **Helping hand**
>
> Once again it is important to **show your workings** in order to ensure you are awarded maximum marks. Since you will need to do the same analysis of costs for both divisions you will save time by **working in columns.** You should always look out for such time-saving devices. Every minute counts when you are in the examination hall! Remember to show your results to the nearest £'000.

Analysis of fixed and variable costs

		Bread		Pastries	
		'000 units	£'000	'000 units	£'000
Option 2 activity and cost		1,500	550	240	283.2
Option 1 activity and cost		1,100	438	210	262.8
		400	112	30	20.4
Variable cost per unit	=	$\frac{£112,000}{400,000}$		$\frac{£20,400}{30,000}$ =	
	=	£0.28		£0.68 =	

Substituting in option 2 :			£'000		£'000
Variable cost	(1,500 × £0.28)		420	(240 × £0.68)	163.2
Total cost			550		283.2
Fixed cost			130		120.0

Forecast profit and loss statements for the year ended 30 June 20X1

Option 1 – increase prices

	Bread	*Pastries*	*Total*
Sale units	1,100,000	210,000	1,310,000
	£'000	£'000	£'000
Sales revenue (1,100 × £0.43)	473	(210 × £1.20) 252	725
Variable costs (1,100 × £0.28)	308	(210 × £0.68) 143	451
Contribution	165	109	274
Fixed costs	130	120	250
Net profit/(loss)	35	(11)	24

Option 2 – reduce prices

	Bread	*Pastries*	*Total*
Sale units	1,500,000	240,000	1,740,000
	£'000	£'000	£'000
Sales revenue (1,500 × £0.39)	585	(240 × £0.90) 216	801
Variable costs (1,500 × £0.28)	420	(240 × £0.68) 163	583
Contribution	165	53	218
Fixed costs	130	120	250
Net profit/(loss)	35	(67)	(32)

(d)

Helping hand

Don't forget to **show your results in a table.** You will lose easy marks if you don't. A clear table will make it easier for you when you come to answer part (f) as well, when you will need to quickly review the results of your calculations.

(i) **Contributions per unit**

Option 1: £(0.43 – 0.28) = £0.15

Option 2: £(0.39 – 0.28) = £0.11

(ii) **Breakeven point**

Option 1: £130,000/£0.15 = 866,667 units

Option 2: £130,000/£0.11 = 1,181,818 units

(iii) **Margin of safety ratio**

	Option 1 Units	*Option 2* Units
Forecast sales	1,100,000	1,500,000
Breakeven point	866,667	1,181,818
Margin of safety	233,333	318,182

Margin of safety	$\dfrac{233,333}{1,100,000} \times 100\%$	$\dfrac{318,182}{1,500,000} \times 100\%$
	= 21.2%	= 21.2%

Bread division **Forecast results for 20X1**		
	Option 1 – increase prices	*Option 2 – reduce prices*
Contribution per unit	£0.15	£0.11
Breakeven point	866,667 units	1,181,818 units
Margin of safety ratio	21.2%	21.2%

(e)

> **Helping hand**
>
> Read the question carefully to ensure you calculate the C/S ratio for the **correct divisions and the correct option.**

$$\text{Contribution to sales ratio} \quad \begin{array}{cc} Bread & Pastries \\ = \dfrac{£165,000}{£473,000} \times 100\% & = \dfrac{£109,000}{£252,000} \times 100\% \\ = 34.9\% & = 43.3\% \end{array}$$

(f)

> **Helping hand**
>
> There are two distinct sections to this part of the question so make sure that your answer is divided into the same two distinct parts. Try to use all of the data and information that you have calculated in parts (a) to (e).

(i) **Bread division**

The forecast profit of £35,000 for next year is the same under both options and represents a **small reduction in profit** compared with £40,000 earned in the year just ended.

Option 1 has a **lower breakeven point** than option 2, but because of the lower level of forecast sales for option 1, **the margin of safety ratio is the same for both options.** This may appear to indicate that each option carries the same level of risk. The major reservation concerning option 2 which should be borne in mind, however, is that the breakeven level of sales is 1,181,818 units which is 98% of the sales achieved during the year just ended.

(1) Does the division have the capacity to produce, sell and distribute the required number of units?

(2) Have the resulting changes in cost behaviour patterns been thoroughly investigated?

(3) Will suppliers be able to meet the increased demand for supplies, particularly in terms of quality and reliability of deliveries?

Option 1 generates the **highest contribution per unit** and the forecast contribution to sales ratio of 34.9% is higher than the ratio for the year just ended. This means that **profits will grow at a faster rate with option 1,** which could be attractive if there are opportunities to increase sales above the forecast levels.

In view of the reservations concerning the high level of breakeven sales with option 2, it appears that **option 1 (increase prices) is the most attractive.** The resulting substantial reduction in sales may cause problems, however.

(1) **The division's competitiveness may be affected** as competitors will have the opportunity to increase their market share.

(2) **The sale of pastries may be affected** by the reduction in demand for bread.

The division should **not be viewed in isolation** and the **effect on the overall company profits** should be considered.

(ii)   **Pastry division**

The forecast contribution from pastries would be considerably less than that in the year just ended if prices were reduced as in option 2. **Losses would therefore be higher** at £67,000 for the year. It appears that **the demand for pastries is not sensitive to the price reduction:** the extra sales volume would not be enough to compensate for the loss in sales revenue per unit.

Option 1, to increase prices, results in increased contribution and a **reduction in losses** compared with the latest year. Demand does not appear to be particularly sensitive to the price increase.

The pastries division is still forecast to incur a loss under option 1, albeit at a reduced level of £11,000. The **substantial contribution of £109,000** indicates that the pastries division is probably a worthwhile activity, however, subject to the earlier comments on the validity of the fixed cost allocation.

Option 1 is therefore the most attractive for the pastry division. The forecast contribution to sales ratio of 43.3% is higher than the 39% achieved in the latest year and so the option will provide opportunities for more rapid profit expansion if sales can be increased. The small reduction in demand for pastries which results from the price increase will probably not have an adverse effect on the demand for bread.

Examiner's marking scheme

			Marks
(a)	Profit and loss statement		10
(b)	Advice to management		5
(c)	Use of high/low method	2	
	Calculation of variable and fixed costs	2	
	Budgeted profit and loss statement per division per option (1 mark × 4)	4	
			8
(d)	(i) Contribution per unit	2	
	(ii) Breakeven point in units	2	
	(iii) Margin of safety ratio	2	
(e)	Contribution to sales ratio		3
(f)	Advice to management		
	(i) Bread division		4
	(ii) Pastry division		4
			40

---

39   NEW PRODUCT LAUNCH (6/01)

A company is currently operating at a level 40% below practical manufacturing capacity due to both a decline in the market for its products and, at the same time, a reduction in its market share.

For the year just ended, the summary absorption costing profit statement is as follows.

	£'000	£'000
Sales revenue		11,200
Production cost of sales:		
Opening stock of finished goods (60,000 units)	540	
Cost of production	8,240	
Closing stock of finished goods (80,000 units)	(720)	
		8,060
Gross profit (before adjustment)		3,140
Under-absorbed fixed production overheads		210
Gross profit (after adjustment)		2,930
Non-production overheads		2,805
Net profit		125

In both the opening and closing stock figures in the above profit statement, fixed production overheads average £2.00 per unit of finished product. Fixed production overheads absorbed into the cost of production in the year totalled £1,820,000. Non-production overheads include variable costs of £710,000 and fixed costs of £2,095,000.

Required

(a) Prepare a marginal costing profit statement for the year just ended.   (7 marks)

(b) Explain, with supporting figures, the difference between the profit in (a) above and that in the absorption costing profit statement.   (4 marks)

(c) Calculate the break-even sales revenue for the year (to the nearest £'000) using the marginal costing data.   (4 marks)

The company is planning to launch a new product (Product Z) in an effort to recover lost sales. Without the new product, activity in each production department would be expected to continue at 60% of practical manufacturing capacity. Annual sales of 245,000 units of Product Z are estimated, at a price of £9.95 per unit.

Estimated costs relating to the new product are to be established from the following information.

Direct materials

0.3 kilos (net) of a new raw material (Material A) will be required per unit of finished product. 10% of the weight of the material input to production is expected to be lost. Material A costs £6.30 per kilo before discount. A quantity discount of 5% is given on all purchases if the average monthly purchase quantity exceeds 4,500 kilos. Other materials are expected to cost £1.47 per unit of Product Z.

Direct labour

Department X: 0.35 hours per unit of finished product at £4.60 per hour.
Department Y: 0.14 hours per unit of finished product at £5.00 per hour.

Production overheads

If Product Z is launched, total overheads in Department X will be absorbed at 130% of direct labour cost. Overhead absorption in Department Y will be established as a rate per direct labour hour based upon the expected utilisation of capacity, and the associated

BPP
PROFESSIONAL EDUCATION

overhead costs, if Product Z is launched. The following figures for Department Y for a year are based upon practical capacity:

Total overheads, £542,400
Direct labour hours, 220,000

Variable overheads in Department X are 40% of direct cost, and in Department Y are £198,000 for a year at practical manufacturing capacity.

Non-production overheads

Non-production overheads are estimated at £0.70 per unit of Product Z for variable overheads, and will be charged at £1.35 per unit for fixed overheads.

Required

(d)   Calculate the estimated total unit cost of Product Z (ie on an absorption cost basis).

(13 marks)

(e)   Discuss the viability of Product Z, at a selling price of £9.95 per unit.   (7 marks)

(f)   Market research indicates that an alternative selling price for Product Z could be £9.45 per unit. Annual sales at this price would be expected to be 305,000 units.

Determine, and comment briefly upon, which of the two selling prices for Product Z would be preferable.   (5 marks)

(40 marks)

39   ANSWER: NEW PRODUCT LAUNCH

(a)

MARGINAL COSTING PROFIT STATEMENT

	£'000	£'000
Sales revenue		11,200
Variable production cost (W1)	6,420	
Add opening stock (W2)	420	
Less closing stock (W2)	(560)	
Variable production cost of sales	6,280	
Variable non-production costs	710	
		6,990
Contribution		4,210
Fixed production overheads (W3)		(2,030)
Fixed non-production overheads		(2,095)
Profit		85

Workings

1   **Variable production cost**

	£'000
Costs of production (absorption costing)	8,240
Less: fixed production overheads absorbed into costs of production	(1,820)
	6,420

2   **Opening stock**

Total production cost per unit $= \dfrac{£540,000}{60,000}$

$= £9$ per unit

Variable production cost per unit $= £9 - £2$

$= £7$

Opening stock value $= 60,000$ units $\times £7$
$= £420,000$

Closing stock value $= 80,000$ units $\times £7$
$= £560,000$

3   **Fixed production overheads**

	£'000
Fixed production overheads absorbed	1,820
Under absorption of overheads	210
	2,030

(b)

Helping hand

Make sure that you can explain how the difference in profits in marginal and absorption costing systems arise.

	£
Absorption costing profit	125,000
Marginal costing profit	85,000
Difference in profits	40,000

The difference in profits reported under the two costing systems is due to the different stock valuation methods used.

When stock levels increase between the beginning and end of a period, as in this situation, absorption costing will report the higher profit (£40,000 in this case).

Stock levels have increased by 20,000 units in the period.

	Units
Closing stock	80,000
Opening stock	60,000
	20,000

Each unit of stock held (under absorption costing systems) includes £2 of fixed production overheads.

Therefore, since stock levels have increased by 20,000 units, the absorption costing profit will be 20,000 × £2 = £40,000 higher than the marginal costing profit.

(c)

Helping hand

Remember that the C/S ratio is the amount of contribution for every £ of revenue earned.

$$\text{Breakeven sales revenue} = \frac{\text{Fixed costs}}{\text{C/S ratio}}$$

$$\text{C/S ratio} = \frac{4,210}{11,200}$$

Fixed costs = £4,125,000

$$\text{Breakeven sales revenue} = \frac{4,125,000}{4,210,000 \div 11,200,000}$$

$$= £10,973,872$$

$$= £10,974,000 \text{ (to the nearest £'000)}$$

(d)

Helping hand

If 10% of the weight of material input to production is expected to be lost, the weight of material required to make 1 unit needs to be divided by 0.9 (100% – 10% as a proportion).

PRODUCT Z – ESTIMATED UNIT COST
ABSORPTION COSTING BASIS

	£	£
Direct materials		
Material A (W1)	1.995	
Other materials	1.470	
		3.465
Direct labour		
Dept X (0.35 hours @ £4.60)	1.610	
Dept Y (0.14 hours @ £5.00)	0.700	
		2.310
Production overheads		
Dept X - Fixed (W2)	1.449	
- Variable (W2)	0.644	
Dept Y - Fixed (W3)	0.290	
- Variable (W3)	0.126	
		2.509
Non-production overheads		
Fixed	1.350	
Variable	0.700	
		2.050
		10.334

Workings

1 **Direct materials**

$$\frac{0.3kg}{0.9} \times £6.30 \times 0.95 = £1.995$$

245,000 units of product Z require 81,667 units (245,000 × 0.3 ÷ 0.9) of material A per annum = 6,806 units of material A per month. Monthly purchase exceeds 4,500 kilos, therefore 5% quantity discount applies.

2 **Production overheads – Department X**

	£
Total production overhead per unit (130% × £1.61)	2.093
Variable production overheads (0.4 × £1.61)	0.644
Fixed production overheads	1.449

3 **Production overheads – Department Y**

	£
Total overheads	542,400
Variable overheads	198,000
Fixed overheads	344,400

Variable overhead per hour $\frac{£198,000}{220,000}$ = £0.90 per hour

∴ Variable overhead per unit   = 0.14 × £0.90
                           = £0.126

Expected utilisation of capacity

The company is operating at 40% below practical manufacturing capacity, ie at 60% of practical manufacturing capacity.

Department Y practical capacity = 220,000 direct labour hours

Current operating levels = 60% × 220,000
                          = 132,000 direct labour hours

If product Z is launched, it will require:

245,000 × 0.14 hours = 34,300 direct labour hours to manufacture 245,000 units.

239

Thus, expected usage of capacity is:

	Direct labour hours
Current operating levels	132,000
Product Z requirement	34,300
	166,300

Fixed overhead absorption rate – Department Y

$$\frac{\text{Fixed overheads}}{\text{Expected usage of capacity}} = \frac{£344,400}{166,300}$$

$$= £2.071 \text{ per direct labour hour}$$

$\therefore$ Fixed overhead per unit $= 0.14 \text{ hrs} \times £2.071$

$$= £0.290$$

(e)

	£
Total cost per unit	10.334
Proposed selling price per unit	9.950
Difference	0.384

Product Z does not appear to be viable at a selling price of £9.95 as the total cost per unit exceeds the selling price by £0.384 per unit (or 3.9% of the proposed selling price).

However, if we were to consider the variable costs associated with Product Z, it is clear that the new product would make a contribution to fixed costs.

MARGINAL COSTING STATEMENT
COST PER UNIT – PRODUCT Z

	£	£
Selling price		9.950
Variable costs		
Direct materials	3.465	
Direct labour	2.310	
Production overheads (0.644 + 0.126)	0.770	
Non-production overheads	0.700	
		7.245
Contribution per unit		2.705

Product Z would therefore make a contribution towards fixed costs of £2.705 per unit.

$$\text{Average C/S ratio for the company} = \frac{£4,210,000}{£11,200,000} \times 100\%$$

$$= 37.6\%$$

$$\text{C/S ratio (Product Z)} = \frac{£2.705}{£9.95} \times 100\%$$

$$= 27.2\%$$

The C/S ratio of product Z is therefore below the company average, however, the product would contribute a total of £662,725 (£2.705 × 245,000) towards fixed costs (based on current sales estimates).

If fixed costs were to remain at the current level then the introduction of Product Z would be viable at a price of £9.95 per unit, and especially since the company is currently operating at 40% below practical manufacturing capacity.

If the company were able to utilise the spare manufacturing capacity that still remains and were able to produce further profitable products without significantly increasing fixed costs then Product Z could become profitable on a full-cost per unit basis. (The fixed costs per unit would be reduced if other products were manufactured.) The company would need to consider how the introduction of new products would affect sales of current products.

It may be concluded, therefore, that it would be viable to launch Product Z since capacity would be more fully utilised and the product would make a valuable contribution towards fixed overheads.

(f) **Product Z – preferred selling price**

Contribution per unit – selling price £9.95	=	£2.705
Total contribution towards fixed costs (245,000 × £2.705)	=	£662,725
Contribution per unit – selling price £9.45 (£9.45 – £7.245)	=	£2.205
Total contribution towards fixed costs (305,000 × £2.205)	=	£672,525

Since total expected contribution is higher at a selling price of £9.45 (£9,800 per annum higher) then the preferred selling price would be £9.45.

This price would also achieve greater market penetration.

However, it should be noted that this preferable price is dependent upon additional sales of 60,000 units per annum (305,000 – 245,000), ie 25% more sales. It should also be noted that the overall gain in contribution is only £9,800 per annum with a fair increase in capacity utilisation. There may also be an increase in working capital and fixed costs associated with these additional sales.

Examiner's marking scheme

			Marks	
(a)	Variable cost of sales	4		
	Contribution	1		
	Fixed production overhead	2		
			7	
(b)	Figures	2		
	Explanation	2		
			4	
(c)	Fixed overheads	1		
	Calculation	3		
			4	
(d)	Material loss	1½		
	Quantity discount	1½		
	Other aspects of materials	1		
	Direct labour	1		
	Production overheads: Dept X	2		
	Dept Y variable	2		
	Dept Y fixed	3		
	Non-production overheads	1		
			13	
(e)	Net loss	1		
	Contribution (£/unit & total)	2		
	Effect on fixed costs, capacity, other sales	3		
	Recommendation	1		
			7	
(f)	Contribution at £9.45	1½		
	Contribution at £9.95	1½		
	Other aspects	2		
			5	
			40	

BPP
PROFESSIONAL EDUCATION

40   PROFIT POTENTIAL (12/01)

A company has, with the aid of management consultants, developed a new product (Product Z) and, at the same time, researched its market potential.

The fee, as yet unpaid, agreed with the management consultants for the work carried out is £70,000. Further research and development costs incurred to date by the company total £96,000.

The sales potential of the new product, indicated by the market research, will depend upon the price charged. At a selling price of £20 per unit, the annual sales volume is expected to be in the range of 150,000 to 200,000 units per annum. If the selling price is set at £18 per unit, sales of between 240,000 and 360,000 units would be expected. Both alternatives would be supported by advertising and promotional expenditure of £180,000 per annum.

Variable production costs are forecast at £12.50 per unit for production up to 200,000 units per annum, reducing to £12.00 per unit on any additional production. Incremental fixed production costs, as a result of the launch of the new product, are expected to be £220,000 per annum.

There is insufficient production capacity available to satisfy the complete range of demand estimates for Product Z. Production in excess of 240,000 units per annum would result in a loss of contribution on Product A at a rate of £5.00 per unit of Product Z.

Variable selling costs are 10% of sales revenue and all products are charged a further 15% of sales revenue to recover the company's general fixed costs incurred across all functions of the business.

Required

(a) Identify, from the information above, an example of:

    (i)   a sunk cost
    (ii)   an opportunity cost
    (iii)   a committed cost   **(3 marks)**

(b) Assess the profit potential from the launch of Product Z using the full range of demand estimates in your analysis.   **(13 marks)**

(c) Advise management regarding the new product launch.   **(4 marks)**

                                                     (20 marks)

40   ANSWER: PROFIT POTENTIAL

Helping hand

In order to be able to identify the effect of product Z on the company's profits, it is necessary to identify separately the **incremental fixed costs** that will be incurred, and the fixed costs that represent an arbitrary apportionment of general fixed costs that will be incurred anyway. This will enable you to highlight **the incremental effect of producing and selling product Z.**

(a) (i)   The further research and development costs of £96,000 represent a sunk cost. This cost has **already been incurred** and **cannot be altered by future management decisions.**

(ii)   If production of product Z exceeds 240,000 units per annum, the **lost contribution on product A** will represent an opportunity cost. The decision to produce at this level of output for product Z would mean that the company will **forgo the opportunity** to earn a contribution from product A, equal to £5 per unit for each unit of product Z manufactured.

(iii)   The management consultants' fee of £70,000 is a committed cost. Although it has not yet been paid it has been **agreed**. It has **arisen as a result of a past decision which cannot now be altered.**

(b) **Profit achievable from the launch of product Z**

Annual sales Volume (units)	150,000		200,000		240,000		360,000	
	£'000	£'000	£'000	£'000	£'000	£'000	£'000	£'000
Sales value	(× £20) 3,000		(× £20) 4,000		(× £18) 4,320		(× £18) 6,480	
Variable production costs:								
150,000 × £12.50	1,875							
200,000 × £12.50			2,500		2,500		2,500	
40,000 × £12.00					480			
160,000 × £12.00							1,920	
Opportunity cost (120,000 × £5)							600	
Variable selling costs (10% × sales revenue)	300		400		432		648	
		2,175		2,900		3,412		5,668
Profit before fixed costs		825		1,100		908		812
Fixed costs:								
Advertising and promotion	180		180		180		180	
Production costs	220		220		220		220	
		400		400		400		400
Incremental profit		425		700		508		412
General fixed costs (15% × sales revenue)		450		600		648		972
Profit/(loss)		(25)		100		(140)		(560)

(c) The following advice takes no account of the **sunk and committed costs** incurred on management consultants' fees and research and development. These costs have **already been incurred** and will not be altered by the launch decision taken in respect of product Z.

The profit statement shows that, over the full range of selling prices under consideration, product Z will **generate sufficient contribution to cover the incremental fixed costs** incurred on its behalf, and will earn an **incremental profit**.

However, at a selling price of £18 per unit the incremental profit **will not be sufficient to cover the company's usual allocation of general fixed costs**. Although product Z is viable in the short term at this price, because it generates an incremental profit, it does mean that the company will be relying on the profit from its other products to cover the general fixed costs. This could threaten the company's profit performance in the longer term.

With the present capacity constraints the company should set the selling price at £20 per unit, thus **avoiding the opportunity cost** of £5 per unit of product Z. Effective targeting of the proposed advertising and promotion costs will be necessary to attempt to achieve the **highest sales volume possible** within the predicted range.

Examiner's marking scheme

			Marks
(a)	Examples (1 for each)		3
(b)	Contribution: selling price £20	2½	
	selling price £18	3½	
	Incremental fixed costs (1 for each)	2	
	Opportunity cost	2	
	Exclusion of sunk costs	2	
	Exclusion of committed costs	1	
			13
(c)	Advice: short-term	3	
	longer term consideration	1	
			4
			20

Mock exam 1

Information for Management
June 2002

Question Paper:	
Time allowed	**3 hours**
ALL FOUR questions are compulsory and MUST be answered	

Level C
Paper 2

DO NOT OPEN THIS PAPER UNTIL YOU ARE READY TO START
UNDER EXAMINATION CONDITIONS

Information for Management
June 2002

Question Paper	
Time allowed	3 hours
ALL FOUR questions are compulsory and MUST be answered	

Level C
Paper 2

ALL FOUR questions are compulsory and MUST be attempted

1   Products X, Y and Z are output from a joint process operation in the following proportions (measured as a percentage of the weight of output which is used as the basis for joint cost apportionment):

Product X	50%
Product Y	30%
Product Z	20%

Products Y and Z are sold without further processing. Product X can either be sold without further processing or it can be further processed and sold as Product FP which is currently the case. A by-product BP results from the further processing operation.

Selling prices are as follows:

Product X	£5.00 per kg
Product Y	£7.50 per kg
Product Z	£3.90 per kg
Product FP	£8.40 per kg
By-product BP	£1.20 per kg

The total weight of output from the joint process in a period was 1,600 kg. Costs incurred in the process in the period were £7,360. Expenditure on the further processing of 800 kg of Product X was £2,580 (including an additional 200 kg of material). Output from the further processing operation was:

Product FP	920 kg
By-product BP	80 kg

50 kg of Product FP were in stock at the beginning of the period at a cost of £317. There were no opening stocks of Products X, Y or Z, or of by-product BP.

Sales in the period were:

Product Y	480 kg
Product Z	320 kg
Product FP	900 kg
By-product BP	80 kg

Required:

(a) **Calculate the gross profit/loss (£ and £ per kg) on each of products Y and Z in the period.**

(6 marks)

(b) **Calculate the gross profit (£ and £ per kg) on Product FP in the period. Note: the FIFO method is used to determine the transfer of production costs to cost of sales.**   (10 marks)

(c) **Discuss the rationale for joint process cost apportionment.**   (3 marks)

(d) **Describe, and comment upon, an alternative method that could have been used to apportion the joint process costs in the situation above. (NB Calculations are not required).**   (4 marks)

(e) **Comment on the profitability of Product Z and advise management of action that could be taken.**   (4 marks)

(f) **Determine whether more profit would have been earned if Product X had been sold without further processing.**   (7 marks)

An enquiry has been received regarding the further processing of 200 kg of Product Z. £310 has been spent to date in establishing that further processing would be feasible. Incremental costs of £670 would be incurred in the further processing of 200 kg of Product Z.

(g) **Calculate the selling price per kg that would make the further processing worthwhile.**

(6 marks)

(40 marks)

2   **Required:**

(a)   **Explain the main influences on the design of planning and control systems.**   (10 marks)

(b)   **Describe the zero-based budgeting (ZBB) method and outline its benefits in comparison with incremental budgeting.**   (10 marks)

(20 marks)

3   A manufacturing company with a single product set its budget for a period on the basis of production and sales of 410,000 units. Budgeting costs were:

	£'000
Variable production costs	697
Fixed production overhead costs	451
Variable administration and selling overhead costs	82
Fixed administration and selling overhead costs	205

A pre-determined absorption rate per unit is established for fixed production overheads.

32,000 units of the product were in finished goods stock at the beginning of the period. During the period, 400,000 units of the product were manufactured and 390,000 units sold. Opening and closing stocks of finished goods are valued at the standard total production cost of £2.80 per unit.

Actual variable costs incurred per unit in the period were as per budget. Actual fixed overhead costs were:

Production	£446,000
Administration and selling	£205,000

The selling price of the product is £3.70 per unit.

Required:

(a)   **Calculate for the period:**

(i)   **the fixed production overhead absorbed;**
(ii)   **the extent to which the fixed production overhead is over or under absorbed;**
(iii) **the fixed production overhead expenditure and volume variances.**   (8 marks)

(b)   **Prepare a profit and loss account for the period, showing clearly the:**

-    **actual sales revenue;**
-    **standard production cost of sales;**
-    **cost variances calculated in (a)(iii) above;**
-    **actual administration and selling costs.**   (9 marks)

(c)   **Calculate the difference in profit for the period if a marginal costing system had been used instead. (Assume that opening and closing stocks would be valued accordingly.)**   (3 marks)

(20 marks)

4   A retailer, operating a number of stores, sells a large number of products which it classifies into three groups. Representative sales and contribution data for the three product groups for a period are as follows:

	Product group		
	1	**2**	**3**
Sales (£'000)	128	440	340
Sales ('000 units)	100	90	200
Contribution (£'000)	64	176	153

Total fixed costs are £340,000 per period.

Floor space in each store is the key limiting factor for the business. The proportion of total floor space occupied by each product group in achieving the above sales is as follows:

Product Group 1	16%
Product Group 2	50%
Product Group 3	34%

Required:

(a)   Calculate the overall contribution/sales (C/S) ratio.   (3 marks)

(b)   Calculate the break-even sales revenue (to the nearest £'000) per period.   (3 marks)

(c)   Determine the viability of an in-store promotion that would decrease all selling prices by 10% leading to an estimated 30% increase in total units sold.   (5 marks)

(d)   Outline other factors that may influence the decision whether to run the promotion.

(4 marks)

(e)   Establish the priority for the allocation of floor space in a new store between the three product groups on the basis of the above representative data and on the assumption that the retailer has the objective of maximising total contribution.   (5 marks)

(20 marks)

ANSWERS TO MOCK EXAM 1

DO NOT TURN THIS PAGE UNTIL YOU
HAVE COMPLETED MOCK EXAM 1

WARNING! APPLYING THE ACCA MARKING SCHEME

If you decide to mark your paper using the ACCA marking scheme (reproduced at the end of each BPP answer), you should bear in mind the following points.

1   The BPP answers are not definitive: you will see that we have applied our own interpretation of the marking scheme to our answers to show how good solutions should gain marks, but there may be more than one way to answer the question. You must try to judge fairly whether different points made in your answers are correct and relevant and therefore worth marks according to the ACCA marking scheme.

2   In numerical answers, do not penalise yourself too much for minor arithmetical errors: if you have followed the correct principles you should gain most of the marks. This emphasises the importance of including workings, which show the marker which principles you were following.

3   If you have a friend or colleague who is studying or has studied this paper, you might ask him or her to mark your paper for you, thus gaining a more objective assessment. Remember you and your friend are not trained or objective markers, so try to avoid complacency or pessimism if you appear to have done very well or very badly.

1

What the examiner said

According to the examiner, 'reasonable marks were often gained on the question as a whole but the answers to the narrative parts ((c), (d) and (e)) and to the more applied calculations (in parts (f) and (g)) often displayed a serious lack of understanding.'

(a)

Helping hand

Don't forget to read the requirements of the question carefully – you are clearly instructed to calculate the **gross profit per kg** as well as the **gross profit** for products Y and Z.

	Product	
	Y	*Z*
	£	£
Sales revenue (W1)	3,600	1,248
Cost of sales (W2)	2,208	1,472
Gross profit/(loss) (£)	1,392	(224)
	÷ 480 kg	÷ 320 kg
Gross profit/(loss) (per kg)	£2.90	£(0.70)

Workings

(1) **Sales revenue – Product Y**

480 kg × £7.50 = £3,600

Sales revenue – Product Z

320 kg × £3.90 = £1,248

(2) **Cost of sales – Product Y**

480 kg × £4.60★ = £2,208

Cost of sales – Product Z

320 kg × £4.60★ = £1,472

$$★ \text{ Joint process cost per kg of product} = \frac{\text{Joint process costs}}{\text{Total weight of output}}$$

$$= \frac{£7,360}{1,600 \text{ kg}}$$

$$= £4.60 \text{ per kg}$$

(b)

Helping hand

Don't forget to deduct the sales revenue from by-product BP when calculating the cost per kg of product FP!

	Product FP
	£
Sales revenue (W1)	7,560
Cost of sales (W2)	6,012
Gross profit (£)	1,548
	÷ 900 kg
Gross profit (per kg)	£1.72

Workings

(1)   **Sales revenue**   = 900 kg × £8.40
                          = £7,560

(2)   **Cost of sales**

Output of Product X   = 50% × 1,600 kg
                      = 800 kg

Product FP

	£
Joint process costs (800 kg × £4.60*)	3,680
Further processing costs (plus 200 kg material)	2,580
	6,260

* See W(2) in part (a).

Output from further processing of 800 kg of Product X and 200 kg of additional material is:

Product FP   920 kg
By-product BP   80 kg

Sales revenue from by-product BP = 80 kg × £1.20
                                 = £96

Cost of producing 920 kg of Product FP   = £6,260 − £96
                                         = £6,164

∴ Cost per kg of Product FP = £6,164 ÷ 920 kg = £6.70 per kg

Cost of sales – Product FP

	Units	£
Opening stock	50	317
Production in period (850 kg × £6.70)	850	5,695
	900	6,012

(c)

Helping hand

Don't forget that there are four main methods of apportioning common costs. Each of the following methods produces significantly different results.

- Physical measurement
- Sales value at split-off point
- Sales value of end product less further processing costs after split-off point
- Weighting

Rationale for joint process cost apportionment

It is important that any joint process costs incurred in a period are apportioned (where relevant) to individual joint products. Once costs common to a process have been apportioned, it is possible to calculate a cost per kg, which in turn can be used to establish the following values in an accounting period.

- Costs of production
- Value of any closing stock
- Value of cost of sales

It follows on that once the above values have been established, a profit (per product) for the period can be calculated.

It is important to remember that the joint process costs which are apportioned to products are not relevant for decision making.

(d) **Sales value at split-off point – alternative method**

With this method, the joint process costs are allocated according to a product's ability to produce income. This method is most widely used because the assumption that some profit margin should be attained for all products under normal marketing conditions is satisfied. The common cost is apportioned to each product in the proportion that the sales (market) value of that product bears to the sales value of the total output from the particular processes concerned.

(e) Product Z has a gross loss of £0.70 per kg (as calculated in part (a)). The reason for this is entirely due to the method that is used to apportion the common process costs (weight of output). However, if an alternative method of joint cost apportionment had been used, for example, sales value at split-off point, then Product Z would have a gross profit per kg (instead of a loss).

Management could consider increasing the selling price of Product Z, but it is not known whether this could cause a reduction in the sales demand.

(f) **Product FP – profit**

	£
Sales revenue (920 kg × £8.40)	7,728
Cost of sales (920 kg × £6.70)	6,164
Gross profit	1,564

Product X – profit

	£
Sales revenue (800 kg × £5)	4,000
Cost of sales (800 kg × £4.60)	3,680
Gross profit	320

Therefore, if product X had been sold without further processing, £1,244 (£1,564 – £320) less profit would have been earned.

(g)

> **Helping hand**
>
> The money that has already been spent to date in establishing that further processing would be feasible is a **sunk cost**. The relevant costs are as follows.
>
> - Lost sales revenue of Product Z (opportunity cost)
> - Further processing costs (incremental cost)

Relevant costs of further processing

	£
Lost sales revenue (opportunity cost) (200 kg × £3.90)	780
Incremental costs of further processing (incremental cost)	670
	1,450

$$\text{Selling price per kg} = \frac{\text{Total relevant costs}}{\text{Number of kg processed}}$$

$$= \frac{£1,450}{200 \text{ kg}}$$

$$= £7.25 \text{ per kg}$$

Note. The costs of establishing whether further processing would be feasible (£310) are **sunk costs**.

However, if the sunk costs of £310 are to be recovered also, the total costs that would need to be recovered = £1,450 + £310 = £1,760. The selling price per kg therefore = £1,760 ÷ 200 kg = £8.80 per kg.

Examiner's marking scheme

		Marks
(a)	Joint cost per kg	2
	Sales	1
	Cost of sales	1
	Gross profit	2
		6
(b)	Product X	1½
	Further processing costs	1
	By-product	2
	Net cost per kg	1½
	FIFO	3
	Sales and gross profit	1
		10
(c)	Stock valuation	1½
	Decision making	1½
		3
(d)	Sales value method	1
	Description	2
	Comment	1
		4
(e)	Consequence of method	3
	No action	1
		4
(f)	Product FP – profit	4
	Product X – profit	2
	Difference in profit	1
		7
(g)	Lost sales of Product Z	2
	Incremental costs	2
	Cost per kg	1
	Sunk cost	1
		6
		40

2

What the examiner said

According to the examiner, 'This wholly narrative question on aspects of budgeting was very poorly answered, the result seemingly of misreading of part (a) of the question by many candidates, and/or a serious lack of knowledge.'

Helping hand

Make sure that you answer the question set – and not one of your own liking. According to the examiner, many candidates explained what planning and control is or how it operates (ie the stages in the budgetary planning and control process). Read the requirements of examination questions carefully.

(a) **Main influences on the design of planning and control systems**

The main influences on the design of planning and control systems can be divided into the following groups.

- Organisational objectives
- The environment

- Organisational structure
- Technology
- Cost effectiveness

Organisational objectives

Different organisations will set their own unique organisational objectives based on what they hope to achieve in the future. Examples of objectives are as follows.

- Target profit
- Target sales
- Market share
- Anticipated growth
- Research and development

The environment

- Degree of predictability
- Degree of competition
- Number of different product markets faced
- Degree of hostility shown by competitors

Organisational structure

- Size
- Lines of reporting
- Responsibility of individuals
- Interdependence of departments
- Degree of centralisation
- Availability of resources

Technology

- Nature of the production process
- Routine-ness/complexity of the production process
- Amount of variety in each task that has to be performed

Cost effectiveness

It is important that the cost of implementing the system is less than the benefits to be gained by implementing the system. It is possible to **partially implement** a system so that critical areas are focused on while other areas have more general (and less costly) controls in place.

(b) **Zero based budgeting** (ZBB) involves preparing a budget for each cost centre from a zero base. Every item of expenditure has then to be justified in its entirety in order to be included in the next year's budget.

ZBB rejects the assumption inherent in incremental budgeting that next year's budgets can be based on this year's costs. Every aspect of the budget is examined in terms of its cost and the benefits it provides and the selection of better alternatives is encouraged.

The basic approach to ZBB has three stages.

Stage 1 – Define decision packages

A decision package is a comprehensive description of a specific organisational activity which management can use to evaluate the activity and rank it in order of priority against other activities. Managers prepare decision packages for the activities within the budget centre for which they have responsibility.

Stage 2 – Evaluate and rank packages

Each activity (decision package) is evaluated and ranked on the basis of its benefit to the organisation. The ranking process provides managers with a technique to allocate scarce resources between different activities.

Stage 3 – Allocate resources

Resources in the budget are then allocated according to the funds available and the evaluation and ranking of the competing packages.

Benefits of the ZBB method

(a) It is possible to identify and remove inefficient or obsolete operations.

(b) It forces employees to avoid wasteful expenditure.

(c) It can increase motivation.

(d) It provides a budgeting and planning tool for management which responds to changes in the business environment; 'obsolescent' items of expenditure are identified and dropped.

(e) The documentation required provides all management with a co-ordinated, in-depth appraisal of an organisation's operations.

(f) It challenges the status quo and forces an organisation to examine alternative activities and existing expenditure levels.

(g) In summary, ZBB should result in a more efficient allocation of resources to an organisation's activities and departments.

Examiner's marking scheme

		Marks
(a)	Main influences (up to 4 for each)	10
(b)	Method	6
	Benefits (up to 2 for each)	6
		max 10
		20

3

What the examiner said

Common errors included the following.

- Part (a)(i) – failing to apply the calculated absorption rate to the actual production volume or including administration and selling overheads in the overhead absorption rate calculation (despite the question asking for 'the fixed production overhead absorbed').

- Part (a)(ii) – incorrect calculation of under-absorbed overhead.

- Part (a)(iii) – not labelling variances as adverse or favourable, and not being able to calculate these basic variances correctly.

- Part (b) – not following the required layout as stated in the question and having difficulty in calculating the profit and loss account items correctly.

(a)

(i)   Fixed production overhead absorption rate (FPOAR)

$$= \frac{\text{Budgeted fixed production overheads}}{\text{Budgeted production (units)}}$$

$$= \frac{£451,000}{410,000}$$

$$= £1.10 \text{ per unit}$$

Fixed production overhead absorbed = Actual units produced × FPOAR

$$= 400,000 × £1.10$$

$$= £440,000$$

(ii)

	£
Actual overhead incurred	446,000
Overhead absorbed	440,000
Under-absorbed overhead	6,000

(iii) **Fixed production overhead expenditure variance**

	£
Budgeted fixed production overhead	451,000
Actual fixed production overhead	446,000
Fixed production overhead expenditure variance	5,000 (F)

Fixed production overhead volume variance

Budgeted production volume	410,000	units
Actual production volume	400,000	units
	10,000	units (A)
× standard fixed production overhead absorption rate	× £1.10	
Fixed production overhead volume variance	£11,000	(A)

(b)

PROFIT & LOSS ACCOUNT
FOR THE PERIOD

	£	£
Sales revenue (390,000 × £3.70)		1,443,000
Standard production cost of sales		
Opening stock (32,000 × £2.80)	89,600	
Production (400,000 × £2.80)	1,120,000	
Closing stock (42,000 × £2.80)	(117,600)	
		(1,092,000)
Standard gross profit		351,000
Fixed production overhead variances		
Expenditure variance	5,000	
Volume variance	(11,000)	
		(6,000)
Actual gross profit		345,000
Administration and selling costs		
Variable (390,000 × £0.20★)	78,000	
Fixed	205,000	
		283,000
Net profit		62,000

★ Variable administration and selling overhead costs per unit = £82,000 ÷ 410,000 = £0.20.

(c)

	Units
Opening stock =	32,000
Closing stock =	42,000
	10,000

Fixed overhead absorption rate = £1.10 (as calculated in part (a)(i)).

∴ Difference in profit   = 10,000 units × £1.10
= £11,000

(**Note.** If a marginal costing system had been in use instead of an absorption costing system, the profits would be £11,000 **lower**. This is because stock levels have increased in the period. Closing stocks would be valued at £1.10 per unit less than closing stocks in an absorption costing system. If closing stocks are valued at a lower figure, costs of sales will be higher and therefore profits lower.)

Examiner's marking scheme				**Marks**	
(a)	(i)	Absorption rate		1	
		Absorption		1	
	(ii)	Under absorption		2	
	(iii)	Expenditure variance		2	
		Volume variance		2	
					8
(b)		Actual sales revenue		1	
		Standard production cost of sales		2	
		Standard gross profit		1	
		Cost variances		2	
		Administration and selling costs		2	
		Net profit		1	
					9
(c)		Stock change		1	
		Valuation		2	
					3
					20

4

(a)

	Product group			Total
	1	*2*	*3*	
	£'000	£'000	£'000	£'000
Contribution	64	176	153	393
Sales	128	440	340	908

Overall contribution/sales ratio $= \dfrac{\text{Contribution}}{\text{Sales}} \times 100\%$

$$= \frac{£393,000}{£908,000} \times 100\%$$

$$= 43.28\% \ (0.4328)$$

(b) Breakeven sales revenue $= \dfrac{\text{Fixed costs per period}}{\text{C/S ratio}}$

$$= \frac{£340,000}{0.4328}$$

$$= £785,582$$

$$= £786,000 \text{ (to the nearest £'000 per period)}$$

(c) **Viability of in-store promotion**

If selling prices are decreased by 10%, total sales revenue will fall by 10%.

Current sales revenue = £908,000 (see part (a))

Reduction (10% × £908,000) = £90,800

Therefore, contribution will fall by £90,800 if selling prices are decreased by 10%.

Contribution after 10% decrease in selling price = £393,000 – £90,800 = £302,200.

If the number of units sold then increases by 30%, this will increase contribution by 30%, ie by £302,200 × 30% = £90,660.

Overall position

	£
Decrease in contribution due to selling price change	(90,800)
Increase in contribution due to number of units sold	90,660
Overall reduction in contribution and profit	(140)

(d) **Factors influencing the decision whether to run the promotion**

- Whether any additional resources are required

- Whether any additional resources are available (if required)

265

BPP
PROFESSIONAL EDUCATION

- The cost of acquiring additional resources (if required)

- How will the retailer's main competitors react?

- Whether new customers (acquired during the promotion) will remain loyal to the retailer after the promotion (and therefore the same level of sales will be maintained)

(e)

> **Helping hand**
>
> In limiting factor situations, remember that if an organisation wishes to maximise total contribution, you need to calculate the **contribution per unit of limiting factor**. In part (e), you therefore need to calculate the contribution earned per m^2 (for example).

	Product group		
	1	*2*	*3*
Contribution (£'000)	64	176	153
If floor space available = 100m^2			
∴ Floor space occupied	16	50	34
Contribution (£'000) per m^2	4	3.52	4.5
Priority for allocation of floor space	2nd	3rd	1st

Since the retailer has the objective of maximising total contribution, the priority for allocating floor space will be determined by the product groups which earn the highest contribution per m^2.

> **Examiner's marking scheme**
>
> | | | **Marks** | |
> |---|---|---|---|
> | (a) | Total sales and contribution | 1 | |
> | | C/S ratio | 2 | |
> | | | | 3 |
> | (b) | Formula | 1 | |
> | | Calculation | 2 | |
> | | | | 3 |
> | (c) | Reduction in selling price | 2 | |
> | | Volume increase | 2 | |
> | | Net effect | 1 | |
> | | | | 5 |
> | (d) | Up to 2 marks for each factor (maximum, 4) | | 4 |
> | (e) | Contribution | 1 | |
> | | Contribution per % of space | 3 | |
> | | Priority | 1 | |
> | | | | 5 |
> | | | | 20 |

Mock exam 2

Information for Management
December 2002

Question Paper:	
Time allowed	**3 hours**
All FOUR questions are compulsory and MUST be attempted	

Level C
Paper 2

DO NOT OPEN THIS PAPER UNTIL YOU ARE READY TO START
UNDER EXAMINATION CONDITIONS

ALL FOUR questions are compulsory and MUST be attempted

1   The output from a manufacturing process is 3.6 tonnes per productive hour. The product is sold for £110 per tonne. Costs of production include:

Direct materials	£45 per tonne of materials input
Process wages	£4,700 per week (for a normal working week of 37 hours)
Rework	£70 per week
Repairs to machinery	£950 per week

10% of materials input are currently lost in the process and some of the output has to be reworked in another department, at times as a result of customer complaints. On average, six hours per week are being lost due to breakdown of machinery leaving only 31 productive hours. Sales are being lost as a consequence.

Investment in new machinery is not feasible at the present time but, with a view to improving the current situation, management has undertaken a value analysis exercise and is introducing quality control and assurance procedures. As a consequence of this, it is now expected that output tonnage can be increased from 90% of materials input to 92% and that the need for rework can be eliminated.

Required:

(a)   Calculate the cost of direct materials per week in the current situation.   (6 marks)

(b)   Calculate the cost of direct materials per tonne of output:

   (i)   in the current situation;
   (ii)   if output tonnage is increased to 92% of materials input.   (5 marks)

(c)   Calculate the increase in weekly profit that will be expected to result from the improvement in materials efficiency and the elimination of product rework.

   (**NB.** Assume:

   -     No change to the current system of machinery maintenance/repairs

   -     Productive hours and process wages remain at 31 hours and £4,700 per week respectively

   -     No additional costs will be incurred as a result of the introduction of quality control and assurance procedures

   -     Additional output can be sold)   (8 marks)

(d)   Define:

   (i)   value analysis;
   (ii)   quality control and assurance.   (6 marks)

(e)   The factory manager has suggested that a system of routine preventative maintenance be considered. This would take the form of a maintenance team, working outside normal working hours. This could be either on a night shift or by Saturday working.

   Incremental costs would be incurred on the routine maintenance team but reductions would be expected in:

   (i)   machine breakdown time with a corresponding increase in productive time;
   (ii)   machine repair costs.

   The table below summarises the forecast effect of the introduction of routine preventative maintenance.

	Routine preventative maintenance	
	Night shift	**Saturday working**
Maintenance team:		
incremental cost per week	£1,200	£600
Machine breakdown time	75% saving	40% saving
Machine repair costs	reduced to £350 per week	reduced by 40%

Required:

Recommend whether routine preventative maintenance should be introduced, and if so whether on a night shift or by Saturday working.

BPP
PROFESSIONAL EDUCATION

(NB. Assume:

- No change to the current levels of material wastage or rework
- Process wages remain at £4,700 per week
- Additional output can be sold) (15 marks)

(40 marks)

2   A company has two production departments (A and B) in its factory. Overheads in each department are currently absorbed into product costs on the basis of machine hours worked.

The production overhead absorption rate in Department A is £5.60 per machine hour. In Department B the absorption rate is to be established from the following data relating to the department for a period.

	£
Allocated production overheads	24,260
Apportionment of factory level production overheads	37,539
Apportionment of service department production overheads	32,911
	94,710
Machine hours worked	11,550

The company is considering the introduction of a revised overhead apportionment system using activity-based costing. The overheads incurred in the factory in the period have been re-classified into activities, and cost drivers for each activity have been identified and measured, as follows.

Activity	Overhead £	Cost driver	Cost driver volume (Depts A and B)
Machine set up	22,224	batches	100
Machine operation	69,255	machine hours	25,650
Inspection and testing	42,816	units produced	446,000
Servicing	39,375	labour hours	18,750
	173,670		

The following information is available for the period relating to Product X, one of the products manufactured in the factory.

8 batches
2,540 machine hours (Department A 1,400; Department B 1,140)
58,068 units produced
2,303 labour hours

Required:

(a)   **Using the existing absorption method:**

    (i)   **establish the production overhead absorption rate in Department B;**   (2 marks)
    (ii)   **calculate the production overhead cost per unit of Product X.**   (3 marks)

(b)   **Using an activity-based approach:**

    (i)   **establish a production overhead absorption rate for each activity;**   (4 marks)
    (ii)   **calculate the production overhead cost per unit of Product X.**   (5 marks)

(c)   **Describe possible outcomes of a change to an activity-based approach to overhead absorption from a traditional absorption costing method.**   (6 marks)

(20 marks)

3   (a)   **Define the term 'price elasticity of demand' and explain its relevance in pricing decisions.**
    (8 marks)

(b)   A company has a single product which is currently sold for £19.60 per unit. Sales volume, in each four-week period, averages 20,000 units. A change in product selling price is being considered.

Analysis of the market has led to the following estimates of the effect that specified changes in the selling price of the product will have on demand.

Selling price	Sales volume
−5%	+6%
−10%	+13%
+5%	−8%
+10%	−20%

Direct production costs should remain at £9.10 per unit if volume per four-week period is 22,000 units or below. If volume increases by more than 10%, a 2% reduction in unit costs would be expected on all production output.

Production overheads of £1,430,000 per annum would be expected to be unaffected by any change in activity. Non-production overheads, currently £923,000 per annum, would be expected to increase or decrease at 50% of the rate of any sales volume change.

Required:

For each of the possible revised selling prices determine the revised sales revenue and profit for a four-week period that would be expected to result. (Assume that there are 13 four-week periods in a year).   (8 marks)

(c)   **State whether, in the situation in (b) above, sales demand is elastic or inelastic and advise management regarding the optimum selling price to maximise profit.**   (4 marks)

(20 marks)

4   A company manufactures a single product and has the following flexible production cost budgets for a period.

Production quantity	12,000 units	15,000 units	18,000 units
Direct materials:			
Material AB	£3,600	£4,500	£5,400
Material CD	£17,760	£22,200	£26,196
Labour (direct and indirect)	£25,700	£29,900	£35,150
Overhead (excluding indirect labour)	£12,400	£13,180	£13,960

The budget includes the following assumptions.

(i)   Each unit of the product requires:

Material AB	0.2 kg
Material CD	0.4 kg
Direct labour	0.2 hours

(ii)   The supplier of Material CD gives a 10% discount on the excess of purchases over 6,000 kg per period.

(iii)   A premium of 25% is paid on the direct labour basic hourly rate on the excess of production over 15,000 units per period.

During the period, the company manufactured 17,000 units of the product and incurred the following production costs.

Direct materials:	
Material AB	£5,025
Material CD	£25,118
Labour (direct and indirect)	£32,889
Overhead (excluding indirect labour)	£13,315

Required:

(a)   **Outline the difference between a flexible budget and a fixed budget.**   (3 marks)

(b)   **Calculate the budgeted costs per kg of Material CD on the excess of purchases over 6,000 kg per period.**   (3 marks)

(c)   **Prepare a statement for the period showing for each of the four items of cost (ie Material AB, Material CD, labour and overhead):**

(i)   **the flexible budget allowance;**
(ii)   **the actual amount incurred;**
(iii)   **the variance.**   (10 marks)

(d)   The purchase price of Material AB in the period was as per budget.

Calculate the material usage variance (in kg) for Material AB.   (4 marks)

(20 marks)

ANSWERS TO MOCK EXAM 2

DO NOT TURN THIS PAGE UNTIL YOU
HAVE COMPLETED MOCK EXAM 2

1

> **Helping hand**
>
> In part (c) it would be perfectly acceptable to produce two separate profit statements to find the increase in weekly profit: one statement showing the **present situation** and one showing the **situation after the improvements**. However, since many items in the statement will not be affected by the changes, we have used an **incremental approach** in our answer. The final result is the same and precious examination time is saved.

(a) Output per week = 3.6 tonnes × 31 productive hours
  = 111.6 tonnes

This represents 90 per cent of the material input

∴ Material input $= \dfrac{111.6}{0.9}$

  = 124 tonnes

Cost of direct materials = 124 × £45 per tonne
  = £5,580 per week

(b) (i) *Current situation*

Direct material cost per tonne of output $= \dfrac{£45}{0.90} = £50$

(ii) *If output tonnage increased*

Direct material cost per tonne of output $= \dfrac{£45}{0.92} = £48.91$

(c)

> **Helping hand**
>
> The cost of maintenance and repairs will not alter, and neither will process wages. Therefore these items are not relevant to the calculation of the difference in weekly profit.
>
> The cost of materials input can also be ignored since this will not alter. The increase in profit is derived from the increase in sales revenue of the extra output, and the saving in rework costs.

Present output = 3.6 tonnes per hour × 31 hours =	111.60 tonnes per week
Increased output $= 3.6 \times \dfrac{0.92}{0.90}$	
= 3.68 tonnes per hour × 31 hours =	114.08 tonnes per week
Increase in output =	2.48 tonnes per week
Increase in revenue = 2.48 tonnes × £110 =	£272.80 per week
Plus saving in rework costs	£70.00 per week
Total increase in weekly profit	£342.80 per week

(d) (i) Value analysis is an approach to cost reduction which reviews the various types of value that a product or service provides, and then seeks ways of reducing costs while maintaining or improving all aspects of value. Four aspects of value are considered: cost value, exchange value, use value and esteem value. The value

BPP
PROFESSIONAL EDUCATION

analysis approach encourages innovation and a more radical outlook for ways of reducing costs.

(ii)   Quality control and assurance is the process of ensuring that products or services meet quality specifications on a consistent basis. It involves setting controls for all stages of the process of product manufacture or service delivery, and then monitoring the process to ensure that the controls are adhered to.

(e)   Since there will be no change to wastage, the output from the process will be 3.6 tonnes per productive hour. The direct material cost per tonne of output will be £50 (from (b)(i)).

Contribution per tonne of output = £110 – £50
= £60

The cost of process wages and rework are not relevant to the decision.

The incremental gain can be calculated as follows.

	Night shift £ per week		Saturday working £ per week
Incremental maintenance cost	1,200		600.00
Less saving in machine repair cost	600	(950×0.4)	380.00
Net incremental cost	600		220.00
Increased contribution from extra output:			
$75\% \times 6$ hours $\times 3.6$ tonnes $\times £60$	972		
$40\% \times 6$ hours $\times 3.6$ tonnes $\times £60$			518.40
Incremental gain	372		298.40

Since both options produce an incremental gain the programme of routine preventative maintenance should be introduced. The night shift basis produces the largest projected gain.

2

Helping hand

When you are answering part (c), remember to consider any potential drawbacks to introducing an ABC system. It is too easy to produce a one-sided answer that discusses only the advantages of a change from a traditional absorption costing method.

(a) (i)   Production overhead absorption rate $= \dfrac{£94,710}{11,550} = £8.20$ per machine hour

(ii)   Production overhead absorbed by Product X:

		£
Department A	£5.60 × 1,400 machine hours	7,840
Department B	£8.20 × 1,140 machine hours	9,348
		17,188

Production overhead cost per unit of Product X $= \dfrac{£17,188}{58,068} = £0.30$ per unit

(b) (i)   **Machine set up**

Production overhead absorption rate $= \dfrac{£22,224}{100} = £222.24$ per batch

Machine operation

Production overhead absorption rate $= \dfrac{£69,255}{25,650} = £2.70$ per machine hour

Inspection and testing

Production overhead absorption rate $= \dfrac{£42,816}{446,000} = £0.096$ per unit

Servicing

Production overhead absorption rate $= \dfrac{£39,375}{18,750} = £2.10$ per labour hour

(ii) Total production overhead absorbed by Product X:

		£
Machine set up cost	= 8 batches × £222.24	1,777.92
Machine operation cost	= 2,540 machine hours × £2.70	6,858.00
Inspection and testing cost	= 58,068 units × £0.096	5,574.53
Servicing cost	= 2,303 labour hours × £2.10	4,836.30
		19,046.75

Production overhead cost per unit of Product X $= \dfrac{19,046.75}{58,068} = £0.33$ per unit

(c) Possible outcomes of a change to an activity-based approach to overhead absorption include the following.

(i) **More accurate product costs**. The more detailed process of tracing costs to multiple activities and their absorption through the use of **multiple cost drivers** should lead to less arbitrary absorption of overheads. Thus managers will be able to make **better informed decisions** such as product pricing, and whether to discontinue a product, armed with a better understanding of the long-run variable costs.

(ii) **Cost control**. The cross-functional analysis of costs should provide a **better understanding of the activities that incur costs**. Added to this, the use of multiple cost drivers rather than a single machine hour rate should create an **awareness of the critical factors that drive costs**. This better understanding of costs will enable managers to focus their cost control activity more effectively.

(iii) **Increased administrative burden**. The work involved in recording and analysing costs and activity levels is likely to increase. The collection of data on multiple cost drivers will require more **detailed recording systems** than with a single machine hour rate. Furthermore the number of cost pools in an activity-based system is likely to be greater than the number of cost centres used to analyse costs in a traditional absorption costing system.

(iv) **There will still be a requirement for arbitrary analysis and absorption**. An ABC system will not produce precisely accurate product costs. There will still be an element of **arbitrary apportionment of costs** between the various activities identified. Also, it is unrealistic to assume that a single cost driver can **accurately trace** all of the activity costs to individual products.

3

> **Helping hand**
>
> Read the question carefully in part (b). The two per cent reduction in unit costs for output above 22,000 units applies to all units produced, not just to the extra output above 22,000 units per period. In order to advise on the appropriate price in part (c), it is a good idea to demonstrate that the current selling price does not produce the maximum profit.

(a) Generally, the higher the price of a good, the lower will be the quantity demanded. The **price elasticity of demand** measures the extent of the change of demand for a good following a change to its price. Price elasticity of demand is measured as:

$$\frac{\% \text{ change in sales demand}}{\% \text{ change in sales price}}$$

Demand is said to be **elastic** when a **small change in the price** produces a **large change in the quantity demanded.**

Demand is said to be **inelastic** when a **small change in the price** produces only a **small change in the quantity demanded.**

A knowledge of the price elasticity of demand (PED) is relevant in pricing decisions because the effect on revenue of a change in price will depend on the PED.

(i) In circumstances of **inelastic demand, prices should be increased** because revenues will increase and total costs will reduce (because quantities sold will reduce).

(ii) In circumstances of **elastic demand, increases in prices** will bring **decreases in revenue** and **decreases in price** will bring **increases in revenue**. Management will then have to decide whether the increases or decreases in costs will be less than or greater than the increases or decreases in revenue.

(b) *Initial workings*

Calculation of costs at the various sales volumes:

Selling price change %		Sales volume Units	Direct production costs £	Production overhead (W1) £	Non-prod'n overhead (W2) £	Total cost £
−5	(20,000 × 1.06)	21,200	(× 9.10) 192,920	110,000	73,130	376,050
−10	(20,000 × 1.13)	22,600	(× 8.918) 201,547	110,000	75,615	387,162
+5	(20,000 × 0.92)	18,400	(× 9.10) 167,440	110,000	68,160	345,600
+10	(20,000 × 0.80)	16,000	(× 9.10) 145,600	110,000	63,900	319,500

Workings

1   Production overheads = £1,430,000 ÷ 13 = £110,000 for a four-week period.

2   For an output volume of 20,000 units, non-production overhead cost = £923,000 ÷ 13 = £71,000 for a four-week period.

Increase in volume %	% change in costs	Total non-production overhead costs £
+6	+3.0	73,130
+13	+6.5	75,615
−8	−4.0	68,160
−20	−10.0	63,900

Table of sales revenue and profit for a four-week period

Selling price change %	Resulting selling price £ per unit	Sales volume Units	Sales revenue £	Total costs £	Profit £
–5	18.62	21,200	394,744	376,050	18,694
–10	17.64	22,600	398,664	387,162	11,502
+5	20.58	18,400	378,672	345,600	33,072
+10	21.56	16,000	344,960	319,500	25,460

(c) The price elasticity of demand is elastic, since the percentage change in demand exceeds the percentage change in selling price. At the current selling price of £19.60 per unit the profit for a four-week period is £29,000.

		£	£
Sales revenue	£19.60 × 20,000		392,000
Direct production costs	£9.10 × 20,000	182,000	
Production overheads	£1,430,000 ÷ 13	110,000	
Non-production overheads	£923,000 ÷ 13	71,000	
			363,000
Profit			29,000

Therefore profit will be maximised at a price of £20.58 per unit (from part (b)), ie a price increase of five per cent is recommended.

4

Helping hand

In part (c) you will need to analyse the cost behaviour patterns in order to determine the flexible budget allowance for each cost. The labour cost is a **semi-variable cost**, consisting of a fixed element and a variable element. The unit cost for direct labour increases by 25% for production over 15,000 units per period. Therefore you will need to apply the high-low method to the cost information provided for the higher output levels, since this is the range within which the actual activity level lies.

(a) A fixed budget contains the budgeted costs and revenues for a single level of activity. It is not designed to change when activity levels alter.

A flexible budget, by recognising different cost and revenue behaviour patterns, is designed to be adjusted to produce realistic budget cost allowances for the actual level of activity achieved.

(b) Number of units produced from 6,000 kg of material CD = 6,000 ÷ 0.4 = 15,000

Therefore the discounted material price applies for production in excess of 15,000 units, and the higher material price is paid for production of 12,000 units.

	Material CD cost per unit for 12,000 units = £17,760 ÷ 12,000	= £1.48
∴	Material CD cost per kg for 12,000 units = £1.48 ÷ 0.4	= £3.70
∴	Material CD cost per kg on the excess of purchases over 6,000 kg	= £3.70 × 0.90
		= £3.33 per kg

(c) *Initial workings*

1   *Material AB*

Budgeted cost per unit = £0.30 at all output levels

$\therefore$ Budget cost allowance for 17,000 units = 17,000 × £0.30 = £5,100

2   *Material CD*

	£
Budget cost allowance for first 15,000 units (given)	22,200
Budget cost allowance for next 2,000 units (2,000 × £3.33 (from (b)) × 0.4)	2,664
	24,864

3   *Labour*

	Production Units	Labour cost £
	18,000	35,150
	15,000	29,900
Increase	3,000	5,250

Variable labour cost per unit, above 15,000 units = £5,250 ÷ 3,000 = £1.75

	£
Budget cost allowance for first 15,000 units (given)	29,900
Budget cost allowance for next 2,000 units (× £1.75)	3,500
	33,400

4   *Overhead*

	Production Units	Overhead cost £
	18,000	13,960
	15,000	13,180
Increase	3,000	780

Variable overhead cost per unit = £780 ÷ 3,000 = £0.26

	£
Budget cost allowance for first 15,000 units (given)	13,180
Budget cost allowance for next 2,000 units (× £0.26)	520
	13,700

Flexible budget control statement for the period: production 17,000 units

	Flexible budget allowance £	Actual cost £	Variance £
Direct materials			
Material AB (W1)	5,100	5,025	75 (F)
Material CD (W2)	24,864	25,118	254 (A)
Labour (direct and indirect) (W3)	33,400	32,889	511 (F)
Overhead (excluding indirect labour) (W4)	13,700	13,315	385 (F)
	77,064	76,347	717 (F)

(A) denotes an adverse variance; (F) denotes a favourable variance.

(d) The purchase price of material AB was as per budget, therefore there was a zero price variance.

The whole of the £75 favourable variance is therefore a usage variance.

Material usage variance (in kg) × standard price per kg = usage variance in £.

Standard price per kg of AB = £0.30 per unit (from (b)) ÷ 0.2 kg per unit
= £1.50 per kg

$\therefore$ Material usage variance (in kg) × £1.50 = £75
Material usage variance (in kg) = £75 ÷ £1.50
= 50 kg

Topic index

This index is provided as a ready reference aid to your revision.

See overleaf for information on other
BPP products and how to order

CAT Order

To BPP Professional Education, Aldine Place, London W12 8AW

Tel: 020 8740 2211   Fax: 020 8740 1184

email: publishing@bpp.com   online: www.bpp.com

Mr/Mrs/Ms (Full name) _____

Daytime delivery address _____

Postcode _____

Daytime Tel _____

Email _____

Date of exam (month/year) _____

	6/02 Texts	2/03 Kits	i-Learn CD* (2/03)	i-Pass CD (2/03)	Virtual Campus enrolment
LEVEL A					
Paper A1 Transaction Accounting	£16.95 ☐	£8.95 ☐	£29.95 ☐		£80 ☐
Paper A2 Office Practice and Procedure	£16.95 ☐	£8.95 ☐	£29.95 ☐	£19.95 ☐	£80 ☐
LEVEL B					
Paper B1 Maintaining Financial Records and Accounts (UK)	£16.95 ☐	£8.95 ☐	£30.95 ☐	£19.95 ☐	£80 ☐
Paper B2 Cost Accounting Systems	£16.95 ☐	£8.95 ☐	£30.95 ☐	£19.95 ☐	£80 ☐
Paper B3 Information Technology Processes	£16.95 ☐	£8.95 ☐	£30.95 ☐	£19.95 ☐	£80 ☐
LEVEL C					
Paper C1 Drafting Financial Statements (Industry and Commerce) (UK)	£16.95 ☐	£8.95 ☐	£30.95 ☐	£21.95 ☐	£80 ☐
Paper C2 Information for Management	£16.95 ☐	£8.95 ☐	£30.95 ☐	£21.95 ☐	£80 ☐
Paper C3 Auditing Practice and Procedure (UK)	£16.95 ☐	£8.95 ☐	£30.95 ☐	£21.95 ☐	£80 ☐
Paper C4 Preparing Taxation Computations and Returns FA2002 (10/02 Text, 2/03 Kit)	£16.95 ☐	£8.95 ☐ £8.95 ☐			
Paper C5 Managing Finances	£16.95 ☐	£8.95 ☐	£30.95 ☐	£21.95 ☐	£80 ☐
Paper C6 Managing People	£16.95 ☐	£8.95 ☐	£30.95 ☐	£21.95 ☐	£80 ☐
INTERNATIONAL STANDARDS					
Paper B1 Maintaining Financial Records and Accounts	£16.95 ☐	£8.95 ☐			
Paper C1 Drafting Financial Statements (Industry and Commerce)	£16.95 ☐	£8.95 ☐			
Paper C3 Auditing Practice and Procedure	£16.95 ☐	£8.95 ☐			

*Now incorporates i-Learn Workbook

SUBTOTAL £ _____

POSTAGE & PACKING

Texts	Mail Order First	Mail Order Each extra	On-line per item	
UK	£5.00	£2.00	£2.00	£ ___
Europe*	£6.00	£4.00	£4.00	£ ___
Rest of world	£20.00	£10.00	£10.00	£ ___

Kits	Mail Order First	Mail Order Each extra	On-line per-item	
UK	£2.00	£1.00	£1.00	£ ___
Europe*	£3.00	£2.00	£2.00	£ ___
Rest of world	£8.00	£8.00	£8.00	£ ___

CDs	Mail Order First	Mail Order Each extra	On-line per-item	
UK	£2.00	£1.00	£1.00	£ ___
Europe*	£3.00	£2.00	£2.00	£ ___
Rest of world	£8.00	£8.00	£8.00	£ ___

Grand Total (incl. Postage)   £ _____

I enclose a cheque for
(Cheques to *BPP Professional Education*)

Or charge to Visa/Mastercard/Switch

Card Number ☐☐☐☐ ☐☐☐☐ ☐☐☐☐ ☐☐☐☐

Expiry date _____   Start Date _____

Issue Number (Switch Only) ☐☐

Signature _____

Register via our website,   www.bpp.com/virtualcampus/cat   and pay on-line

REVIEW FORM & FREE PRIZE DRAW

All original review forms from the entire BPP range, completed with genuine comments, will be entered into one of two draws on 31 July 2003 and 31 January 2004. The names on the first four forms picked out on each occasion will be sent a cheque for £50.

Name: _____   Address: _____

_____

Date:_____   _____

How have you used this Practice & Revision Kit? *(Tick one box only)*	During the past six months do you recall seeing/receiving any of the following? *(Tick as many boxes as are relevant)*
☐ Home study (book only)	☐ Our advertisement in *ACCA Student Accountant*
☐ On a course: college _____	
☐ With 'correspondence' package	☐ Other advertisement _____
☐ Other _____	☐ Our brochure with a letter through the post

Why did you decide to purchase this Practice & Revision Kit? *(Tick one box only)*	**Which (if any) aspects of our advertising do you find useful?** *(Tick as many boxes as are relevant)*
☐ Have used complementary Interactive Text	☐ Prices and publication dates of new editions
☐ Have used BPP Texts in the past	☐ Information on Practice & Revision Kit content
☐ Recommendation by friend/colleague	
☐ Recommendation by a lecturer at college	☐ Facility to order books off-the-page
☐ Saw advertising in journals	☐ None of the above
☐ Saw website	
☐ Other _____	

Have you used the companion Interactive Text for this subject?   ☐ Yes ☐ No

Your ratings, comments and suggestions would be appreciated on the following areas

	Very useful	Useful	Not useful
Introductory section (How to use this Practice & Revision Kit)	☐	☐	☐
'Do You Know' checklists	☐	☐	☐
'Did You Know' checklists	☐	☐	☐
Possible pitfalls	☐	☐	☐
Questions with help	☐	☐	☐
Helping hands	☐	☐	☐
Content of answers	☐	☐	☐
Mock exams	☐	☐	☐
Structure & presentation	☐	☐	☐
Icons	☐	☐	☐

	Excellent	Good	Adequate	Poor
Overall opinion of this Kit	☐	☐	☐	☐

Do you intend to continue using BPP Interactive Texts/Kits?   ☐ Yes ☐ No

Please note any further comments and suggestions/errors on the reverse of this page. The BPP author of this edition can be emailed at lynnwatkins@bpp.com

Please return to: Lynn Watkins, BPP Professional Education, FREEPOST, London, W12 8BR

REVIEW FORM & FREE PRIZE DRAW (continued)

Please note any further comments and suggestions/errors below

FREE PRIZE DRAW RULES

1   Closing date for 31 July 2003 draw is 30 June 2003. Closing date for 31 January 2004 draw is 31 December 2003.

2   Restricted to entries with UK and Eire addresses only. BPP employees, their families and business associates are excluded.

3   No purchase necessary. Entry forms are available upon request from BPP Professional Education. No more than one entry per title, per person. Draw restricted to persons aged 16 and over.

4   Winners will be notified by post and receive their cheques not later than 6 weeks after the relevant draw date.

5   The decision of the promoter in all matters is final and binding. No correspondence will be entered into.